Animal Advocacy and Environmentalism

Animal Advocacy and Environmentalism

Understanding and Bridging the Divide

Amy J. Fitzgerald

polity

First published in 2019 by Polity Press

Polity Press
65 Bridge Street
Cambridge CB2 1UR, UK

Polity Press
101 Station Landing
Suite 300
Medford, MA 02155, USA

ISBN-13: 978-0-7456-7933-4
ISBN-13: 978-0-7456-7934-1(pb)

A catalogue record for this book is available from the British Library.

Library of Congress Cataloging-in-Publication Data

Names: Fitzgerald, Amy J., author.
Title: Animal advocacy and environmentalism : understanding and bridging the
    divide / Amy J. Fitzgerald.
Description: Cambridge, UK ; Medford, MA, USA : Polity Press, 2018. | Series:
    Social movements | Includes bibliographical references and index.
Identifiers: LCCN 2018019595 (print) | LCCN 2018036300 (ebook) | ISBN
    9781509533756 (Epub) | ISBN 9780745679334 | ISBN 9780745679341 (pb)
Subjects: LCSH: Animal rights movement. | Animal welfare. | Environmentalism.
    | Green movement.
Classification: LCC HV4708 (ebook) | LCC HV4708 .F5825 2018 (print) | DDC
    179/.3--dc23
LC record available at https://lccn.loc.gov/2018019595

Typeset in 11 on 13 pt Sabon by
Servis Filmsetting Ltd, Stockport, Cheshire
Printed and bound in the UK by CPI Group (UK) Ltd, Croydon

For further information on Polity, visit our website:
politybooks.com

For Milo Eugene,
with love and hope

Contents

Abbreviations

AAM – Animal Advocacy Movement
AZA – American Association of Zoos and Aquaria
CAFO – Confined/Concentrated Animal Feeding Operation
CAZA – Canadian Association of Zoos and Aquaria
EAZA – European Association of Zoos and Aquaria
EM – Environmental Movement
GCC – Global Climate Change
IAA – Industrial Animal Agriculture
IQ – Inverted Quarantine
ToP – Treadmill of Production
WAZA – World Association of Zoos and Aquaria

Introduction

As an animal[1] advocate and environmentalist, the animal advocacy movement (AAM) and environmental movement (EM) have intersected in my personal life for years, yet I did not really start thinking about the relationship between the two until I was a graduate student. One event in particular that occurred about fifteen years ago stands out in my mind as crystallizing my interest in the relationship between the two movements. I was at an academic environmental studies conference, and the organizers had arranged for a preeminent cognitive ethologist to give a presentation to the entire assembly over dinner about his research on animal interactions. I was quite impressed that they had invited a keynote speaker to talk about animals at an environmental studies conference; in my experience, there was not much of a dialogue between academics interested in environmental issues and those interested in animal issues, save for a few notable exceptions.

During his talk, he transitioned from discussing his research on companion animals to discussing the cognitive capabilities of animals raised for human consumption, complete with photographs, as dinner was served. Those who had not requested the vegan option were served a very large helping of meat. I prepared myself for a very awkward social situation: the keynote speaker was discussing the complex minds and lives of animals as their flesh was being served. To my surprise, the attendees engaged in carefree dining, the presenter seemed unfazed, and he received strong applause upon the completion of his talk. On the one hand,

1

I was pleased that the conference organizers had invited an animal advocate as their keynote speaker, but on the other hand, I was perplexed by the (lack of) response to his message. That event solidified my interest in the seeming divide between the EM and the AAM.

A few years later, after assuming my new position as an assistant professor, I was invited to speak at an event hosted by my new university. It was a dinner event attended by university donors and faculty to welcome a guest speaker to campus; she was a feminist, politician, environmentalist, organic farmer. I was asked to talk about my research on animal abuse and interpersonal violence. The attendees were seated at tables enjoying their drinks as I began to discuss my research. As I transitioned into a discussion of my work on the negative community effects of slaughterhouses, focusing on environmental degradation and increased crime rates, dinner was served (earlier than scheduled, as I recall). In came the serving staff with platters of meat, passing right in front of me as I tried to continue speaking while ignoring the awkward social situation I was sure was brewing. This time I was partially correct about the awkwardness: while some people dined on the meat and continued to listen to me speak about the problems associated with animal agriculture, a number of others looked uncomfortable and picked at the food on their plates. I was worried that I had offended several university donors, particularly given that I was a new faculty member. After the meal, however, a few attendees approached and thanked me for making a connection for them that they had not made before. Later the organizers apologized profusely for the timing (but not explicitly the content) of the meal.

The lesson that I have taken from these two experiences – in addition to learning to politely decline requests to give talks during meals – is that there are many people (such as academics who study the environment and university donors interested in hearing about environmentalism and organic farming) who are receptive to pro-environmental messages but are also capable of either blocking out pro-animal messages or coping with the cognitive dissonance that results. I do not think that the audiences at these two talks were unique. I think that these two experiences illustrate how insular the EM and the AAM have been. The purpose of this book is to bridge this divide through developing a better understanding of the historic, philosophical, and political rifts between the EM and the AAM. I hope to suggest ways that the two can be brought into closer alignment, while being sensitive to the extant differences. It is a way to make a broader case for what many of us know from our personal lives: environmental, animal, and human wellbeing are interrelated.

Why this book?

Besides my own personal interest, why is writing a book focused on animal advocacy, paying special attention to its relationship with environmentalism, warranted? There are two parts to answering that question: the first is explaining why animal advocacy is important, and the second is detailing why addressing the relationship with environmentalism is particularly important. These are discussed in turn below.

The scope of current (ab)uses of animals globally is immense. I argue herein that the "animal issue" is a massive looming social justice issue that we must grapple with. There are ethical reasons why we should be concerned with the wellbeing of other animals (Adams and Donovan 1995; Donovan and Adams 2007; Regan 2004; Singer 1990), but, in addition, the wellbeing of animals can be entwined with the well-being of people and the environment. For instance, there is growing evidence of a connection between animal abuse and interpersonal violence, albeit a more complicated one than previously theorized (Arluke et al. 1999; Ascione and Shapiro 2009; Ascione et al. 2007; Barrett et al. 2017; Beirne 2011; Currie 2006; Fitzgerald et al. 2009; Flynn 2011). Also, severe environmental degradation is often a consequence of modern animal agriculture (Centner 2006; Clay 2004; Donham et al. 2007; Edwards and Ladd 2000; Ladd and Edwards 2002, Magdoff et al. 2000; Steinfeld et al. 2006). In short, the harms perpetrated against animals are worthy of consideration in their own right ... and also because they often expand to harm human wellbeing.

There are also conceptual connections between the subjugation of nonhuman animals and various groups of people. The socially constructed culture/nature dichotomy has been identified as an important mechanism for linking these forms of oppression. There are three features of this and other oppressive dichotomies (such as mind/body) that make them particularly problematic. First, they are hierarchical, and the dominant category (culture) is rendered normal and is privileged over its constructed opposite (nature). Second, they are structured as being antagonistic, as "disjunctive pairs in which the disjuncts are seen as exclusive (rather than inclusive) and oppositional (rather than complementary) and that places higher value (status, prestige) on one disjunct than the other" (Warren 2000, 46). As a result, culture and nature are viewed as opposite and mutually exclusive categories. Finally, these dichotomies are undergirded by a logic of domination that justifies the subordination of one group (i.e., nature) by the other (i.e., culture) (Warren 2000). This domination can be explicitly violent, but can also manifest itself more subtly, such as in the form of paternalism (Mackinnon 2004).

The culture/nature dichotomy rationalizes and perpetuates the belief that humans are unique and vastly different from (and superior to) nonhuman animals: humans are believed to belong exclusively to the realm of culture, whereas other animals and organisms are considered simply as nature (Noske 1989). However, membership in the realm of the cultural has not been afforded equally to all humans: hegemonic conceptions of masculinity have been associated with culture, whereas women and subordinated masculinities (e.g., those who belong to racialized and/or impoverished groups) have been largely associated with nature. Nature and those associated with it have been constructed as the Other and of lesser value than those associated with culture. Kheel (1993) sums it up as follows: "Nature, which has been imaged as female, has been depicted as the 'other', the raw material out of which culture and masculine self-identity are formed" (p. 244). This othering process undergirds numerous forms of human oppression (such

4

as sexism, racism, and classism) as well as the oppression of non-human animals and degradation of the environment. The result vis-à-vis nonhuman animals and the environment is thoroughgoing anthropocentrism, as well as speciesism.

In short, *anthropocentrism* refers to the notion that humans are ascendant over all other species (see Arluke and Sanders 2008 for a discussion of different gradations). *Speciesism* is related to anthropocentrism in that it refers to prejudice or discrimination based on species, although there is not total agreement on the scope of the concept (see Fjellstrom 2002). The term was originally coined by Richard Ryder and intended as "a deliberate 'wake-up call' to challenge the morality of current practices where non-human animals are being exploited in research, in farming, domestically and in the wild" (Ryder 1975, 1). He used the term to facilitate his argument that physical characteristics, such as those that define species, are not relevant in making moral decisions. Speciesism is therefore conceptually analogous to other forms of discrimination based on perceived physical differences, such as racism and sexism.[2] The comparison, however, is not without controversy; some argue that it could trivialize the suffering of specific human groups (see Cushing 2003 for a description of this perspective), while others assert that species is a fundamentally different physical characteristic than sex or race because it is associated with qualities important to ethical decision making, such as intelligence (e.g., Brennan 2003; Steinbock 1978). Yet the scientific dividing lines on qualities such as intelligence are continually shifting, and selection of such qualities and associated thresholds are increasingly being recognized as rather arbitrary.

Although crude and simplistic articulations of parallels between these forms of oppression can be problematic and used to trivialize the suffering of human groups, I do think that there are practical and theoretical reasons to attend to these connections. The history of associating some human groups with nature instead of culture is unsavoury, but should not be glossed over. As David Pellow and I have argued, "in order to redress oppression rooted in the culture/nature dichotomy we cannot simply attempt to 'elevate' certain human groups from the nature side of the dichotomy to the culture side. Instead, we must deconstruct the entire dichotomy" (Fitzgerald and Pellow 2014, 30). Doing so requires challenging the anthropocentrism and speciesism that are used to rationalize the constructed chasm between culture and nature; this book is intended to contribute to that dialogue.

The second part of the original question that needs to be addressed is this: Why pay special attention on these pages to the relationship between animal advocacy and environmentalism? As will be detailed in this book, these two social movements have much in common. Both articulate challenges to anthropocentrism and are confronted by common sources of resistance. Further, their concerns are often grouped together under the umbrella of environmental ethics (Pojman 2016; Sutherland and Nash 1994). Yet, somewhat surprisingly, there has been relatively little written on the relationship between animal advocacy and environmentalism and its respective social movements. Some academic works (discussed below) have been written on specific aspects of the divide between the EM and AAM movements, but a need remains for holistic analyses of the relationship between the two and what form it might take in the future.

Decades ago, Eugene Hargrove (1992) compiled previously published articles and chapters tackling the issue of animals within environmental ethics in an edited volume, *The Animal Rights / Environmental Ethics Debate*. Notably, it did not include the work of scholars advocating animal rights or liberation perspectives. In his introduction to the volume, Hargrove asks the question, "Will animal liberation and animal rights unite harmoniously with environmental ethics and live happily ever after?" (1992, xxi). He follows up with this response: "To be honest, it does not seem very likely. As I see it, environmental ethics will continue to be an unpleasant thorn in the side of animal welfare ethicists, even though they themselves have no plausible solutions to the problem of what to do, and not do, with sentient wild animals" (xxi–xxii). I would suggest that the social, political, and environmental landscapes have changed quite significantly in the twenty-five or so years since Hargrove made his prediction, and that partnership between these two movements is in fact feasible.

This feasibility is beginning to be mapped out in the literature, such as in Lisa Kemmerer's (2015a) recent edited volume, which compiles perspectives on, and experiences with, collaboration between the two movements as told by a wide array of international activists and academics.

Years earlier, Ted Benton (1993) explored why there had not been much cross-pollination between radical leftist movements (particularly those grounded in socialism) and the EM and AAM in *Natural Relations: Ecology, Animal Rights and Social Justice*. Nevertheless, in his book he makes a strategic decision to focus on socialism and animal rights, noting that the EM and AAM ought not be lumped together and that the connections between environmentalism and socialism were already being articulated elsewhere. Therefore, while his book provides a discussion of the distinctions between environmental and animal rights perspectives, due to the scope of the book he was unable to delve into the details thereof.

More recently published monographs have explored specific points of connection between the two movements. *Evolution, Animal "Rights," and the Environment* (Reichmann 2000) focuses specifically on the application of "rights" to animals and the environment from a philosophical perspective. Lisa Kemmerer's recent book, *Eating Earth* (2015b), examines the environmental impacts of consuming animals via industrial animal agriculture (IAA), fishing, and hunting. Aimed at environmentalists, the book makes the case for why those concerned about the environment ought to adopt a plant-based diet. Additionally, a book I authored, *Animals as Food: (Re)connecting Production, Processing, Consumption, and Impacts* (Fitzgerald, 2015), focuses specifically on IAA, and traces the impacts through the commodity chain, with special attention paid to the negative environmental effects. These books, however, do not provide a holistic assessment of the trajectories of the broader EM and AAM, and where they might most usefully intersect.

Some environmentally focused volumes have addressed substantive animal issues, such as seal hunting (Wenzel 1991) and whaling (Kalland 2012; see also Marietta and Embree 1995; Zimmerman 2005; White 2008), but again the focus has been on a specific issue instead of on the environmental and animal advocacy movements more generally. The reverse is true of monographs and edited anthologies on the animal advocacy movement (AAM); on those pages there has tended to be little discussion of the EM. The exceptions include acknowledgements that the same cultural ferment facilitated the environmental and animal rights movements (Jasper and Nelkin 1992), juxtapositions of the perspectives advocating for the moral consideration of individual animals against positions articulated within environmental ethics (Fellenz 2007), and a comparative analysis of animal advocacy vis-à-vis environmentalism in the US and France (Cherry 2016). I would suggest that ecofeminists (e.g., Eckersley 1992; Gaard 2017; Warren 1997; Adams 1994; Noske 1989) have been the most consistent in articulating the intersections between concern for the environment and non-human animals, although their focus has been primarily philosophical.

Noting these gaps, a few authors have commented on the neglect of animals within environmental discourses and vice versa, although they have not been optimistic about a closer relationship between the two movements and associated areas of academic interest. In his contribution to an edited anthology, Steven Yearley (2002, 277) concludes, "environmental concern coexists uneasily with concern for every last animal." In her article on the omission of animals specifically by environmental sociology, Hilary Tovey (2003) explains that in the relatively few instances that animals are addressed in that literature, it is as "wild" animals and in the form of populations of generic types – not as individual subjects. Consequently, variations within categories are overlooked. It is also important that the numerous domesticated animals in contact with human societies are omitted from their purview. Tovey aptly observes that "the lack of interest among environmental sociologists in domestic and domesticated animals seems paradoxical. It contrasts starkly with levels of interest among the general public" (2003, 203).

There have been some promising developments in the field of green criminology. In a paper published in *Criminology*, Piers Beirne (1999) argued for a nonspeciesist criminology that would meaningfully examine criminal and non-criminal harms perpetrated against animals instead of conceptualizing them merely as property and their abuse as an instrumental marker of aggression against people. The nonspeciesist criminology project appeared to find a home in the field of green criminology that was taking shape at the time. The definitions of green criminology that emerged generally make reference to an intersecting focus on harms perpetrated against animals and the environment; for instance, Beirne and South (2007) define it as "the study of those harms against humanity, against the environment (including space) and against non-human animals committed both by powerful institutions (e.g., governments, transnational corporations, military apparatuses) and also by ordinary people" (xiii).

Moreover, one of the three broad theoretical frameworks recognized within green criminology is specifically devoted to addressing the victimization of animals. This species justice perspective utilizes an anti-speciesist lens to examine harms against animals, and understands animal wellbeing as being distinct from human interests. The other two green criminology frameworks – environmental justice and ecological justice – respectively focus on environmentally mediated harms to people, which are shaped by one's social and geographic location and viewed as an extension of human rights, and harms against the environment, providing space for understanding the intrinsic value of the environment (White 2008).

To date, however, the field has been populated mainly by works undertaken within the latter two frameworks. Further, it appears as though species justice has been subsumed under ecological justice in much of the literature. Consistent with this approach, Nurse (2016) writes, "species justice considers the responsibility man [sic] owes to other species as part of broader ecological concerns" (17). Likely owing to this conceptualization, when animals are included in green criminology the focus tends to be on illegal actions against wildlife animals, such as poaching. Exploring the harms visited upon wildlife, such as Nurse's (2013) work, is important, and clearly demonstrates how environmental and animal interests intersect; however, green criminological work ought to also thoroughly explore the victimization of animals in their own right, including the victimization of domesticated animals, that which is not environmentally mediated, and that which is entirely legal and institutionalized. These forms of victimization represent a large proportion of the harms inflicted upon animals, and correspondingly are the focus of the AAM; true species justice will require confronting them.

These limitations are likely at least partially owing to the shortage of cross-pollination between the EM and the AAM. Moreover, to date there has been little analysis of the chasm between the two realms. Yet this absence does not in and of itself necessarily warrant a book on the subject. A more compelling justification, I think, is the fact that these social movements and associated academic literatures share much in common and could benefit from coalition building. For instance, the source of the greatest harms against the environment and animals – the sociopolitical economic system – are shared. Likewise, the resistance to these movements is analogous in many respects. This book details the potential sites of cooperation and capacity-building between the EM and the AAM. It would be naïve to explore this promise without also attending to the historic and current divisions between the two movements; therefore, this book engages in that analysis as well.

Just as other authors (e.g., Benton 1993, discussed above) have had to make difficult decisions about what to include and exclude in their books, I have had to do so here. Benton decided to focus his book on socialism and animal rights, as he felt that the connection between environmentalism and socialism was satisfactorily addressed elsewhere. On these pages, I attend to the historic, current, and potential relationships between the AAM and the EM. I spend more time teasing apart the different perspectives within the AAM, its composition, and examining recent developments in that movement than the EM because I anticipate that the average reader will be less well-versed in these matters than they are the EM, as that movement is more populous and there has been more written on the subject (see, for instance, Brulle 2000; Dowie 1995; Gottlieb 1993; Gould, Schnaiberg, and Weinberg 1996; Merchant 2013; Scarce 1990; Szasz 2007). Moreover, although I integrate research and illustrative examples from a variety of geographic regions, I focus mainly on the national and social movement contexts that I know best: Canada and the United States.

Why the divide between animal advocacy and environmental movements?

As alluded to thus far, to date there have been concrete and theoretical divides between the AAM and the EM. It is certainly fair to ask why discussions about the environment and the EM have paid such little attention to the animals that share the environment with us, and why the tension between the two movements and areas of academic research has at times been extremely acrimonious. To begin to answer this question we must look back to philosophical deliberations that took place nearly forty years ago.

In 1980, philosopher J. Baird Callicott declared in an academic article that the differences between the EM and the AAM were irreconcilable. Callicott launched several critiques against the animal rights/liberation movement, including that a widespread shift to vegetarianism would be an ecological disaster and that domesticated animals "have been bred to docility, tractability, stupidity, and dependency. It is literally meaningless to suggest that they be liberated" (Callicott, 1980, 53). To say that his article was tantamount to filing divorce papers between the two movements would be an understatement. Eight years later, Callicott wrote another article, "Animal Liberation and Environmental Ethics: Back Together Again" (1988), and stated that he regretted the "acrimonious estrangement" between the two movements that his previous article had caused. Coming close to a rare academic about-face, Callicott wrote, "Animal welfare ethicists and environmental ethicists have overlapping concerns. From a practical point of view, it would be far wiser to make common cause against a common enemy – the destructive forces at work ravaging the nonhuman world – than to continue squabbling among ourselves" (1988, 163). He proceeded to suggest that mutual sympathy between the two movements could forge a meaningful relationship. However, his revised argument received less attention and appeared to have less traction. Why is that the case? Well, there are a number of factors, beyond Callicott's remarks, that have contributed to the divide between the two movements and associated areas of academic interest. These factors will be fleshed out in the subsequent chapters, but they warrant brief introduction here.

Different levels of analysis

Those interested in animal issues and environmental issues tend to engage at different levels of analysis. The EM adopts a holistic view and is focused on ecosystems (Catton 1980; Dowie 1995; Gottlieb 1993; Tovey 2003). In contrast, the AAM tends to focus more at the individual level (Eckersley 1992; Jasper and Nelkin 1992; Regan 1980). The tension between the two perspectives has resulted in many debates; for instance, should one intervene to assist an injured wild animal or is doing so interfering with ecosystem functioning? The debates often entail environmentalists accusing animal advocates of being shortsighted, only caring about "cute" animals (e.g., domestic pets), and not caring about the numerous, perhaps less cuddly, species currently at risk. The tension between these two discourses is perhaps best illustrated with regard to the issue of hunting (Jasper and Nelkin 1992), the focus of Chapter 2.

As a result of these analytical differences, advocacy discourses related to the environment and animals are different in a fundamental way: much of the AAM has been framed, implicitly and explicitly, around a discourse based on rights (for alternative conceptualizations see Curtin 1996; Donovan 1990; Hawkins 1998; Plumwood 1996). This rights-based discourse, which has been critiqued as being too individualistic (Curtin 1996) among other things, has further separated environmental and animal-related concerns. More specifically, the language of rights generally lacks relevance in discussions of the environment, and additionally the individualizing discourse of "animal rights" may preclude broader environmental thinking among animal advocates. Thus, the different levels of analysis and resultant discourses have created a formidable, although not insurmountable, divide between the social movements and academic research related to the environment and animals.

Gender

Another, admittedly more speculative factor that may contribute to the divide between the two movements and areas of study is gender composition. Some scholars, including Rocheleau et al. (1996) and Shiva (1989), have observed that the environmental sciences have been dominated by men. There are also gendered differences related to animal concern. For instance, research has found that historically and currently, most animal advocates are women (Herzog 2007; Munro 2001; Jasper and Nelkin 1992; Peek et al. 1996; Kruse 1999); that altruism has a significant positive effect on being vegetarian (Kalof et al. 1999), and women tend to exhibit higher degrees of altruism than men (Dietz et al. 2002; Kalof et al. 1999; Kalof 2000); and that among the general public, women tend to be more concerned about animal issues than men (Broida et al. 1993). It is possible that the dominance of men in environmental studies has contributed to the downplaying of animal interests, and that the preponderance of women in the AAM has made it possible to dismiss interest in animals as "sentimental."

Science

The EM and the AAM have had different relationships with science, both historically and today. Environmentalism has been closely linked with scientism; the movement was born out of growing scientific evidence that humans were harming the environment. Today's EM continues to leverage scientific evidence to make its case (although there have, of course, been cases where environmental advocates have challenged scientific orthodoxy). The AAM, however, has had a different, and even antagonistic, relationship with science. The modern AAM has its roots in anti-scientism, a response to the macabre experimentation on animals in the nineteenth century. Public exposure of these experiments spurred many women into animal activism, as many had had their own negative experiences with the scientific – particularly the medical – establishment (Tuohey and Ma 1992). Statistics from the late twentieth century indicate the negative perceptions of science by animal advocates have persisted: 52 percent of a sample of animal activists reported believing that science does more harm than good. The proportion of a sample of the general population who shared that belief was only 5 percent (Jamison and Lunch 1992).

Radicalism

In their classic, detailed examination of the AAM, Jasper and Nelkin (1992) distinguish among three groups that comprise what they refer to as the animal rights movement: welfarists, pragmatists, and fundamentalists. They assert that the pragmatists and fundamentalists constitute the radical wing of the movement. While I disagree with aspects of their categorization and labels, I agree with their point that what many consider to be the radical positioning within the movement (which Jasper and Nelkin refer to as the "animal rights crusade") has come to represent the entire movement in the minds of most people (see also Sorenson 2016).

Environmentalists may thus be wary about aligning themselves with the concerns of animal advocates because the animal "rights" movement in particular has developed this (not necessarily deserved) reputation for radicalism and the use of so-called terrorist tactics (see Best and Nocella 2004). There may therefore be an unwillingness among the masses who self-identify as environmentalists and the environmental organizations that rely on their donations to closely associate with the AAM.

Although the EM also has its own radical flank that utilizes direct action techniques (see Scarce 1990), the entire movement has not been identified with it to the degree that the AAM has. In fact, many of the large and most popular environmental organizations are reform-oriented, and have become institutionalized (Brulle 2000) and thus legitimized in the eyes of many (and impotent in the eyes of others). The reputation of animal advocacy, which I hope to challenge in this book, has no doubt at least partially contributed to reluctance on the part of environmentalists to building coalitions.

The focus of the book

This book explores these factors that have contributed to the continued divide between the environmental and animal welfare/rights/liberation movements and their associated fields of academic pursuits. I utilize case studies of what are arguably the most contentious issues (hunting, zoos, and fur) between the two movements to illustrate how the divisions are manifested and have been articulated, and to demonstrate that there is hope for cooperation between these two movements even on these most contentious issues. This comparative case study approach is also useful for elucidating the nuanced differences within the AAM, while also demonstrating that there is much that animal advocates share in common, which has particular value in this context because disunity within the movement has likely been an impediment to greater progress (Munro 2012; Nurse 2013). The book also provides a much-needed exploration of how the divide between animal advocacy and environmentalism can be expected to narrow due to demographic changes, changing areas of emphasis within the AAM and the EM, and growing recognition that the challenges and resistance being faced by these two movements are actually quite similar. It is my position that changes in the AAM and the EM currently underway or on the horizon hold the potential to bring the movements into closer alignment.

For its part, the EM has passed through three generally acknowledged phases over the past several decades. The first focused on the environment as a resource, and conservation and preservation were key among the recommended strategies. The second phase, largely in response to Rachel Carson's *Silent Spring* (1962), focused on the problems caused by chemicals and pollution. The third phase is said to have been ushered in by the acknowledgement that environmental problems do not recognize political or species boundaries, and that many of the most pernicious problems, such as climate change, are global and trans-species (Norton 2000).

In the context of these growing global risks, sociologist Ulrich Beck infamously declared, "poverty is hierarchic, smog is democratic" (Beck [1992] 2007, 36). That is, not only do environmental hazards not respect political boundaries, they also do not discriminate by class. We are all at risk. This realization has swelled the ranks of those who identify as environmentalists. I will demonstrate herein that just as the EM has gained so much support because there is increasing evidence that harms against the environment also harm all people, the AAM is poised to gain growing support as it becomes increasingly apparent that many harms against animals are also associated with negative impacts on the environment and people. In this way, some animal issues will be refracted through environmental issues.

There is, however, a risk to gaining movement support because individuals are concerned about their own wellbeing. Andrew Szasz (2007) has diagnosed this problem as *Inverted Quarantine* (IQ) in his book, *Shopping Our Way to Safety: How We Changed from Protecting the Environment to Protecting Ourselves.* He explains that the popularized EM has become focused around a commodified and individualized response to risk. Instead of buying organic food because it is better for the environment and the animals that inhabit it, for instance, many consumers are motivated by concern for their own health and that of their family. Szasz (2007) argues that this individualized, consumerist response to environmental threats is the opposite of a social movement, and results in a "political anesthesia." People feel that they are protecting themselves, which makes them less concerned about the larger, systemic causes of the problems and redressing them. He writes, "I conclude that mass flight into inverted quarantine decreases the likelihood – and defers the day – that something substantive is done about those hazards" (2007, 172).

Yet he is not entirely pessimistic. Szasz (2007) points out that there have been times in the past, such as during the nuclear shelter panic in the US, when in the end people rejected the impulse of the

IQ. So it is possible that it could be rejected in the end vis-à-vis the environment. He also mentions, but does not go into much detail about, the potential of time spent in the IQ to expose people to teachable moments. He alludes to the possibility of crossover from individualized response to broader engagement in his discussion of food, writing that while some people who purchase organic products do not consider themselves environmentalists, "as they shop in the organic food store and read the labels and the posted information, such folks spend time in the 'discursive space' of the EM, exposed to its worldview and ideology" (2007, 203). He nonetheless argues that this educative process will not be sufficient to overcome the impetus of the IQ.

I argue throughout this book that, like the EM, the AAM is also confronted with the problematic of the IQ. However, as will be elaborated upon in the next chapter, research indicates that the AAM is unique relative to many other social movements because many of its associated concerns contain an emotional pull, and many people are recruited into the movement through being exposed to these affective elements. Therefore, it is possible that the IQ could have a more positive effect on the AAM as the teachable moments vis-à-vis animal issues that one is exposed to while in the IQ might resonate at the emotional level and require less explanation and convincing. The IQ phenomenon, for all of its faults, could help to advance the AAM and bring it into closer alignment with the EM at the micro level.

This trend that Szasz diagnoses in the EM is part of a larger process of neoliberalization. Although some attention has been paid to how this process is affecting environmentalism, as far as I can tell, attention has not been paid in the literature to how it has affected the AAM up to this point in time, and how it may do so in the future.[3] In fact, one critique of the literature is that it has been exceedingly anthropocentric, resulting in understanding nature as a resource. By way of a corrective, Bakker (2010) identifies aspects of nature that ought to be examined, such as human bodies and genetically modified organisms. I would add animals more generally to that list; when they have been addressed in this area of literature, as with the green criminology and environmental sociology literatures, it has been in the form of wildlife-as-resource. Bakker goes on to recommend a non-anthropocentric analysis, writing, "scholars of neoliberal nature should adopt a non-anthropocentric view of the agency of nature, and interrogate the status of non-humans as political subjects. In this way, we might produce better accounts of the interrelationships between ecological processes, non-humans and humans – whereby agency is both enabled and constrained" (718). This goal remains to be achieved.

The phenomenon of pet keeping might be particularly instructive in this respect, as it is "part of a dual process: the intensification of nature accumulation and hyper-commodification of consumption under neoliberal regimes of capital accumulation" (Bakker 2010, 718). Yet this is one aspect of neoliberalization that may work to the advantage of the AAM: as more people come into contact with pets, even if it is because of accumulation and commodification, their circle of compassion might grow to include other animals (Bulliet, 2005; Nast 2006). There are currently several factors facilitating an increase in pet ownership in developed countries, such as a decline in family size, aging populations, increasing consumerism and alienation, and a desire to be mobile that may preclude having children (Nast 2006).

The impact of consumerism more generally on animals and the environment has certainly been negative in many ways (see Nash 1989). However, as Beers (2006) points out, the impacts are more nuanced than generally assumed. She breaks down the three sectors where spending increased the most after World War II – automobiles, home, and recreation – and how each affected animals. Animals and the environment were certainly harmed by the expansion of car culture, whereas the increase in consumerism in the home sector had mixed impacts. While it harmed some animal habitats, the increasing suburbanization fostered a desire to "get back to nature" among many residents. The increase in recreation also brought people closer to nature, although, as discussed in Chapter 2, this has come at a cost.

These complexities all warrant increased research attention. The impacts of neoliberalization on animals certainly need to be better fleshed out. Nonetheless, there have been a few steps in the right direction. For instance, the impacts of neoliberalization on animal agriculture (see Haggerty, Campbell, and Morris 2009), wildlife tourism (e.g., Duffy 2014), and studying animals and other marginalized populations (Fraser and Taylor 2016) have been examined. Yet the impacts on the AAM – particularly its relation to the EM – remain unexamined. This book is intended to begin to fill that gap.

The impacts of neoliberalism on the environment and the EM have been more thoroughly examined. How the neoliberal promotion of free markets has affected the environment has perhaps been best captured in the Treadmill of Production (ToP) concept and theory (see Schnaiberg 1980; Gould, Pellow, Schnaiberg 2008). In short, it points to the expansion imperative of capitalism, coupled with investment in technologies to increase production, as causing environmental harm through producing negative environmental outputs, extracting resources from the environment, as well as removing environmental sinks. It is theorized that the biophysical limits of the environment will eventually cause a crisis in the ToP. In the interim, the environment continues to be degraded in the interests of economic expansion.

The concept has been used, with various levels of specificity, to describe socioenvironmental phenomena that involve animals, such as the expansion of industrial animal agriculture (IAA) (Horrigan et al. 2002; Nibert 2012; Novek 2003; Stretesky et al., 2014). However, to date, the consequences of these macro forces on animal wellbeing more generally, and the AAM more specifically, have not been articulated. This book begins to explore what the Treadmill of Production (ToP) might mean for animal advocacy, how the forces it describes may serve to bring the AAM and the EM closer together, and how attending to animal issues can serve to further illustrate its conceptual value.

Not only are factors external and internal to the AAM and the EM potentially bringing them closer together, making an examination of the relationship between the two prudent and timely, there are sound theoretical reasons for attending to the connections between environmental, ecological species, and social justice. For this reason, this book employs an analytical framework that is thoroughly intersectional in that it attends to not only sexism, racism, classism, heterosexism, and ableism, it also addresses the anthropocentrism and speciesism that also affects those groups that have been lumped together on the nature side of the culture/ nature dichotomy. Some have, for example, engaged in this work under the banner of (critical) ecofeminism (Gaard 2017), while others have described it as a total liberation frame (aligned with the field of critical animal studies) (e.g. Nocella et al. 2014)).

This book takes up the challenge of strategizing for change by focusing on the ways that greater cooperation between the environmental and animal advocacy movements would be mutually beneficial. I am not alone in thinking that cross-pollination between the movements would be useful, although not without challenges (see Pellow 2013). For instance, Mary Anne Warren (2000) argues that the movements are complementary and that each makes up for the shortcomings of the other. She specifically points to lack of concern among animal advocates about issues of species threats and extinctions, and a lack of concern among environmentalists about the wellbeing of domesticated animals. She concludes, "Only by *combining* the environmental and animal rights perspectives can we take account of the full range of moral considerations which ought to guide our interactions with the non-human world" (Warren 2000, 185). This book not only advocates for collaboration between the movements, it demonstrates that it is in fact feasible, even in the face of historic divides, and that there are some social forces that may even help to make it happen.

The composition of the book

The first chapter of the book provides the historical and philosophical background necessary to understand the perspectives and debates within the AAM, and its relation to the EM and environmental perspectives more generally. The subsequent three chapters detail three topical areas where there have been strong disagreements between many proponents of the EM and the AAM. These chapters provide illustrations of the concepts and tensions introduced here and discussed in more detail in the next chapter. While Chapter 1 draws heavily upon work done within the disciplines of history and philosophy, Chapters 2–4 integrate the work that has been done in sociology, anthropology, criminology, geography, and political science to analyze the topics (sport hunting, zoos, and fur) under examination. Chapter 5 focuses on industrial animal agriculture and argues that, facilitated by unfolding social forces, this issue holds a great deal of promise for bringing the two movements closer together. The final chapter highlights the mutual forms of resistance that the two movements are encountering, and ties together the arguments made in the previous chapters to suggest that greater collaboration between the movements is not only theoretically preferable, it is achievable.

Over twenty years ago, Anne Sutherland and Jeffrey Nash (1994) argued based on their in-depth research on the animal rights movement that the movement had radical potential. They wrote at the time that "the new forms of moral protest that animal rightists espouse, while still concerned with the plight of animals, seem to use animals as a call for fundamental changes in Western culture's view of nature" (172). Nonetheless, it continues to be cast as a single-issue and rather insular movement, often deservedly so (Pellow 2013). The overarching goal of this book is to demonstrate that the fundamental changes that the AAM and the EM are advocating for vis-à-vis culture and nature are much more closely aligned than often depicted, particularly by those with a vested interest in maintaining a wedge between the two and leveraging one side against the other.

1

The Animal Advocacy Movement(s)

This chapter lays the foundation for understanding the animal advocacy movement (AAM) and its connections to other movements, particularly the environmental movement (EM). It begins by tracing the development of a coherent AAM and the different threads within it. A similar detailed examination of the EM is not possible here due to space constraints, but is available elsewhere (see Dunlap and Mertig 2014; Brulle 2000; Gottlieb 1993; Dryzek 2005).

After examining the development of the AAM and its constituent perspectives, insights from the social movement literature are integrated to better understand the strategies and tactics that the AAM has used, and to situate it relative to other social movements. Next, the chapter turns to detailing the theoretical distinctions between the AAM and EM most specifically. I argue in this chapter that the failure to take an intersectional approach that considers both the harms perpetrated against animals and the environment (not to mention humans), as well as their common sources, is currently a limitation of both of the mainstream movements. That is, there is a need to deconstruct the culture/nature dichotomy as a whole instead of attempting to elevate individual groups of victims (i.e., animals, the environment, human social groups) into the cultural consciousness.

The history of animal advocacy

Understanding where animal advocacy stands today in and of itself and relative to other movements requires an understanding of the origins of the movement. Unfortunately, such a historical understanding is often lacking. In the words of Beers, "when it comes to the AAM, an historical amnesia effectively erases the significant legacies today's animal activists and society as a whole have inherited from their mostly forgotten predecessors" (2006, 2–3).

Like many other social movements, such as the women's movement and the EM, the AAM has unfolded in waves or phases over time, each of which was catalyzed by a number of factors. The first wave of the movement focused on issues of animal welfare and cases of extreme cruelty against domesticated animals, often pets. It was made possible by changing attitudes about animals, which began to shift perceptibly in sixteenth- and seventeenth-century Western Europe. Up to that point in time, people had encountered animals in instrumental contexts, such as animals used as food and those used for labour. A multitude of factors began to reshape the relationship between people and (some) animals: Industrialization and urbanization simultaneously moved people further away from the instrumental use of animals; growing sentimentalization around middle-class nuclear families paved the way for some animals to be considered part of that social institution; and companion animals became a means to reconnect people to the nature that they were being slowly detached from (Jasper and Nelkin 1992; Thomas 1996).

The protective attitudes towards animals taking shape at this time were ultimately not restricted to species of animals that served as pets; they also spread to other species, particularly those being subjected to public harm. The first legislation ever introduced to protect animals in Britain was introduced in the early nineteenth century to protect bulls from bull baiting (using dogs to attack bulls as entertainment). Although that specific bill failed to get the necessary votes to become law, in 1822 the first legislation to protect animals was passed; it was aimed at protecting animals produced for food and working animals from "unnecessary" cruelty (Kean 1998; Jasper and Nelkin 1992).

The "unnecessary cruelty" concept was and still is debated within the movement. What is *unnecessary* and what is *cruelty*? In other words, what ends can justify subjecting animals to suffering? Differing answers to these questions divided the movement into two factions in the nineteenth century – the humane movement and the antivivisection movement (Jamison and Lunch 1992; Beers 2006) – although as Beers argues, in practice there was crossover between these neat categories. The humane movement responded with more conservative answers to the questions posed above, accepting animal suffering as necessary in some contexts, such as for the good of science. The anti-vivisection movement, in contrast, developed out of a critique of the amount of suffering being inflicted upon animals under the banner of science.

These respective movements attracted somewhat different members. The animal welfare movement was dominated by social elites that considered kindness to animals important to personal moral development (Jasper and Nelkin 1992). In contrast, the anti-vivisection movement was comprised of more socially disadvantaged groups. People from lower socioeconomic status groups and women, in particular, empathized with the plight of animals within scientific institutions because they also saw themselves as vulnerable to the growing power of science (Tuohey and Ma 1992; Jamison and Lunch 1992). The ascendancy of science, at the time and into the present, is a double-edged sword: it provided increasing evidence of the continuity between humans and animals, but this continuity made the use of animals as human models in experiments attractive (Tuohey and Ma 1992). Emphasizing the role that anti-scientism played in the development of the AAM, Tuohey and Ma (1992) assert that the movement "did not emerge out of a philosophy of natural rights, nor even a sentimental feeling for animals" (81), but instead can be traced back to a desire to protect the moral and religious status quo of the time from the growing power of science. This is perhaps somewhat overstating the case; however, I think it fair to say that the desire to protect against scientism played a role in the development of the AAM that is often under-appreciated in the literature.

Although there was certainly agitation on behalf of animals in the subsequent years of the nineteenth century and the first half of the twentieth century, and various organizations to protect animals (such as the Royal Society for the Prevention of Cruelty to Animals (RSPCA)) were founded (see Beers 2006, especially Chapter 5), the movement did not surge ahead again in many Western countries until after World War II. Rapid social changes at this time laid the foundation for broader questioning of the treatment of animals. In particular, the growing emphasis on the nuclear family and domesticity brought an increasing number of animals into homes as pets. Surely many animals were included into homes as objects to round off the image of the perfect family, but affection towards these creatures grew dramatically in spite of the sometimes utilitarian function they served. The subsequent protest movements of the 1960s and 1970s (particularly the environmental, feminist, antinuclear, and peace movements) developed a critique of instrumentalism that the AAM was able to extend to the use of animals. The civil rights and feminist movements also fomented rights-based discourses that animal advocates were able to extrapolate from (although the discourse of rights was not entirely new to the AAM), in addition to borrowing from their critique of institutionalized harms (Jasper and Nelkin 1992).

The combination of the adoption of a critique of instrumentalism and a rights-based discourse by some animal advocates and organizations pushed the movement in a more radical direction than the earlier animal welfare movements had: instead of critiquing individual forms of extreme cruelty, the movement initiated a more comprehensive critique of institutionalized and instrumental forms of harm (Shapiro 1994; Jasper and Nelkin 1992). This is not to imply that some animal advocates had not been articulating this position earlier; however, there is general consensus that it was not until the 1960s that this perspective began to be expressed and enacted more broadly as a movement. This shift in perspective was also related to changing perceptions of animal subjectivity. In Jasper and Nelkin's words, "The gradual radicalization of the animal protection movement thus followed changing images of animals; from pitiful objects of charity, to innocent beings with interests of their own, and – finally – to autonomous individuals with a right to their own lives" (1992, 69–70). Of course, it is good to remember that the definition of "radical" is highly subjective; for Jasper and Nelkin, the transition from animal welfare to "animal rights" and arguments in favour of the abolition of harmful uses of animals is deserving of the term. For others, there is nothing radical about those propositions.

Intellectual ammunition

The critiques of instrumentalized uses of animals were woven together and articulated by several philosophers. This gave animal advocates the intellectual ammunition they needed to complement the growing concern for some species of animals. In the literature, these philosophers have been referred to as the midwives of the movement (Jasper and Nelkin 1992). The main philosophical perspectives will be discussed shortly.

In addition to the catalyzing role of philosophers, the movement was propelled forward by the emergence of a growing number of animal organizations and victories in some of the important campaigns they mounted. In the late 1970s, animal advocates (led by Henry Spira) compiled evidence of troubling experiments being performed on cats at the American Museum of History and began a series of protests. Success was theirs in under two years: the experiments were stopped. Another visible victory came in the early 1980s when Alex Pacheco (co-founder of People for the Ethical Treatment of Animals) blew the lid off experiments being performed by Edward Taub on monkeys in Silver Springs, Maryland. The experiments were stopped and Taub was eventually found guilty of six counts of animal cruelty; however, the convictions were not upheld because of jurisdictional issues (Jasper and Nelkin 1992). The reversal of these convictions notwithstanding, the successful campaigns helped to propel the movement forward.

The advancement of the movement at this time was not occurring in a vacuum. In addition to drawing on some ideological aspects of other social movements, it also drew heavily on other social movement strategies, particularly from the EM. These included direct mail fundraising, using the legal system, and direct action techniques that garnered a lot of free publicity (Jasper and Nelkin 1992; Beers 2006). The use of legal strategies brought the AAM and the EM together in the 1970s on issues of species extinction and protecting whales and dolphins.

Another strategic decision the AAM had to make, and continues to have to make, is where to focus its attention. Through the 1980s, the AAM retained much of its focus on vivisection, although this began to change in the 1990s. This shift in priorities has been documented empirically. Plous (1998) surveyed activists at a national animal rights event held in 1990 and again in 1996 and noted a significant change in which issue advocates thought the movement should focus on. In 1990, the majority of activists considered animal research to be the most significant issue to be tackled, but by 1996 the most important issue identified was animal agriculture. That the focus of the movement was on animal research up until the 1990s is not entirely surprising, given its historical roots in the anti-vivisection movement and that the most significant campaign successes up to that point in time had been on the issue of animal research.

The diversity of concerns addressed today by the AAM as well as the diversity of its constituencies are both challenges and potential sources of strength. The movement has been able to effect concrete changes in some types of animal (ab)use and to influence perceptions of the public on a number of issues. In addition to successes related to animal research (e.g., reducing the number of animals used in research and improving their living conditions, popularizing alternatives to dissection), the movement has made fur less popular and has secured improvements in the living conditions of some animals used as entertainment (Jasper and Nelkin 1992; Jamison and Lunch 1992; Luke 2007), to name a few. The movement has been able to realize these successes at least partially by uniting very diverse constituencies. Jasper and Nelkin (1992) observe, the movement has attracted the support of people not often allied in concern and activism. Young punks dressed in voguish black demonstrate alongside the elderly matron with a poodle; conservatives (common in animal welfare organizations) march next to radical feminists. For all these men and women, animals are an important part of their social and environmental community. (p. 170)

It should be also noted, however, that, to date, the movement has not been what one would call diverse in terms of racial/ethnic composition (Pellow 2013).

The relative diversity of perspectives and constituencies can also pose ideological and logistical challenges. Additionally, the wide variety of issues the movement as a whole addresses also affects the buy-in it receives from various groups and the public. As Einwohner (2002) observes in the context of the US,

> The animal rights movement occupies a somewhat contradictory position... In some ways, the movement's goals have been accepted by the public; for instance, polls show that Americans oppose the use of animal testing for cosmetic products... At the same time, however, the American public has been much slower to show support for the movement's other goals... Americans therefore are capable of multiple – and somewhat competing – attitudes about animals. (p. 509)

Moreover, it is not just people in the US who have complicated and sometimes conflicted attitudes about animals: this is endemic to Western societies.

In addition to the challenges posed by the variety of issues taken up by the movement, the diversity of constituencies, and the fact that the public is capable of holding conflicting attitudes about animals, the movement faces other significant challenges. The most significant include that the scope of the harms inflicted upon animals is immense, the industries that are responsible for inflicting a great deal of this harm are extremely powerful, there is strong resistance to change, many uses of animals are justified on religious and historic grounds, and legally animals are considered property (see Wise 2000). Faced with these challenges, various tactics have been recommended, and the tactical decision-making has been influenced by philosophical considerations. The ways that philosophical approaches to animal ethics are parsed varies, but one delineation I find particularly useful because of the amount of ground it covers is that articulated by Martha Nussbaum (2001; 2006). She identifies four main philosophical approaches, examined in turn here, followed by a brief discussion of other approaches worthy of examination.

The contractarian approach

The contractarian approach is grounded in the work of Immanuel Kant. Kant argued that people ought not to engage in animal cruelty, primarily because it makes one more likely to be cruel to other people. He therefore envisioned our duties to animals as being indirect. A more recent application of this perspective has been developed by John Rawls, who argues that there cannot be reciprocity in relationships between people and animals, and therefore we do not have a direct duty of justice vis-à-vis the treatment of animals (Nussbaum 2001); nonetheless, we may have indirect duties to them.

Although the contractarian approach has not been drawn on heavily by animal advocates, there are some elements of it apparent in animal advocacy discourses, such as the anthropocentric notion that harm to animals is problematic because it can make the perpetration of harm against people more likely. This thinking was particularly evident in the early animal welfare movement. The perspectives more commonly used by animal advocates today assert that we do have more of a direct duty to animals (although not fully direct, in some cases) than Kant and Rawls envisioned; utilitarianism is one such perspective.

Utilitarianism

Jeremy Bentham, the first Western philosopher since Porphyry to address the morality of the (ab)use of animals (Nussbaum 2001), was a proponent of utilitarianism. His writings spanned the eighteenth and nineteenth centuries, wherein he argued that although there are important differences between people and animals, there exists a moral obligation to minimize the suffering of animals. He famously wrote, "the question is not, *Can they reason?* nor, *Can they talk?* but, *Can they suffer?*" (Bentham 1789). Nussbaum (2001, 1526) also credits him as being "the first major legal thinker to suggest that animals should have legal protection from cruelty."

Peter Singer popularized the utilitarian approach in the modern AAM. Singer, a preference utilitarian, wrote *Animal Liberation* (1990), which is generally accepted as *the* book that catalyzed the modern AAM. After the empathy for animals that had built up with the animal welfare and anti-vivisection movements began to wane, a new basis for concern for animals was needed, and Peter Singer's book served exactly that purpose (see Tuohey and Ma 1992). In this book and elsewhere, Singer builds on Bentham's work, arguing that we must give animal interests equal consideration in our moral calculations, and that doing so requires us to treat animals as well as we treat cognitively similar humans. Failure to give equal consideration to the interests of cognitively similar animals results in speciesism. He explains that we cannot "say that all human beings have rights just because they are members of the species *homo sapiens* – that is speciesism, a form of favouritism for our own that is as unjustifiable as racism" (1987, 4). The implication of this reasoning is profound. According to his logic, most of the ways we currently treat animals are unethical. Nevertheless, his reasoning does not define all uses of animals as unethical: in some cases, such as certain instances of animal experimentation, the infliction of harm upon animals could be justified if, taking both human and animal interests into consideration, the benefits outweigh the harms (Singer 1990).

Singer's work has become synonymous with "animal rights." The irony is that he does not advocate a rights-based approach. He actually argues that interests or preferences provide a better mechanism for animal advocacy than rights. Although it may seem like a mere semantic issue to some, the difference between these approaches is important. Singer's utilitarian approach aims at maximizing the benefits for the individuals involved, while a rights-based approach (discussed in more detail shortly) prioritizes the rights of individuals not to be harmed over the maximization of benefits.

Due to the attention Singer's work and the utilitarian approach more generally have received, a number of rebuttals and critiques have been articulated. Some commentators have disagreed with Singer's equal consideration of human and animal interests. For instance, Tuohey and Ma (1992) assert that human and animal suffering are inherently different because only humans are able to attribute meaning to their suffering. Others have focused on the limitations of the utilitarian perspective itself, pointing out that it requires rather complex calculations in order to determine the ethics of a specific action.

Nussbaum (2001) also points out several limitations regarding what this perspective means for the actual wellbeing of animals. First, it is not clear how this approach can deal with deprivations of which animals are not aware. Second, the perspective favours more cognitively sophisticated animals. Nussbaum does not necessarily see this as a problem in and of itself, but suggests that this prioritization should be deliberated. Finally, the perspective appears to view individuals as "containers of satisfactions" that can be replaced. Therefore, individuals are not respected as much as the maximization of the greater good is, perhaps enabling the birth of animals into exploitative institutions (such as animal agriculture or science) to be interpreted as a positive if it adds to the aggregated good (Nussbaum 2001). The rights-based approach focuses on redressing some of these limitations.

The rights-based approach

This perspective, which is most commonly associated with the works of Tom Regan, asserts that individuals have intrinsic value, and that rights flow from this intrinsic value. The type of rights addressed varies by author. Tom Regan (2004) focuses primarily on moral rights. In his work, he draws a useful distinction between moral agents and moral patients. Moral agents (i.e., mentally competent adult humans) have the capabilities necessary for making rational, moral decisions. Moral patients (such as non-human animals), on the other hand, lack the ability for such decision-making. Nonetheless, moral patients, he argues, ought not to be considered a means to an end. Doing so would be an unjust violation of that individual's rights.

Whereas utilitarians advocate for taking the greater good into consideration in moral decision-making, advocates of the rights-based perspective argue that even the greater good cannot justify violating the rights of individuals. Rights-based advocates are not, however, suggesting that animals be granted all rights equivalent to those that humans enjoy. Some rights, such as voting rights, would not make sense if extended to animals. They are instead advocating for basic rights, such as the right to life and freedom, which humans enjoy. Although, like human rights, there may be qualifications.

The rights-based approach has also been subject to critique. A general but relatively common critique of the concept of animal rights is that humans are unique in their capacity for moral decision-making, and extending rights to animals is nonsensical in that they cannot be held responsible for their harmful actions. Machan (2012, 14) articulates this critique as follows: "Animals are not moral agents and cannot have rights like human beings any more than they can be guilty of moral wrongs or crimes ... for such reasons as medical research or feeding the hungry, people may use animals, just as trees, fruits or lakes." This type of critique, however, overlooks the distinction between moral agents and moral patients that Regan articulates.

There are other critiques that I think carry more weight. One salient criticism levied against rights-based approaches is that, in the words of Nussbaum (2001, 1535), "they are a little loose and vague." This approach is often articulated at an abstract level and it can be difficult to discern exactly how it would be applied in practice, although developments in the field of animal law are beginning to provide a glimpse into what the application of specific rights to animals might look like. Another related concern is that the rights-based approach has been applied to animals in an overly broad sense in that distinctions in rights are not made based on the varying capacities of different species. Nussbaum (2001) argues that this is one area where the utilitarian approach is preferable to the rights-based because it takes the capacity of the animal into consideration in its moral deliberations. In other words, it is a more fine-tuned approach, compared to the somewhat broad brush being used by rights-based advocates.

Another critique, one most specifically related to the topic of this book, is that the rights-based approach could compromise ecological wellbeing. Franklin (2005) has explored this point, and he argues that in cases of conflict between the more specific interests of animals and the broader interests of the environment and human wellbeing, the environment/human side should be prioritized. He suggests that doing so is more in line with the utilitarian approach, but seems at odds with the rights-based approach. Franklin (2005) points to Regan's assertion that in a scenario where a choice has to be made between protecting the last two remaining animals of one species (let's say crickets) versus one animal whose death would be of greater consequence to that individual (let's say a cat), then the most ethical choice would be to protect the rights of the individual animal (the cat in this example). Here we can see where the individualism of the rights-based approach to animals can be at odds with the holism of environmentalism.

The neo-Aristotelian approach

Nussbaum (2001) refers to the fourth perspective she delineates as neo-Aristotelian. She explains that Aristotle was particularly interested in the capabilities and functioning of organisms. Nussbaum describes the insights derived from the application of these conceptualizations to non-human animals as follows: "Every creature strives for a good, which is the exercise and maintenance of its characteristic form of life" (2001, 1535). In short, animals ought to be treated in ways that allow them to actualize their capabilities. The notion that problems arise when people and animals are thwarted from meeting their potential can also be traced back to the work of Karl Marx (Nussbaum 2004).

It is this perspective that Nussbaum herself advocates. She argues, "animals are subjects who have entitlements to flourishing, and who thus are subjects of justice, not just objects of compassion" (2004, 307). She envisions this perspective as sharing some common ground with the previous three perspectives discussed. More specifically, in focusing on individual capabilities, this perspective would treat animals as ends instead of means, which is consistent with the Rawlsian and rights-based approaches, although not necessarily the utilitarian. It also diverges from the utilitarian approach in that it includes harms that individuals are not (yet) aware of within its purview, whereas utilitarianism does not necessarily include those harms in its calculations of the greater good.

What this perspective does share with the utilitarian approach is that it does not deal in absolutes: subjecting an individual to harm is not necessarily wrong. For utilitarians, harm can be justified in the interests of the greater good. From a neo-Aristotelian approach, what an outsider may perceive as harm may be tolerated if it does not negatively impact an individual's ability to live up to its capabilities (Nussbaum 2001). For instance, ownership and confinement of an animal is not necessarily unethical, according to this perspective, as long as that animal is able to flourish in line with his/her capabilities.

Nussbaum (2004) suggests that an advantage of this approach is that while it is concerned with the wellbeing of individuals, it also concerns itself with wellbeing at a larger aggregate level, such as species, because harms at that level can negatively impact capabilities at the individual level. She recommends further developing this perspective by examining and clarifying the capabilities of groups of animals, and states that the focus should be on the wellbeing of animals deemed capable of suffering. Although she is not adverse to the use of rights language to ensure that individual capabilities are satisfied, she argues that "the language of rights needs articulation and clarification via the language of capabilities" (2001, 1538). To this end, she provides a list of ten things animals are entitled to (e.g., life, emotions) (see Nussbaum 2004). Access to these entitlements would enable animals to actualize their capabilities. Whether an individual has the ability to flourish would be assessed within the context of their species.

The critiques of this perspective have ranged from the very specific to the very broad and general. In terms of the latter, Singer (2002), among others, has argued that the neo-Aristotelian approach Nussbaum articulates does not provide a unique ethical approach. More specifically, Nussbaum is critiqued for not providing a mechanism for evaluating the importance of various capabilities. For instance, humans generally have the capability to play a musical instrument. Does this capability translate into an entitlement to have access to opportunities to do so? Clearly, this could be problematic.

The feminist approach

There is another perspective that, although Nussbaum does not explicitly address it in her categorization, is worthy of consideration. Feminist theorists and activists argue that the philosophical perspectives described above have, to varying degrees, distanced themselves from emotion and kinship in articulating their bases for ethical concern for animals. Josephine Donovan (1990) singles out Singer and Regan as being guilty of this, writing, "Regan's and Singer's rejection of emotion and their concern about being branded sentimentalist are not accidental; rather, they expose the inherent bias in contemporary animal rights theory toward rationalism, which, paradoxically, in the form of Cartesian objectivism, established as a major theoretical justification for animal abuse" (351). Conversely, feminists such as Donovan (1990), Carol Adams (1994), and Mary Midgley (1998) argue that the emotional connectedness between people and animals should form the foundation of our ethical obligations to them. They have also critiqued rights-based discourses for promoting individualism, which undercuts a focus on community and communal wellbeing (Donovan 1990). Feminists further question the efficacy of rights, pointing out that even the institutionalization of women's rights has not ended their victimization, so it seems unlikely that it would be able to do so for animals (Mackinnon 2004).

Feminists who adopt an intersectional lens in analyzing the (ab)use of animals argue that women and animals have been similarly situated with respect to the constructed culture/nature dichotomy: both have been more closely associated with the bodily and the nature side of this dichotomy, whereas the cultural has been the realm of (particularly white) men. As discussed in the Introduction, both sides of this binary have not been treated equally: the cultural has been privileged over nature. This has negatively affected women and animals, as well as the environment. Solutions, therefore, are not to be found by more closely aligning with the cultural side; instead, the dichotomy itself and its associated negative impacts must be challenged (Donovan 1990; Fitzgerald and Pellow 2014). There is some affinity here between the feminist position on animal ethics and environmentalism in that both emphasize holism over individualism and the concerns of both are positioned on the nature side of the culture/nature dualism.

While the other perspectives have rather clear rules for determining the proper treatment of animals, the feminist perspective emphasizes community and caring, and has accordingly been critiqued as being abstract and vague. The connection between the oppression of women and animals, as well as other denigrated groups, has also been critiqued for devaluing women by connecting them with nature and for essentializing women (Jackson 1993; Stange 1997), although the latter critique really only pertains to a very narrow articulation of this perspective.

Each of these perspectives has its strengths and limitations, and they are still works in progress. As Nussbaum explains, "our major philosophical theories in this area are still relatively undeveloped, and we have not defined very clearly the conceptual framework we should use to articulate philosophically what sympathy tells us in our lives" (Zool, 1511–1512). Nevertheless, these perspectives have all been successful in providing intellectual inspiration for the AAM. Their resonance with the general public in practice, however, is likely limited (Posner 2004), and some commentators have suggested more "pragmatic" approaches to determining how we should treat animals. For instance, Dutch scholars Kupper and

Buning (2011) recommend public deliberations where differing values vis-à-vis animals could be expressed. It should be noted, however, that having a majority group deliberate the treatment of a minority group could be problematic.

Alternatively, public education about the current treatment of animals in various contexts (e.g., as food, scientific subjects) could go quite a distance in fostering empathy, which Posner (2004) argues would translate into a greater willingness to spend more on products and in-kind responses from companies. He argues that the practice of pet keeping should propel the cause forward. Similarly, Tuohey and Ma (1992, 88) locate the successes of the movement thus far in pet keeping instead of philosophical works.

Even though they may not be garnering a lot of attention among the public, these philosophical perspectives have directly and indirectly informed the different threads within the AAM. Each of these factions brings with it different strategies for improving the wellbeing of animals. It is these camps within the movement, to which we now turn, that members of the public are more likely to be familiar.

The threads within the animal advocacy movement

There are a few ways that the threads or camps within the AAM have been parsed in the literature (for example, see Jasper and Nelkin 1992; Munro 2012). Three distinct groups tend to be singled out, although the terminology used to describe them varies. Each of these groups is examined in turn below, making explicit how they are connected to the philosophical perspectives discussed in the previous section.

There is rather widespread agreement on the first category: animal welfarists. Welfarists accept most uses of animals, but nonetheless advocate for minimizing their suffering. Their strategies for achieving that goal are reformist; that is, they do not seek to overthrow or drastically change the current system. Instead, they seek to work within the system and advocate strategies such as public education and legislative changes (Jasper and Nelkin 1992;

Munro 2012). They also tend to concern themselves exclusively with species of animals where sentience has been demonstrated (Anderson 2004). The contractarian perspective discussed in the previous section is connected with aspects of this approach, such as objection to extreme cases of animal cruelty but not necessarily a problematization of institutionalized forms of animal harm.

Different terms are used in the literature to identify the second group of animal advocates, although there is general agreement on the characteristics of this group. Jasper and Nelkin (1992) refer to this group as pragmatists; others refer to them as animal liberationists (Munro 2012). This group seeks to place more limits on the use of animals than the welfarists, but are willing to allow the use of animals if the benefits outweigh the drawbacks. From this perspective then, there could be circumstances where keeping animals in captivity or testing on them could be acceptable. They also draw distinctions along species lines for determining what protections ought to be in place. For instance, primates would be more entitled to protections than birds. The utilitarian position is often associated with this faction of the AAM because of its weighing of benefits and drawbacks to determine what is ethical. Nussbaum's capabilities approach could also fit here because of its deliberate examination of what each species needs in order to flourish.

The final group is variously referred to as the fundamentalists (Jasper and Nelkin 1992), animal rightists, or abolitionists (Munro 2012).[4] They argue that like people, animals have intrinsic rights. They therefore disagree with any use of animals that results in harm and advocate for the immediate abolition of the use of animals instead of gradual, incremental changes. Because abolition of animal uses is unlikely to occur through reformist measures (at least in the short term), proponents of this perspective employ strategies external to the system, such as protests. The animal rightist philosophical position discussed above is most closely aligned with this perspective. To date, the AAM has been most generally associated with this thread within the movement.

The more decidedly radical animal advocacy groups would, at least conceptually, belong to this latter thread of the movement. In the pursuit of abolition of the use of animals, some groups have turned to direct, illegal actions. The most notorious of these groups is ALF – the Animal Liberation Front. The group has its origins in Britain, although it is loosely organized. For instance, cells are self-organized and individuals can claim to be affiliated with the group without any formalized connections. Further, those acting on behalf of the organization do not always take credit for their actions. Therefore, there is no way to know truly how many actions the organization has really undertaken. One thing that is apparent is that people have rarely been harmed in the execution of ALF actions. There has only been one known assassination committed in the name of animal advocacy: in 2002, Pim Fortuyn, a right-wing politician in the Netherlands, was killed by an activist, apparently targeted due to his support of animal use industries (Munro 2005). As a whole, the movement has been decidedly anti-violence, with few activists surveyed endorsing violence (Munro 2005). The most commonly used tactic in the movement is demonstrations, and most people are recruited into the movement via very mainstream activities, such as being given educational materials or through advertising.

So which approach is preferable?

As with the philosophical positions discussed earlier, there has been much debate over which of the threads of animal advocacy is preferable conceptually and strategically, and some of the debate has been quite heated. The animal welfare position has been criticized conceptually for failing to problematize and challenge speciesism. But proponents of this perspective argue that the reformist strategies of animal welfarism are the most effective and expedient way to make positive changes in the lives of animals, regardless of theoretical limitations (e.g., Posner 2004). Further, Favre (2004) has argued that the debate over the efficacy of animal welfarism is what is holding the movement back; he writes, "It is a burden of the animal rights movement that so many of its leaders will support only the purest philosophical position, regardless of political feasibility" (236).

Others believe that the animal liberationist position is preferable because it provides a mid-range perspective between what some perceive as the extremes of the welfarist and rightist positions. They also believe that it is through this middle-ground positioning that the movement is most likely to forge allegiances with other movements because "Animal liberationists frame speciesism as a social problem comparable to sexism and racism and other forms of intraspecies exploitation and so are amenable to coalition-building with progressive social movements such as social justice, consumer, public health and environmental groups" (Munro 2012, 172).

Finally, some point to the abolitionist thread of the movement as the most likely to make real changes in the way animals are treated. They reason that working within the current system, as the welfarist and liberationist perspectives do to varying degrees, is unlikely to result in fundamental change to the uses of animals within society, and that the only real way to do so is to challenge the system itself. Further, they point to animal welfare tweaks as not only unlikely to result in significant changes but also as actually perpetuating the system (see Francione 1996; 2010).

Quite commonly in popular discourses, including those in the media, the AAM is reduced to this third group and the nuances within the movement are glossed over. More problematically, there is a perception that animal advocates are "radical" and even dangerous. Munro points to the media in particular as perpetuating this gross overgeneralization: "In the UK and North America, where animal rights activities are most in evidence, the media typically frame the campaigns as the actions of violent extremists or terrorists, and in so doing support the backlash against animal rights by animal-user industries" (2012, 174). This perception can lead to the claims of the movement being easily dismissed in the minds of some.

It should be noted, however, that perceived radicalism among a portion of a social movement could also have positive consequences. In the 1980s, Herbert Haines coined the term "radical flank effect" and theorized that the existence of a radical faction within a movement could have positive impacts on an extant moderate faction by making it seem more reasonable and influencing the public and government to cede to some of the their demands in order to hold off the more radical faction. Some of his research bore this out (Haines, 1984, 32). There are other insights from the more general literature on social movements that can be useful in analyzing the AAM and assessing what the best strategies might be.

Understanding animal advocacy as a social movement

Compared to other social movements, the AAM has received relatively little research attention (for a notable recent exception, see Cherry 2016). Munro (2012) goes so far as to suggest that it is "one of the most misunderstood and understudied social movements of our era" (177). The information we do have about the movement is in some cases partial and provisional. Three areas where the research has focused, and where I think conclusions can be safely drawn, include (1) membership in the movement, (2) how the movement can be classified in the context of other social movements, and (3) what strategies have been usefully employed by the movement. Each of these clusters of research are discussed in turn below.

Who are animal advocates and activists?

First, it is important to make a distinction between who advocates and activists are, because these can be two distinct roles. Advocates or supporters are a larger segment of the population concerned about animal issues: these are the individuals who support the goals of the movement. Activists are a smaller subset of this population: they are the individuals who are more involved in the movement and expend more resources on it.

The sociodemographic characteristics of movement supporters appear significantly different from those of its constituent activists. Animal activists tend to be white with backgrounds of fairly high socioeconomic status (Munro 2012; Lowe and Ginsberg 2002), whereas supporters are less likely to be white, middle-aged, and well educated (Jerolmack 2003; Franklin et al. 2001). Thus, support for animal rights appears to be more dispersed across the population than is activism for the cause (Jerolmack 2003; Franklin et al. 2001; Uyeki, 2000) and the voices of the movement (i.e., authors and leaders) have tended to come from privileged backgrounds. They have been critiqued for failing to be reflexive about their positioning and privilege, and for leaving some groups feeling unrepresented and marginalized (Harper 2012; Pellow 2013).

Activism and support for the AAM is quite gendered, although it has become less so in recent years. From 1990 to 1996, the proportion of female activists at a given national US animal rights event dropped from 80 percent to 76 percent in Plous's (1998) sample and 77 percent to 74 percent in Galvin and Herzog's (1998) sample. Despite evidence of a slow shift, the research still indicates that there is a large and statistically significant difference between men and women in participation rates. Supporters of the movement also tend to be female, and among the general public women tend to display more pro-animal attitudes (Herzog 2007).

Research has also documented commonalities in the reasons given for joining the movement. Lowe and Ginsberg (2002) found in their sample that the most commonly reported reason was that the adoption of an ethical vegan/vegetarian diet made the movement attractive to them (64 percent). The second and third most common reasons are that they had been drawn in by companion animal issues (29 percent) and the use of animals in experiments (28 percent), respectively.

Many animal advocates also share an affinity with the EM. When asked to rank social movements according to favourability in one study, animal advocates ranked the EM most favourably, followed by the feminist movement (Jamison and Lunch, 1992). Interestingly, however, examination of a nationally representative sample in the US found that when other variables are controlled for, the relationship between support for environmentalism and animal advocacy becomes insignificant for men (Kruse 1999). The author of the study concludes that this finding "provides some support for an ecofeminist perspective that seeks to link the oppression of women, animals, and nature to promote both pro-environmental and pro-animal activism among women" (Kruse 1999, 193). In addition to overlap among some supporters of the AAM and the EM, the two movements also share some general social movement characteristics.

What type of movement is the animal advocacy movement?

The EM and the AAM have both been categorized as New Social Movements (NSMs) (Marangudakis, 2002; Mertig and Dunlap, 2001). These social movements are different from movements that emerged prior to the 1960s in that those movements were more class-based and policy oriented. The NSMs, conversely, are said to be post-citizenship and post-materialist movements because their goals are not necessarily political and participants do not stand to gain personally from the movement. Instead, participation is said to be altruistic (Munro 2012; Lowe and Ginsberg 2002). Others (e.g., Barker and Dale 1998; Calhoun 1993) recommend tempering claims that these movements are dramatically different from earlier movements, pointing out that movements in the late eighteenth and nineteenth century contained many of the elements purported to be distinctive to the NSMs, including a focus on identity politics, articulating specific demands instead of utopian notions of widespread fundamental social change, and the "politicization of everyday life" (Calhoun 1993, 398).

There is also a debate over whether NSMs are truly detached from class-based foundations (which would set them squarely apart from many earlier social movements) or if NSMs are comprised mainly of people situated in a "new class": highly educated and employed in white-collar jobs, but not necessarily high-income (Mertig and Dunlap 2001). In their comparative examination of Western European countries and the US, Mertig and Dunlap (2001) found that membership in this new class only predicted statistically significant support for environmentalism or several other NSMs in Norway. Moreover, when they looked at income as a measure of class, they found that it was a better predictor of NSM membership, including environmental and animal rights, although generally in the negative direction, meaning that lower income is associated with higher membership, which runs counter to what has generally been assumed.

As discussed earlier, AAM activists have tended to be less diverse than supporters. Within the EM, mainstream environmental activists (e.g., those concerned with conservation issues) have tended to be middle- and upper-class whites; however, the environmental justice wing of the movement that has taken shape over the past few decades has been more representative of the working class and people of colour (Agyeman et al., 2016). Nevertheless, coalition building between the environmental and animal advocacy movements, as advocated herein, would need to draw on critical environmental justice / ecofeminism / total liberation perspectives, grounded in the importance of inclusion and intersectionality, in order to avoid replicating the sociodemographic limitations of earlier activism within both movements (see Pellow 2013).

What strategies has the movement employed?

Research indicates that NSMs are less inclined to use violence to achieve their campaign goals than previous social movements were. This is a strategic decision, as it is believed that governments and the media are less inclined to support causes associated with violence, and that they will be met with repression by the state (Munro 2005). The AAM also fits in as a NSM in this respect as it has been mostly nonviolent. It should be noted, though, that not using violence does have drawbacks. The difficult situation this poses for the movement is aptly described by Munro (2005, 79): "On the one hand, animal rights activists need the media to promote their call for the compassionate treatment of animals; on the other, the media need dramatic footage and headlines which violence and threats of violence provide, albeit… as a moral cost to the movement."

Munro (2005) also provides a useful categorization of the most common strategies within the movement. He identifies two main categories: publicity and interference. Publicity strategies include persuasion (e.g., pamphleting) and protest (e.g., picketing, vigils). Interference strategies in turn include noncooperation (e.g., boycotts) and intervention (e.g., monkey wrenching). There is not a vast amount of research to draw on here, but based on what has been published, it appears that support in the movement for illegal actions in the latter category above declined in the 1990s (Plous 1998; Gavin and Herzog 1998).

The movement has also had to strategize about which goals to prioritize. Due to the myriad ways in which animals are used and harmed worldwide, there are many areas where the movement could focus, and there are no easy answers to where it should focus. Some would point to where the largest number of animals are harmed; others would point to where victories might be easily and quickly won. Historically, animal testing was prioritized within the movement, but over time it has been eclipsed by concern regarding animal agriculture. Plous (1998) noted a statistically significant increase from the proportion of activists she surveyed in 1990 and six years later who ranked animal agriculture as their top priority, increasing from 24 to 48 percent. Much of this gain was at the cost of the issue of animal testing.

Some would argue that this is an effective shift in priorities because more animals are harmed by animal agriculture. Yet based on her research findings, Einwohner (1999b) argues that potential for success is a critical consideration, especially for a movement with limited resources. In her study she examined campaigns against hunting, experimentation, circuses, and fur, and concludes, "The possibilities that exist for changing these practices are shaped by two factors: the extent to which the practices are seen as *necessary* by those who engage in them; and the extent to which the practices are defined as *central* to individuals' lives" (171). The circus and fur campaigns enjoyed relative success, which Einwohner attributes at least partially to opportunities: these practices are rather peripheral in the lives of participants. Conversely, the hunting and experimentation campaigns were not as successful; these practices enjoy structural support, participants are highly committed, and alternatives are limited. As well, hunters and experimenters are more cohesive and powerful groups, and their practices are less successfully challenged than those of less powerful groups are. She concludes, in short, that "not all political issues are created equally" (Einwohner 1999b, 179). Brian Luke (2007) makes a similar point in asserting that the AAM has enjoyed successes in realms of animal use that are primarily related to women's interests and consumerism, such as fur and cosmetics testing.

The movement also needs to be strategic about recruiting new members. This is another area where the extant research can be quite helpful. One thing that sets the AAM apart from many other social movements[5] is that recruitment through friends or family is not very common (see Jasper and Poulsen 1995); Lowe and Ginsberg (2002) report that in their survey of animal advocates only 9 per cent were recruited that way. It should be noted, however, that vegetarians/vegans are commonly recruited through social networks (Maurer 2002), and because for many people their first foray into animal advocacy is abstention from animal products, this indirect route of recruitment could be more important than alluded to by the 9 percent statistic cited above. A much larger proportion (58 percent) were motivated to join by material they read or saw. More than three-quarters of participants considered books and pamphlets effective in recruiting, and 60 percent felt videos were effective. Jasper and Poulsen (1995) found even greater numbers reported the importance of reading among their sample: 72 percent reported it was very important and 19 percent indicate it was somewhat important to their recruitment into the movement. More up-to-date research, including an examination of the impacts of social media, is needed.

Visual materials are particularly useful for the AAM, particularly shocking images (Jasper and Nelkin 1992). Such representations can be referred to as moral shocks and mind bombs. These shocks are described as "an event or situation [that] raises such a sense of outrage in people that they become inclined toward political action, even in the absence of a network of contacts. These are usually public events, unexpected and highly publicized" (Jasper and Poulsen 1995, 498). The AAM is certainly not alone in using shocking imagery to recruit members, but it does rely on it quite heavily given that it cannot rely on recruitment through exist-ing networks as much as other movements can. Animal issues also lend themselves quite easily to this type of strategy because the images send a simple message: it is easy to interpret how the animal captured in the image is feeling. As they say in the litera-ture, they are good "condensing symbols" (Jasper and Poulsen 1995, 495).

Nonetheless, there is a fine line between successful and coun-terproductive shocks. A study of the response of members of the public to advertisements by People for the Ethical Treatment of Animals (PETA) found participants reacted negatively to several types of ads, most specifically those that challenged their cultural beliefs, religious beliefs, or patriotism, and those drawing connec-tions between the treatment of animals and the treatment of people (e.g., slavery). In short, the findings suggest that moral shocks are useful up to the point of challenging the values and behaviours of the recipients, which is certainly tricky when it comes to animal issues. The author concludes, "it could be that moral shock cam-paigns are ineffective when promoting vegetarianism, because condemning meat consumption (as opposed to other violations of animal rights) inevitably forces people to confront their own behaviour" (Mika 2006, 932).

Complicating matters further, the ads that research participants responded most positively to also receive the least amount of attention from participants (Mika 2006). This places these social movement organizations in a difficult predicament, which leads the author of the study to pose this question: "Is it preferable to get noticed in a negative way or not at all? The latter seems to hold virtually no potential for recruiting members. The former may not fare much better, but holds at least some potential for being part of a long process of conversion and recruitment" (Mika 2006, 933). Her conclusion is that animal advocacy groups need to tailor their advertising to the specific audience they are targeting.

Further evidence of the importance of considering the audi-ence in campaign strategizing is provided by Einwohner's (1999a; 1999b; 2002) work. Her ethnographic research on anti-hunting and anti-circus campaigns documented an important identity interaction between the activists and their targets. Although the gender and class composition of the activists was similar in both campaigns, the targets (hunters) of the anti-hunting campaign made significant class- and gender-based assumptions about the activists, likely because they were more conscious of their own relatively homogenous gender and class than were the more heterogeneous circus attendees. The result was that hunters focused on the gender and class statuses of the activists, which deflected attention away from their message, whereas the circus attendees were more receptive to their message because less of an "us versus them" dynamic was created (Einwohner 1999a). Thus, the content of the message and the way it is delivered are not the only important considerations: who is delivering the message vis-à-vis the target is also important.

Another strategy for recruiting promoted by some activists is to appeal to other movements. At its base, the AAM is grounded in a critique of instrumentalism. It shares this with many other movements, particularly the EM, as well as society more broadly. Jasper and Poulsen (1995) suggest this as a good starting place, and one that can unite movements: "Fear, anxiety and outrage against instrumentalism are common themes to modern societies and make good starting points for many framing efforts" (503). Findings from a survey of animal advocates indicate that not only are activists interested in more harmony within the movement, they are also interested in working with environmental organizations (Galvin and Herzog 1998).

Academics have also voiced their support for coalition-building between movements, even though some have suggested that there can be challenges to maintaining a common identity in a movement once others are included. Pellow (2013) has noted both the challenges and the potential for productive alliances between the environmental justice movement and AAM, and Warren (2000) has argued in favour of building bridges between the AAM and EM more generally, stating, "a harmonious marriage between these two approaches is possible, provided that each side is prepared to make certain compromises" (p. 172). Munro (2012) points out that such a union could be particularly advantageous to the AAM because it has goals that are large, numerous, and geographically diverse. In their classic book on the AAM, Jasper and Nelkin (1992) go so far as to assert that coalition building with other movements "could prove crucial to the future of animal rights" (53). Therefore, strategically, it might make good sense to build coalitions, most especially with the EM. Nevertheless, practically speaking, several things must be taken into consideration, including the historic divide between the movements.

Sources of discord between the animal advocacy movement and the environmental movement

As discussed in the Introduction, there is a long history of division between the environmental and AAMs that was articulated by philosopher J. Baird Callicott in his 1980 article, wherein he concluded that the differences between the movements were irreconcilable. Nevertheless, eight years later he declared in another article that the differences between the movements could – and should – be overcome, and that the energy expended on philosophical debates between the movements should instead be devoted to bettering the environment and the animals therein. That article received much less attention. I also introduced four characteristics that I think have set the movements apart: they employ different levels of analysis, the AAM has been quite gendered, the AAM has had a much more antagonistic relationship with science than the EM, and the AAM has been depicted as being much more radical than the EM. I would like to close this chapter by interrogating each of these purported differences in light of the material just discussed, and in doing so, chart a way forward for these two movements.

The claim that the movements employ different levels of analysis is accurate, to a degree. In this chapter, we discussed at length the philosophical differences within the AAM. The animal rightist and abolitionist perspectives can certainly be at odds with the holism of environmentalism. The topic of invasive species is instructive in this regard. If a non-native species of fish is introduced to a body of water, it can pose serious environmental problems. It may out-compete other species of fish for food sources, or introduce diseases to the native fish populations. Environmentalists and environmental scientists may advocate for killing the invasive fish to stem the problems. The goal of the environmentalist is to preserve the larger ecosystem. An animal advocate adopting a purist animal rightist/abolitionist perspective would argue that such a cull is unethical because it violates the rights of the individual fish that will be killed. In short, the wellbeing of the system does not outweigh the rights of the individual.

Other perspectives within the AAM, however, could be reconciled with the environmentalist approach here. The wellbeing of the larger ecosystem could be taken into consideration in the utilitarian calculation aimed at maximizing wellbeing while minimizing harm. If the proliferation of the invasive fish species is going to cause several other species of fish to starve to death, then the decision to institute a cull may be ethical from this perspective. However, it should be emphasized that, as Singer (1974; 1990) argued, the interests of animals are to be weighed in this calculation alongside those of humans. Therefore, it would not be ethical to institute a cull to eliminate the invasive species if the reason for doing so is simply that people do not like the way it tastes and its dominance in this body of water is therefore an inconvenience to fishers.

The neo-Aristotelean capabilities perspective articulated by Nussbaum (2004) can also be consistent with the environmental perspective here. She explicitly states that the wellbeing of larger aggregate levels, such as species, are of interest to this perspective because harms at that level can negatively impact the ability of individuals to flourish and fulfil their capabilities. The feminist perspective also lends itself to more of an environmental approach in a situation like this because it tends to emphasize holism over individualism, complete with its focus on how the culture/nature dichotomy negatively impacts those associated with the nature side (Donovan, 1990; Fitzgerald and Pellow, 2014). Therefore, the divide between the movements caused by different levels of analytic focus is not as wide as one might think; however, if the

AAM is associated strictly with the animal rightist/abolitionist perspective then the divide would appear potentially unbridgeable.

Related to the differing levels of analysis favoured by the two movements is the thorny issue of "rights," which has been a particularly strong point of contention between the EM and the AAM. There are two aspects of the discourse of rights that has set the two movements apart. The first is that the AAM has been painted with the broad brush of rights-based claims in popular discourse. As demonstrated herein, however, some within the movement do not actually advocate a rights-based platform, although – to add to this confusion – many do use the term "rights" as a short form for what they are advocating, even though they may not be proponents of a rights-based strategy per se.

Additionally, the environmental position has been depicted as being irreconcilable with a rights-based approach. Yet, in recent years, scholars have increasingly argued that a rights-based approach may be useful in protecting human health and wellbeing, and the environment by extension (see, for instance, Hayward 2004; Bullard 2000; Boyle and Anderson 1998). At the time of this writing, the Canadian government is considering including language about citizens having a right to a healthy environment in the Canadian Environmental Protection Act.

I have also proposed that the gender composition of environmental science and the AAM may have played a role in sustaining a divide between the movements. The environmental sciences have been dominated by men (Rocheleau et al. 1996), although the EM has not been as gendered. The AAM, however, has been populated mainly by women (Herzog 2007), and concern about animal issues among the public has tended to be gendered feminine as well. In turn, concern about animal issues has been commonly derided as sentimental. As discussed in this chapter, however, the composition of the movement has been shifting in recent years, with more men becoming involved. As more men become involved, the perception of concern for animals as being "merely sentimental" may lose its salience. Further, as more women enter science, technology, engineering, and math (STEM) fields, such as environmental science, we may observe more concern for animals permeating disciplinary boundaries. That is not to say that there are essential differences between men and women that will be responsible for these changes, but instead differential socialization and structural positioning have shaped and been shaped by how gender is socially constructed.

As discussed in this chapter, there has been a perceptible shift in the target priorities of the AAM. Whereas targeting the use of animals in research had been a priority, there has been a shift to focusing on industrial animal agriculture (IAA). This, of course, does not mean that all activists and organizations are focused on this specific issue, but instead that there has been a shift at the aggregate level. This may serve to ease the perception that the AAM is anti-science, as will efforts to engage with the scientific community via the ongoing establishment of centres for alternatives to animal models in science internationally, which may in turn open more opportunities for working with an EM that has largely been connected very closely with science. Chapter 5 focuses specifically on what the shift to focusing on IAA could mean for the AAM and its relationship with the EM.

Finally, I asserted in the last chapter that the AAM has been associated with its "radical" fringe more than the EM has been. Further, the association with radicalism might have dissuaded some environmentalists from also aligning themselves with the AAM. There is reason to think, however, that this is becoming less of an issue as animal advocacy, for better or worse, employs illegal tactics less often and is becoming more mainstream. Recent successful ballot initiatives in the US, banning gestation crates for pigs and battery cages for chickens, indicate that public support for at least some animal causes is increasing. In Canada, the province of Quebec, which has one of the worst legal track records for animal welfare in the Western world, recently passed a bill that formally recognizes animals as sentient beings (*Globe and Mail* 2015). There are also pieces of legislation in place in the UK that recognize animal sentience (World Animal Protection 2014). Political parties devoted specifically to animal advocacy have emerged, such as the Animal Welfare Party in the UK and the Party for the Animals (Partij voor de Dieren) in the Netherlands. This type of institutionalization, which may make some animal activists shudder, may resonate well with the mainstream EM.

This chapter has demonstrated that while there has been a historic divide between the EM and the AAM, this divide is certainly not insurmountable, and, in fact, there are several reasons why changes internal and external to both movements may be serving to narrow this divide. Additionally, there is much variation within the AAM, and its relationship with the EM is often much more nuanced than is often depicted. Although there are still noteworthy divides between the two movements, they do share much in common. Rollin (1988) articulates this simultaneous tension and potential as follows:

> Those who give primacy to animals have tended to deny the moral significance of environments and species as direct objects of moral concern, whereas those who give moral primacy to environment-ecological concern tend to deny or at least downplay the moral significance of individual animals. Significant though these differences are, they should not cloud the dramatic nature of this common attempt to break out of a moral tradition that finds loci of value only in human beings, and derivatively, in human institutions. (p. 125)

Both movements – particularly in their challenge to anthropocentrism – are potentially revolutionary. This synergetic potential may have been dampened by perceived insurmountable differences between the two, but the analyses of three specific cases where the two movements have been notoriously at odds – sport hunting, zoos, and fur – conducted in the next three chapters provides evidence that the synergetic potential remains nonetheless, and that a view to the larger social context makes actualizing it appear even more likely.

2

Sport Hunting:
Environmental Stewardship,
Cultural Ritual, or Blood Sport?

A lion died on July 1, 2015. This may not seem like big news, but it was at the time. Several factors in this case made it newsworthy, at least in many Western countries. This lion had a name: Cecil. He was a relatively rare black-maned lion and reportedly lived primarily in a national park in Zimbabwe. Cecil was apparently a favourite among park tourists. He was also being tracked as part of study of wildlife in the area. What was even more noteworthy was the way Cecil died. A trophy hunter from the US killed him, apparently after luring Cecil out of the park.

Once news of Cecil's death spread (particularly via social media) people began picketing outside of the hunter's dental practice in Minnesota. He was forced to close his practice until the furor died down. The hunter ultimately was not charged with any crimes, but two of his guides were charged with using bait to lure Cecil out of the park to his death (Dzirutwe 2015). The incident sparked an international discussion about the ethics and environmental impacts of trophy hunting. It also at least indirectly spurred legal changes in some countries.

The US Endangered Species Act was modified to include southern and east African lions as threatened species. This new designation would make importing trophies from these hunted animals into the US significantly more difficult. France instituted an outright ban on lion trophies, and Britain announced a ban that began in 2017. Private companies also made changes in response to the outcry over the incident: dozens of airlines announced that they would no longer carry hunting trophies for customers (Goode 2015).

Although many lauded and celebrated these actions, some voiced concern that these restrictions would ultimately harm conservation efforts funded through hunting licenses, as well as locals who depend on the direct and spin-off revenue generated by the activity. Who is right? There is no quick answer to that question. At the heart of it lies a debate about the ecological and economic utility of sport hunting, as well as the ethics of killing animals for sport. This chapter provides an entrée into this debate – a debate that has been central to the divide between the EM and the AAM, perhaps since the inception of both.

The chapter begins with an examination of different types of hunting, the history of sport hunting, and the motivations behind it. We then move into a discussion of environmental ethics related to hunting, and how and why animal advocates can find themselves at odds with some environmentalists on the topic. Subsequently the various reasons for and against sport hunting are detailed, and finally we discuss how the animal advocate and environmentalist positions on this issue might now be closer together than in the past, more so than has generally been assumed.

What is hunting?
(And why is the question important?)

There are many different types of, motivations for, and meanings associated with hunting. Failure to pay attention to these nuances risks conflating very different forms of hunting. As will be demonstrated in this chapter, these differences are important to articulating and better understanding the animal advocacy and environmentally informed positions on hunting.

Simply put, human hunting entails the predation and killing of wild animals. The act and the perceptions of it are shaped by at least three considerations: the techniques used, the type of animal hunted, and the motivation for the hunt. The latter two are most relevant to this chapter. Consideration of the type of animal hunted focuses on how "wild" the hunted animal is; for instance, some argue that even the killing of partially domesticated animals (such as those raised on game farms) should not be labelled hunting (Cahoone 2009). The purpose of or motivation behind hunting can be divided roughly into subsistence, commercial, and sport hunting. The goals of subsistence and commercial hunting (sustenance and income, respectively) are fairly straightforward. The definition of sport hunting is a little more difficult to nail down. The term was created to refer to the ethical, fair chase of an animal, and to differentiate it from commercial hunting (Heffelfinger et al. 2013), and by the more affluent to distinguish their activity from that of the rural poor (List, cited by Cahoone 2009). Use of the term "sport" to refer to hunting has more recently been problematized. It implies an even playing field that does not exist in hunting (see Kheel 1996). Other terms have been suggested, such as the cumbersome "neo-traditional cultural trophic practice" (Cahoone 2009).

This chapter is primarily focused on sport hunting, recognizing that the term is imperfect. It does, however, usefully exclude the killing of animals undertaken for profit and undertaken out of necessity for food. Although those motivations for hunting are important, they are beyond the purview of this chapter, as it is on the issue of sport hunting that the EM and the AAM have most significantly diverged. In order to understand the roots of this divergence it is necessary to at least briefly examine the history of sport hunting.

A brief history of sport hunting

Sport hunting in Western Europe was historically associated with the nobility (Dunk 2002; Franklin 1998). It was eventually instrumentalized as a tool in class-based protest and rebellion among the working class (Cartmill, 1993; Franklin 1998). In fact, one of the first things the revolutionary government in France did in the late eighteenth century was to remove the class-based restrictions on hunting (Dunk 2002). In North America, hunting was mainly used for acquiring food and killing pests, until approximately the 1830s, when English colonizers began promoting hunting as sport and recreation (Dunlap 1988; Muth and Jamison 2000). Hunting as a sport quickly became popular in the US, thanks to a confluence of factors: people had access to public lands for hunting, unlike in England where the wealthy controlled hunting access (Dunlap 1988; Muth and Jamison 2000); it was facilitated by narratives of rugged individualism and nationalism (Franklin 1998); it became an escape from modernization (Franklin 1998); increasing disposable income and leisure time made it more accessible (Franklin 1998; Kheel 1996); and Darwin's work on evolution in the nineteenth century made hunting more attractive to those desiring to reconvene with their "animal sides" (Franklin 1998).

Perspectives on sport hunting continue to vary geographically. Franklin (1998, 361) refers to the "nostalgic quality" of hunting in the US and Australia, which he suggests is connected to their histories of nation-building in sometimes challenging environments. In France, Britain, and the Netherlands, where hunting was associated with social elites, it has elicited more resentment. Perceptions of hunting are also shaped by how it has been regulated by the state. In Britain, hunting generally remained accessible only to those who could hunt on their own property and thus was largely a private activity. In the Netherlands, however, hunting regulations implemented in the 1950s made hunters responsible for conservation of lands and game species. As a result, hunting there has become more closely linked with conservation (Franklin 1998) and hunters are therefore more likely to be viewed favourably by the public. The connection between sport hunting and conservation, however, was borne somewhat out of necessity (although there is a philosophical grounding for it as well, discussed below). The situation in the US is a useful case in point.

The growing popularity of sport hunting, coupled with significant land access, extremely limited regulations, and increasingly advanced weaponry, resulted in dramatic wildlife population declines in the US by the 1870s (Dunlap 1988). Some species, such as the passenger pigeon, were extinguished completely. In response, a number of wildlife conservation laws were passed early in the twentieth century. The Federal Aid in Wildlife Restoration Act added an 11 percent tax on hunting weapons and ammunition. The proceeds were earmarked for conservation efforts; funds from this tax and hunting licenses have since their inception funded wildlife conservation projects to the tune of $12 billion (Card, 2012). This has been used to frame sport hunting as environmentally friendly, and even as an environmental necessity, by sport hunters, their organizations, hunting businesses, and government regulators in the US and elsewhere.

Ecological justifications for sport hunting have become increasingly important in recent decades, and have given rise to what Kheel (1995; 1996) refers to as the "holist hunter." Empirical research in diverse geographic locations has documented the pervasiveness of the "holist hunter" narrative. Among the hunters whom she interviewed and observed give testimony during public hearings, Einwohner (1999b, 176) notes that most framed their activity as an environmentally necessary form of "wildlife management." They also in turn depicted critiques of their activities by activists as anti-science, overly emotional, and originating in urban instead of rural realities.

Research conducted with hunters in six countries in Europe and Eastern Africa found that most participants labelled themselves as conservationists and believed that species and habitats would suffer without hunting. Even when other reasons for their activities (such as the desire for trophies, or for fun) were given, the participants argued that their main motivation was conservation. The authors acknowledge that it is difficult to know if, in doing so, hunters are communicating their true motivations, or if they are being strategic in framing their activity as environmentally important (Fischer et al. 2013). McLeod (2007) points to the latter in his research on duck hunting in New Zealand, writing that hunters "are increasingly finding that they must justify an activity their grandparents practiced without compunction" (151). Environmental utility has grown into a particularly powerful justification.

Justifications for sport hunting are becoming ever more important against the backdrop of declining participation. In Canada, the province of Quebec is concerned about the cultural impacts of the decline, and along with the federal government has examined ways to increase participation, including Hunter Apprenticeship programmes where children 12 years and up can hunt with adults (Dunk 2002). In the US, states such as Michigan created task forces to investigate how to protect and recruit more people into the activity (Fitzgerald, 2005a). Women, long underrepresented in the sport, have been the focus of targeted recruiting.

Academics have also contributed to the hunter-as-environmentalist narrative. In the wildlife management literature, the term "conservation hunting" has been adopted "to reflect the benefits to wildlife management and conservation and to the associated local wildlife–wildlife user relationship resulting from regulated recreational hunting programs" (Freeman and Wenzel 2006, 22). Philosophers have been making these connections for quite some time. We will turn to an examination of the philosophical writings on the subject shortly in order to better understand the grounding of the tension between animal advocates and some (but certainly not all) environmentalists on the subject of sport hunting. Before doing so, however, it is useful to draw some distinctions between the three groups under analysis here.

Sport hunters, environmentalists, and animal advocates

The EM, particularly the conservationist strand, has in general historically supported sport hunting and argued that the activity is a useful form of maintaining ecological balance. The large institutions of the movement and many of their key figures have long legacies of supporting hunting. For instance, the National Wildlife Federation was founded by famous hunter and writer, Aldo Leopold (Luke 2001). Another large organization, the Nature Conservancy, permits hunting and fishing on some of its land (Card 2012).

The relatively close relationship between hunters and the EM underwent some changes in the mid-twentieth century as the focus of the EM and the public's perception of hunting began to shift.

The hunting community points to the release of Disney's film *Bambi* in 1942 as marking a shift in public sentiment toward their sport. They suggest that the general messages viewers received from the film were that nature is a peaceful place and that humans are a dangerous force (Cartmill 1993; Muth and Jamison 2000), and more specifically that hunters are villains to be feared. They also point to increases in pet ownership, or what some refer to as the "cult of the pet" (Muth and Jamison 2000, 847), particularly among urban residents (Boglioli 2009), as affecting the public's attitudes towards animals and contributing to anthropomorphism that has harmed hunting. Increasing urbanization was also accompanied by a shift from utilitarian valuations of wildlife to more of a protectionist orientation (Dubois and Harshaw 2013).

The hunting community also points to the popularization of what they consider dubious science as contributing to anti-hunting sentiments. They argue that animal advocates have interpreted evolution "as dissolving the boundaries between humans and the nonhuman animal world" and that they have bought into "a science that is so heavily interpreted and popularized that conservation professionals may not even recognize it. It is the science that has been mediated through television 'documentaries,' news magazines, and popular books; a science that tells us that elephants weep from emotional deprivation" (Muth and Jamison 2000, 847). At the same time that anti-hunters are critiqued for accepting some scientific findings, they are depicted as anti-science and overly emotional (Paulson 2012).

While public sentiments towards hunting were changing, the mandate and composition of the EM were as well. In the 1960s, the movement began to shift away from a focus on conservation to toxics and pollution in the wake of Rachel Carson's *Silent Spring*. According to Card (2012), this marked the beginning of a cultural rift between hunters and environmentalists. He points to increasing urbanization, ascendancy of other issues of import to environmentalism (such as global climate change), controversies over guns, and the rise of the animal rights movement as pulling the EM and hunters apart.

While animal advocates may feel that the connection between

the EM and hunting advocates has been too close, to be fair, as indicated above, many hunting advocates feel that the contemporary EM has not paid enough attention to the potential benefits of hunting. In this vein, Paulson (2012, 60) states, "sustainable hunting remains a fringe area within global conservation advocacy." He asserts that environmental NGOs (non-governmental organizations) are particularly concerned about how supporting hunting will be perceived by donors, and therefore (publicly) limit their support. Against the backdrop of these social changes and tensions, the debate over sport hunting in the environmental ethics literature has continued to rage.

Environmental ethics and hunting

The morality of sport hunting is a key issue in environmental ethics – according to King, "because environmental ethics has emerged in contemporary philosophy as a response to the destructive consequences of human interventions in the natural world, hunting stands out *prima facie* in need of moral justification" (1991, 61). The debate that has ensued is about as lively and profound as academic debates get, and it has spilled over into the EM more generally. At the heart of the debate are two different worldviews and associated notions of where moral standing is properly located. On the one side are animal advocates, who argue that individual animals have moral standing (e.g., Regan 2004; Francione 2010). On the other side are ecocentrists who prioritize the wellbeing of the ecosystem over individual (animal) interests (see Wade 1990) and biocentrists who argue that nature has intrinsic value and therefore can trump the interests of individual animals, or humans for that matter (Halsey and White 1998).

Cahoone (2009) concisely sums up the differences between the environmentalist and animal advocacy perspectives as follows:

> Unlike the animal rights/welfare views, ecological ethics must hold that: the ecosystem, on which all members depend, and the species-roles in

that ecosystem, are more valuable than the individuals occupying them; the good of a complex organism, e.g., its ability to feel pain or be a "subject" of its life, can be trumped by the ecosystem role of less complex organisms, including vegetation and terrain or aquatic ecosystem features; wildness, as opposed to domestication, is a good; and even death, as the transfer of chemical energy among organisms, can be a good. (p. 69)

Animal advocates have certainly conceptualized animal death as a negative, particularly if it involves suffering. In contrast, some environmentalists argue that attempting to mitigate suffering and death can actually lead to ecologically destructive decision-making (Everett 2001). This is one of the main divisions between the respective movements.

In addition to arguing that hunting is natural and that it positively affects the environment directly by balancing animal populations, some argue that it also fosters pro-environmental sentiments more generally and indirectly. Jensen (2001) suggests that hunting can make people more environmentally virtuous, foster a sense of responsibility for one's actions, and can also generate interest in environment-related careers (Jensen 2001).

The "predator argument" is a relatively strong and more direct argument that environmentally focused hunters have used to demonstrate the ethical nature of their activity.[6] This argument has several derivations: one has been forcefully argued by philosopher J. Baird Callicott (1989), among others (e.g., Cahoone 2009). He argues that if we accept the argument that animals have rights, then we are morally obligated to intervene to prevent predator animals from killing prey. By extension, the argument goes, if it is moral for animals to eat other animals, then why would it be immoral for humans to do so? It is asserted that hunting is natural human activity. However, these and similar arguments overlook the fact that humans have been "self-domesticated," and therefore cannot be appropriately equated with natural predators (King 1991). Additionally, those who have interpreted hunting as natural behavior tend to be male hunters and philosophers (for an exception, see Stange 1997), thus representing only part of the picture.

Relatedly, Cahoone (2009) argues that hunters serve an environmental function by taking the place of natural predators and keeping animal populations under control. He also suggests that the claim by animal advocates that this type of predation is unethical is the most environmentally threatening aspect of animal advocacy. It is worth noting, however, that Cahoone, like many pro-hunters, does not go on to question why natural predators are largely absent in the first place. Moreover, hunting is not going to solve the overpopulation of some species of animals. Instead, it is "a logical extension of the instrumental and anthropocentric relation to nature which made a managed environment necessary in the first place" (King 1991, 82).

Others argue that hunting is ethical because in most cases death by a hunter results in less pain than death by an animal predator or by starvation (see Cahoone 2009; Dizard 1999). Cahoone (2009) does admit that hunting likely causes a more painful death than what he refers to as a "painless" death for domesticated animals killed for meat, although he does not appear to take into consideration the suffering endured by animals in IAA prior to their death.

The opposing view on the ethics of sport hunting tends to be painted with a broad brush by sport hunters. For instance, Gunn (2001) states that animal advocates accept killing animals only when it is a matter of human survival. Yet, as discussed earlier, from an animal welfare perspective, sport hunting may be justifiable in the absence of suffering, or at least if the suffering is minimized. There is also some potential leeway from a utilitarian perspective. Someone could argue from this perspective that the pleasure of hunting outweighs the pain of the victim in the case of a "clean kill"; however, as King (1991) points out, it is hard to determine how it weighs up against the harm caused to those connected to the victim. Peter Singer (1993) has stated that he could envision hunting being morally justified if the hunted animal population has exceeded the amount of food that can sustain it. It is the animal rights perspective that would have more of a resolute position on sport hunting. According to that perspective, just as we would not approve of the hunting of humans, the hunting of animals must be deemed unethical. From this perspective, the ecological status of a species is not relevant in determining the ethics of hunting. To this end, Rollin (1988) states, "Killing *any* ten Siberian tigers is no different than killing the *last* ten."

Even though not all environmentalists agree with sport hunting and not all animal advocates are diametrically opposed to it, the activity is still a wedge issue in the environmental ethics literature, marking it in opposition to animal advocacy. It will likely continue to be an issue of concern for the foreseeable future, at least partially because the population of predator animals has been decimated in so many regions that hunting and/or organized culls are viewed as inevitable in regulating prey species (Gunn 2001). In light of this, it is worth evaluating the specific environmental claims made in favour of sport hunting and those against as articulated by animal advocates.

Hunting as an environmental good

I focus here on what I consider to be the strongest pro-hunting arguments vis-à-vis environmental and animal wellbeing, aspects of which have already been introduced. There are three such arguments: that hunting is beneficial because it results in less pain and suffering and environmental degradation than IAA, that it generates revenue that aids conservation efforts, and that it directly supports conservation via population management. Each argument is examined in turn below.

Hunting versus agriculture: Less harm?

Many academics and hunters make the argument that hunting is a better way of procuring meat because at least the hunted animals experienced freedom instead of being confined in what are colloquially referred to as factory farms and referred to in the literature as confined/concentrated animal feeding operations (CAFOs) (Pardo and Prato 2005; Gunn 2001; Cahoone 2009). This argument does tend to assume the necessity of meat consumption. Beyond that, they are certainly correct that there is no freedom inside CAFOs; however, the death of domesticated farmed animals is regulated (although imperfectly), whereas the death of the hunted animal is not and s/he may suffer quite substantially in the absence of a "clean" kill shot.

A more unusual argument, and one that is not as vulnerable to the animal advocate claim above that meat eating is unnecessary in many regions, is that hunting results in less environmental destruction and animal deaths than the production of vegetable crops. The largest threat to wildlife is habitat loss, not hunting, and industrial agriculture (both meat and plant) is particularly destructive to wildlife habitats (Knezevic 2009). Further, the mass production of vegetables results in animal deaths through the land clearing process, the use of pesticides and fertilizers that contaminate the land and water, the use of machinery to prepare the land and harvest the plants, protecting the crops from wildlife, and via the use of energy forms (such as fossil fuels) that are harmful to animals (Cahone 2009). Of course, precise calculations of the number of animal lives taken as a result are not possible. Nonetheless, Cahoone (2009) concludes, *"it is very likely that agricultural production kills more animals than deer hunting per unit of nutrition"* (81; emphasis in original). He does concede that organic agriculture fares better, but points out that it is not immune to causing animal deaths either, as it still requires habitat loss and some form of crop protection.

Although we cannot determine the exact amount of environmental degradation and animal deaths attributable to industrial agriculture versus hunting, the above argument is a good reminder that industrialized agriculture is not innocent. Admittedly, hunting may be an easy target for animal advocates because there is a direct connection between participation and animal deaths, but there are many other forms of harm that are indirect or separated by time and space that also warrant critical attention. Hunting may also receive more critical attention because many of the hunted species are of the cute and cuddly variety (e.g., deer), whereas the animals harmed more directly by agriculture (e.g., rodents killed in the fields by machinery) may not be. Pro-hunters (e.g., Card 2012) have sought to juxtapose what they believe to be a sentimentality for cute animals among animal advocates against their more "rational" conservation of all species. As will be demonstrated in what follows, however, hunters are rather vulnerable to the critique that they protect some species over others as well.

Hunting revenue as conservation funding

In some countries, such as Canada and the US, sport hunting generates revenue via taxes on hunting supplies and licensing fees that is allocated to conservation efforts. Broadly speaking, this is referred to as the North American Model of Wildlife Conservation (Muth and Jamison 2000). It is celebrated in the wildlife management literature for having restored wildlife populations that were at risk prior to its adoption. One group of researchers writes,

> During the twentieth century, there arose a system of wildlife conservation in North America with an infrastructure supported by a unique environmental ethic so effective and exemplary that it defied political and historical expectations. It was remarkable that wildlife would be given such high priority in a culture where capitalism, free enterprise and private property rights are held in high esteem. (Heffelfinger et al. 2013, 389)

They go on to write, "Game populations are renewable resources that literally pay the bills for a far-reaching, comprehensive system of sustainable wildlife conservation that has proven itself superior to any other widely implemented model" (402). As a result of this perceived success, they say, other countries are being urged to adopt this model.

The amount of money generated from hunting taxes and fees is significant. Statistics from 2006 in the US, for instance, indicate that the tax on hunting, fishing, and weaponry purchases contributed $233 million to state wildlife agencies; hunting licenses generated an additional $612 million; and hunters made $313 million in donations. This adds up to approximately $1.2 billion in revenue for one year. In Canada, one yearly calculation put the tax revenue of hunting at $384 million (Heffelfinger et al. 2013).

In addition, hunters sometimes pay extremely high license fees to hunt rare and highly sought after animals. For instance, in the late 1990s, a hunter paid more than one million dollars for special licenses to hunt rams in Alberta, Canada (Coltman et al. 2003).

There are several ways that this revenue is used for conservation. First, it is used to pay for conservation officers and a substantial proportion of agency budgets. In the US and Canada, most of the wages paid to conservation officers are said to be funded by hunting and fishing taxes and fees. It is estimated that three-quarters of wildlife agencies' budgets are derived from those taxes and fees (Heffelfinger et al. 2013). Second, the monies support conservation through the purchase of land. In the province of British Columbia alone, for instance, every year $5–6 million from the revenue is used to purchase or restore lands. In the US, $58.5 million was allocated to the states and used to acquire 12.2 million acres of land between 2005 and 2009 (Heffelfinger et al. 2013). Third, the revenue is used to fund research. Heffelfinger and colleagues (2013) report that in the US in 2009, for instance, approximately $57 million was allocated to state wildlife agencies for research. These and similar figures have contributed to hunters having the reputation, at least in some circles, as "the largest organized group working to save wildlife" (Dunlap 1988, 51).

Hunting also has more indirect economic impacts. Money spent on lodging and transportation is one such example. These impacts are slightly more difficult to estimate. Findings from a Canadian survey in 1996 indicated that hunters spent $823 million related to their pursuit and contributed to 14,200 jobs. In the US, hunters spent $24.7 billion in 2006, which had a larger economic spinoff impact of $66.7 billion and contributed to almost 660,000 jobs (Heffelfinger et al. 2013). On the flipside, hunting interests estimated that the ban on fox hunting in the UK would cost 5,000 to 8,000 jobs (Pardo and Prato 2005), although it is unclear what the ultimate impact was.

The above statistics are often recited in the hunting literature without reference to the other side of the equation: the costs of hunting. These costs may include loss of other tourism dollars, for instance. An analysis of duck hunting in Southern Australia enumerates many associated costs, but concludes they do not outweigh the revenue generation, although these results cannot necessarily be generalized to other geographic locations and to other types of hunting (Bennett and Whitten 2003). What is incontrovertible is that sport hunting does generate a significant amount of money that is allocated for conservation efforts, and in the absence of the willingness of the state to provide similar funding, fiscal dependence on the activity has been the result.

Additional contributions are claimed in the context of developing countries. Hunting by tourists is said to stimulate the local economy and provide jobs that otherwise would not exist (Freeman and Wenzel 2006), jobs less environmentally harmful than livestock farming (Gunn 2001). For instance, tourism brought $1,250 million into the Tanzanian economy. Although this entire amount is not attributable to hunting, Benjaminsen and colleagues (2013) assert that most of it is wildlife-related tourism, a sizable proportion of which is hunting. It is also argued that having this economic value associated with wildlife provides an incentive for local populations and governments to conserve these animals (Paulson 2012), and provides a valuation that can be entered into cost–benefit calculations in making decisions about permitting development projects (Freeman and Wenzel 2006). This logic is used to rationalize even the controversial trophy hunting of big game animals, as articulated here by Freeman and Wenzel (see also Gunn 2001):

> Trophy hunting provides an excellent basis for developing conservation hunting programs. A conservation hunting program contributes to the short- and long-term viability of a wildlife population by generating incentives and a management system to support, and if required, restore, associated habitats and ecosystems. (2006, 22)

These arguments are not without their critiques. In some locations, the prioritization of preserving wildlife populations for tourists to hunt has resulted in the eviction of some human populations from their land and has banned their own subsistence hunting. This is one area where neoliberalism seems to be having mixed impacts.

It has had a positive effect in the context of oppressive regimes because power has been redistributed from the state, and more collective control over natural resources has resulted. However, there is a tipping point where local communities begin to experience dispossession as the natural resources increase in value (Benjaminsen et al. 2013). In short, as hunting by tourists has become increasingly profitable, the role of the state and private guide companies has increased at the expense of the autonomy of the local peoples. There are also concerns that trophy hunting in particular causes problems for the hunted species, discussed in detail shortly.

Hunting as environmental equalizer

Those who support hunting as a form of environmental management also argue that there is a more direct relationship between hunting and conservation: hunting of some species is required to keep their populations in check. They point to research indicating that when the population of large mammal species is greater than their habitat can sustain, it results in population declines due to drops in reproductive rates and increases in mortality. Hunting can therefore be useful because "reducing densities lessens competition and increases the population growth rate by improving reproduction and survival" (Heffelfinger et al. 2013, 401). Nonetheless, this can result in a vicious cycle, where populations increase because of hunting, thereby requiring greater population management.

Hunting is not only said to potentially benefit the hunted population, it is also claimed to be necessary in cases where a large population of one species threatens the wellbeing of another. This has particularly been the case with invasive species that are introduced to an ecosystem and then outcompete the native populations. In such scenarios, doing nothing can result in environmental degradation (see Gunn 2001 for a discussion of the ethics of killing invasive species). Targeted instrumental hunting, referred to as a cull, is not without its opponents, particularly in some regions. A survey of a sample of citizens in the province of British Columbia, Canada documented 90 percent opposition to culling predators, even to protect endangered species (Dubois and Harshaw 2013). Culls can also create significant animosity in human communities, as illustrated by Dizard's (1999) account of a town in Massachusetts in conflict over a deer cull that a state agency deemed necessary to protect a reservoir supplying citizens with water.

Culls are also used to manage disease among wildlife.[7] For example, a cull of canines was undertaken in the Serengeti National Park because the distemper they carried was threatening the lion population (McCallum and Hocking 2005). Animal advocates have recommended treating or vaccinating individual animals. The same survey of residents in British Columbia discussed above found that the majority of respondents (approximately 70 percent) opposed culls in general. Instead, they supported treating or quarantining sick animals, a strategy not favoured by the conservation professionals surveyed (Dubois and Harshaw 2013). Addressing illness and risk with individual animals is more time and resource intensive, and the impacts can be more difficult to observe and document. Nonetheless, some successful cases have been documented, such as the vaccination of foxes in Europe and raccoons in the Northeast United States against rabies (McCallum and Hocking 2005).

There are also studies indicating that culls may not be as effective as presumed. Harrison and colleagues (2010) argue that there is ample scientific evidence that culls can be quite problematic. Most specifically, they can have unintended consequences and have high price tags. The authors examined the efficacy of culling mountain hares to control louping ill virus in red grouse, and conclude that culls do not produce the desired outcome. Another failed cull detailed in the literature involved a cull of badgers in Britain to control transmission of bovine tuberculosis to cattle, which actually proved counterproductive because the removal of some badgers caused increased movement among the remaining ones in the resultant territorial vacuum, and further spread the disease (McCallum and Hocking 2005).

Finally, it has been suggested in the literature that hunting fosters a desire for conservation among participants and makes them more ecologically minded. There is some empirical research to support this claim. A study by Oldfield and colleagues (2003) using interviews and aerial photos, and controlling for income, found that landowners who participate in bird hunting and/or are supportive of it maintain significantly more trees on their land. Further, those who have hunted in the past plant significantly more trees than nonhunters do. They conclude that if hunting were banned, it could negatively affect conservation on private lands, requiring the state to provide funds to incentivize property owners to engage in conservation measures.

Hunting as environmental and animal harm

Too often, the arguments in favour of hunting, such as those just discussed, are presented without consideration of the arguments against. This section provides exactly this needed context. It focuses on three arguments against sport hunting related specifically to environmental wellbeing that I consider the most persuasive. Of course, the most persuasive argument against hunting for animal advocates is likely to be that it results in the pain and death of individual animals. That morally grounded argument was discussed earlier in this chapter and will therefore not be detailed again here in the interests of providing space for other lines of argument that speak specifically to environmental impacts.

A problematic conservation structure

Recall that one of the arguments put forward by proponents of hunting is that their activity generates a significant amount of revenue for wildlife conservation. That cannot be disputed; however, there are also associated costs (discussed in the last section), and the money comes with strings attached. The North American conservation model has caused conservation agencies to become beholden to hunting interests and focus on the conservation of species that hunters covet. Doing so can destabilize instead of balance ecosystems because certain species (e.g., deer) are propped up while predator species (e.g., wolves) are decimated (Baker 1985; Fitzgerald 2005a). An illustration of the propping up of preferred populations and negative environmental impacts can be found in the state of Michigan. Michigan's Department of Natural Resources implemented a plan to achieve a five-fold increase in the deer population by clear-cutting parts of state forests to create the ideal habitat for the animal. They successfully reached their goal of bringing the population up to one million deer (Baker 1985).

These policies may sound good for the species that are bolstered, but it diverts attention and resources from a more holistic analysis and treatment of ecological issues facing an area; or in other words, "more wildlife might be protected less effectively now than ever before" (Luke 2001, 6). Even proponents of the current conservation model (e.g., Muth and Jamison 2000) admit that the focus on game species is a flaw. There are also aspects of hunting that some conservation professionals think should be changed, such as the use of dogs to hunt black bears, which the majority (57 percent) of a sample of over 3,000 conservation professionals in the US disagreed with (Muth and Jamison 2000). The strength of the hunting lobby, however, precludes making changes in many instances.

Boglioli (2009) documents another case of hunting interests trumping conservation goals in his ethnographic research on coyote hunting in Vermont. There, coyote hunting derbies are held with the stated goal of controlling what is argued to be an overpopulation of coyotes that is threatening the deer population. Some nonhunters, and even hunters, oppose the coyote hunting derbies primarily because the animals are not consumed and because prizes are awarded. For its part, the Fish and Wildlife Service (FWS) has not officially opposed the hunts because there is no evidence that the hunts harm the overall coyote population. Boglioli (2009, 209) points out that this

> position contradicts the most important stated purpose of the coyote tournaments: killing coyotes to increase the deer population. Among wildlife managers, however, it is common knowledge that coyotes

actually reproduce at a higher rate when they are confronted with intensive attempts to control their numbers... the coyote tournaments may actually increase the coyote population.

The FWS also reports that the deer population has not been negatively impacted by the coyotes, which also undercuts the purpose of the hunts. In spite of all of this, the FWS has not intervened in the hunts, even though in private they are negative about the hunts (Boglioli 2009).

Thus there is reason to question whether this conservation model, in giving so much power to hunting interests, is serving the needs of the environment, much less the wildlife. It may also do a disservice to the nonhunting public interested in enjoying wildlife in other ways, as it can negatively affect species that people are interested in observing, and can keep people out of wildlife areas during hunting season (Franklin 1998). This conservation model may even harm some species intended to be "protected" via hunting, which would seriously undercut one of the stated environmental benefits of hunting.

Hunting contributes to "evolution in reverse"

Hunters generally target the largest and strongest individuals of hunted species, as they make the most attractive trophies. This leaves the weaker individuals left to procreate, creating what Teale refers to as "evolution in reverse" (cited by Kheel 1995, 96). This argument is not without its detractors, including Heffelfinger and colleagues (2013), who argue that targeting the largest male animals simply results in the removal of the oldest males, not necessarily those with strong genes that would be beneficial to pass on. They do admit, however, that hunting can skew the age and sex of a population.

The empirical research indicates that sport hunting can have negative consequences for some animal populations. Two studies in different geographic locations provide evidence of the potential impacts. A study of bighorn sheep in Alberta, Canada undertaken over 30 years documented evolutionary changes resulting in a decrease in average weight and horn sizes (referred to as "micro-evolutionary response to selection"). The researchers explain that rapidly growing, large horns are heritable, and due to hunting, animals with these characteristics lived shorter lives and therefore had fewer opportunities to reproduce, resulting in this evolutionary change. They compare what was observed in the sheep with the increase in tuskless elephants in Africa, believed to be associated with the poaching of elephants with tusks. The researchers speculate that these types of evolutionary changes could also negatively affect disease-resistance traits in the population, concluding that "sport hunting is one of the most pervasive and potentially intrusive activities that affect game mammal populations globally" (Coltman et al. 2003, 656).

Another study documented negative impacts of sport hunting on animal species that have a propensity for committing infanticide when the number of adult members in a population decreases (Packer et al. 2009). Simulation models the researchers ran indicate that hunting is associated with population declines in these species. They assert that such declines have been observed over the past 25 years among populations of large cats (e.g., lions, cougars) in African countries, as well as states in the US where sport hunting of these populations is common.

Even researchers who have not documented negative impacts of hunting on the species they study leave the door open to the possibility. In their discussion of the impact of hunting on polar bears in Canada, Freeman and Wenzel (2006) write, "There appears to be no evidence that non-resident trophy hunting of polar bears in the Canadian Arctic is detrimental to polar bear conservation or has caused any significant negative impacts upon indigenous communities where bears are still hunted for subsistence" (28). They go on to admit, however, "Questions arise concerning the possible long-term effects of selectively removing more large male bears than females from polar bear populations. However, little research has been directed to this issue at this time" (28–29). Perhaps one reason that little research is conducted on these potential species impacts is that hunting interests fund so much of the research on wildlife.

As discussed earlier, the hunting community is generally quick to accuse animal advocates of being emotional and anti-science, while presuming that science-based evidence is on their side (Paulson 2012). They strategically frame the hunting debate as a battle over science instead of morals. When it comes to the well-being of some species, however, the science may be on the side of animal advocates. The impact on other species is unclear, pointing to the need for funding research specifically on the long-term effects of hunting on species.

Hunting tourism can harm local people and environments

As noted earlier, sport hunting in developing countries has been framed by some as being beneficial to local human and animal populations. Yet the literature on hunting conservation programmes in developing countries does contain some cautionary notes. The case of Tanzania is illustrative. In their recent examination of hunting and wildlife policies there, Benjaminsen and colleagues (2013) explain, "The last decade has seen a steady chipping away at the promise of community-based conservation espoused in the 1990s across Africa." The Tanzanian government has consolidated its power over wildlife, companies have been given rights to conduct hunting expeditions, and community members have been left with little voice in what happens. Additionally, there is ample evidence of corruption in the industry and hunting quotas violations.

Tanzania's experience is part of a broader trend of governments recentralizing control over wildlife because of its economic value, even through violent means, in southern and eastern Africa (Benjaminsen et al. 2013). For their part, animal advocates have articulated widespread scepticism regarding hunting conservation programmes in developing countries for years. Even proponents of sport hunting tourism admit that some negative impacts are borne by local communities, as illustrated by the following statement by Paulson (2012, 55):

> research has almost uniformly shown increased survival of game animal populations as a result of the harvest of trophy animals. However,

previous research has also demonstrated that such management models often change traditional socio-environmental relationships and lead to undesirable outcomes on locals, including uneven levels of equity in economic benefits.

Changes in socioenvironmental relationships, by extension, can have long-term negative environmental consequences. Once again, greater research is needed to unpack what the short and longer-term impacts of sport hunting are on animal species, local human communities, and the broader environment.

Where to from here?

After reviewing the arguments for and against the claim that hunting is environmentally beneficial, it may seem that there is no hope for bringing pro-hunting environmentalists and animal advocates closer together on the issue of sport hunting. In fact, some observers (e.g., Dizard 1999) have been quite pessimistic about this possibility. Nonetheless, I see some potentially productive ways forward.

Cultural considerations

Cultural considerations are related to the environmental considerations detailed above in important ways. In Indigenous cultures, for example, hunting is important beyond food provision: it has symbolic and traditional value, and can be part of a connectedness with the environment. Freeman and Wenzel (2006), for instance, argue that polar bear hunting by Inuit in the Arctic helps them to preserve important cultural connections to the environment.

The AAM is often depicted as being insensitive to such cultural connections to hunting, and in some instances this critique has been well-deserved (see King 1991). However, pro-hunters (and certainly many nonhunting environmentalists) are quick to paint the AAM with a rather broad brush and cast the whole movement as culturally insensitive. To this end, a quote by one animal advocate in reference to an Inuit hunt – "to me, Inuit culture is a dying one. I see my job as helping it go quickly" (cited by Muth and Jamison 2000, 845) – is cited by many hunting advocates in the literature as illustrative of the insensitivity of the whole movement. It is a gross overgeneralization.

On the other hand, the cultural importance of hunting has been claimed by others who do not have as clear a historical tradition. Some authors (e.g., Cahoone 2009) have argued that if some Indigenous populations can use cultural tradition to justify hunting, then non-indigenous populations in rural areas should be able to do so as well. This cultural argument has been used in some recent policy debates over sport hunting. It was used to defend foxhunting against those seeking to ban it in the UK (see Pardo and Prato 2005) and by rural white men in Ontario, Canada in defence of the spring bear hunt (Dunk 2002).

To be sure, this appropriation of the language around cultural traditions to justify sport hunting has not gone unchallenged. In opposition to the claim of the cultural importance of the spring bear hunt to rural white men in Ontario, Dunk (2002) writes that such hunting is "a product of industrialization and the postwar Fordist compromise that brought relative affluence to unionized, male workers, in the transportation, mining and forest industries" (57), and is not grounded in cultural traditions. Kheel (1995) has been similarly critical of the selective appropriation of aspects of Indigenous cultures by white hunters to justify their activity. The issue of power is important here. Sport hunters do not share with ethnic/racial minority cultures a relative lack of power; as a group, sport hunters are quite powerful, as evidenced by their ability to shape wildlife policies.

A truly intersectional, ecofeminist perspective that foregrounds power imbalances helps to understand that appropriating cultural traditions to justify hunting animals for sport is problematic, as is denigrating cultures that have long and culturally significant traditions of hunting animals. It is important for the AAM to acknowledge that hunting is an important cultural tradition for *some* groups, and that not all hunting has the same animal welfare, environmental, and social impacts. That is, social justice must be taken into consideration alongside animal and environmental justice (see Kitossa 2000; Pellow 2013). Ecofeminism is useful in making these connections. That is not to say, however, that it has all of the answers. As Gaard (2001) acknowledges, while ecofeminists have the tools needed to address cross-cultural animal and/or environmental issues, concrete strategies for improvements have been harder to come by.

To that end, a good place to start would be for animal advocates to begin by critically examining the harms perpetrated within their own culture instead of weighing in on the cultural practices of others, while also speaking out in the face of attempts to appropriate others' cultural traditions to justify one's actions and/or negatively impacting other cultures in an attempt satisfy one's desires (e.g., trophy hunting) (for further discussion of the complexity of such cultural arguments, see Kim 2015). The recommended strategies Gaard (2001) provides for ecofeminists more generally would also be useful for animal advocates to employ. The first is to critically evaluate how activists select targets: although the actions of those with less relative power may be attractive targets, it does the larger goal of social justice (that includes species and environmental justice) a disservice. Focusing on those who perpetrate more wide-ranging and significant harms, such as corporations, although challenging, can also be strategic and more conceptually consistent. Gaard also recommends challenging instead of reifying dualisms, such as the culture/nature dualism discussed throughout this book, and fostering relationships with what she refers to as "border crossers." In short, just as it is problematic to ignore the nature side, and privilege the culture side, of the constructed culture/nature dichotomy, it is also harmful to ignore the cultural in attempting to protect that constructed as natural.

Considering nature

It should be apparent after reading this chapter that animal advocates and environmentalists have been divided in many ways over the issue of sport hunting. Each side has some valid points worth considering. Hunting advocates are correct that their sport provides considerable funding for conservation activities and that without their support (through taxes, license fees, and donations) these efforts would have to be funded in alternative ways, presumably by the state. Yet states taking on greater responsibility for conservation seems unlikely given the larger context of a trend towards diminishing state involvement in securing public goods under neoliberalism.

Nevertheless, animal advocates are also correct in pointing out that the conservation efforts undertaken are not necessarily aimed at ensuring ecological health as much as they are at ensuring a large population of species that are preferred prey for hunters. Even some hunting advocates acknowledge that the publicly funded agencies responsible for overseeing wildlife and the environment need to be more responsive to the needs of the public and even animal advocates. From this perspective, Muth and Jamison write,

> it will be important that conservation professionals and sportsmen and women work to forge a middle ground on wildlife management issues that is responsive to evolving public sentiments. One avenue for achieving this goal is for the conservation community to identify common ground with moderate organizations in the animal protection movement and to work together with them toward progressive accomplishments in advancing the cause of wildlife conservation. (2000, 849)

The reference to evolving public sentiments makes it clear that it is in their own best interests to support pro-environmental policies and not simply those that will benefit hunting conditions.

There is also empirical evidence indicating that the argument that hunting is needed to maintain ecological wellbeing is overstated. There is evidence that for some species, at least, sport hunting results in less healthy and robust populations, providing some support for the "evolution in reverse" hypothesis. There is also evidence that some species do not respond as expected to culls, and that the widespread killing of some populations can result in unintended, and in some cases directly counterproductive, consequences. Animal advocates would do well to draw on this empirical research and advocate for more say in decision-making regarding wildlife policies. Also, because so much research on conservation is funded by hunting interests, animal advocates and environmentalists should advocate strongly for other sources of research funding, and keep the sources of funding in mind when reviewing the extant literature. I am not suggesting that research funded by hunting interests necessarily draws erroneous conclusions, but I am suggesting that such funding can have an impact, even at the most basic level of determining what research questions get asked. There are a number of writers (e.g., Loftin 1984; Varner 1994) who are sympathetic to the argument that killing animals is wrong, but who nonetheless state that hunting may be necessary for environmental reasons and may even ensure the death of fewer animals in the long run. Determining if this is in fact the case is going to require ample, high-quality research that is not myopically geared towards the needs of hunters.

Another argument by pro-hunting environmentalists that is not easily refuted is that hunting provides a more ethical and environmentally sustainable method for procuring meat. My assessment is that they are correct on both counts: hunted animals (in general) do not experience the extreme confinement and the associated litany of welfare problems that animals produced for food do in industrial animal agriculture (IAA). Their quality of life is likely better, although the quality of their death is surely variable. The environmental impacts of IAA (detailed in Chapter 5) are also immense and certainly dwarf hunting locally. Many animal advocates would likely counter that meat consumption is neither necessary nor desirable. Nevertheless, in the *current* context where the vast majority of the population consumes meat, regulated and responsible hunting is likely preferable. I have qualified this statement with the words *regulated* and *responsible* in recognition that not all hunting is undertaken responsibly or to procure meat, and to flag the fact that science not beholden to hunting interests will be needed to determine sustainable hunting quotas and seasons. In the presence of these elements, animal advocates may want to cede some ground to pro-hunting environmentalists in the short term for the aggregated benefit of animal and environmental wellbeing.

Instead, focusing the critique of hunting on cases linked to environmental harm makes logistical, philosophical, and strategic sense. The number of people who identify as environmentalists vastly outnumbers those who identify as animal advocates, so this tactic may mobilize more sympathizers for the cause. This was the case in an anti–duck hunting campaign in Victoria, Australia. Instead of using moralistic language, the group leveraged environmental concern by highlighting the need to conserve threatened species and to protect the environment from the lead shot in the cartridges, and they were ultimately successful in reducing the amount of duck hunting (Munro 1997).

I am aware that some animal advocates may not like the thought of selecting specific types of hunting to oppose. In fact, perhaps the only thing they may like less is my next proposal: there may be common ground to be found with pro-environment hunters. I am not alone in this thought. In his article in the *Wildlife Society Bulletin*, M. Nils Peterson (2004) argues for greater engagement between hunters, environmentalists, and animal advocates, suggesting that they have more in common than might be expected. All three constituencies share a professed love of wildlife that sets them apart from the rest of the population, or as Peterson (2004) puts it, "This shared ethical space is missing from the apathetic moderate majority and is needed to challenge the growing consumptive materialistic paradigm of human existence" (319). Of course, many animal advocates will understandably question how much hunters love wildlife if they are engaged in killing wild animals. However, we cannot overlook the possibility that some hunters, perhaps those who genuinely engage in hunting with the goal of promoting ecological sustainability, do care more about and know more about wildlife than the general population. There may therefore be some common ground here where these constituencies can come together, such as around issues of habitat destruction, species extinction, and the harmful impacts of IAA. The interests of all three groups are also threatened by the impacts of the Treadmill of Production (ToP) (discussed in the Introduction), and this could be a point of synergy.

In analyzing harms to animals, the role of the ToP has not

really gained traction. Perhaps this is because animals, as inputs to the treadmill, have been conceptualized as a renewable resource. Therefore, their use does not pose the same problem for the tread-mill structure as does the use of resources understood as being nonrenewable, such as fossil fuels. Speciesist assumptions aside, the treadmill of production (ToP) perspective is aimed at analyz-ing how the treadmill is exceeding existing biophysical limits, a process expected to worsen until ultimately it culminates in a coupled socioeconomic and environmental crisis. Because the supply of animals is seemingly endless, a supply shortage, with its attendant consequences for the treadmill, is unlikely.

Nevertheless, the ToP perspective can be utilized to elucidate the intersecting interests of animal advocates, environmentalists, and hunters. A key element of the ToP is the expansion imperative (see Schnaiberg 1980; Gould, Pellow, Schnaiberg 2008). This expan-sionist ethos is responsible for significant habitat destruction. More and more land is converted to serve the needs of production, notably the production of meat, which is increasingly recognized as *the* driver of habitat loss (Machovina et al. 2015). This habitat loss poses a risk to wildlife that animal advocates, environmental-ists, and hunters alike have a vested interest in.

There may also be some utility in using the ToP concept to analyze the state of wildlife management. Investment in technologies aimed at increasing production is symptomatic of the treadmill, and the increases in production that it enables further harm the environ-ment. If "technologies" are broadly conceptualized, the perspective can be useful for analyzing the production of certain species to be hunted. As discussed in this chapter, species that are prized as game are propped up while those constructed as a threat (predators) are whittled down. The treadmill analogy fits well here: conditions are modified (removal of predators, habitat modifications) to encour-age increased (re)production of certain species of animals so that they can be hunted. In the short term, it works in the interests of hunters, but as the evidence detailed in this chapter demonstrates, there may be long-term ecological consequences in the form of population collapses and maladaptive evolutionary changes. In the very least, the long-term consequences are uncertain.

The welfare of domesticated animals may be another site of common interest to animal advocates, environmentalists, and hunters. Peterson (2004) and some other pro-hunting environmentalists voice concern about the wellbeing of animals, and are willing to extend protection to domestic animals. He recommends extending ethical protections to animals on the grounds of relatedness instead of sentience; that is, he argues we owe more of an ethical duty to animals that we share our lives with than those we do not (also see Scruton 2002). This is in line with Callicott's position that ethical consideration should be extended to domesticated animals, but not wild animals. Paraphrasing his reasoning, wild animals are situated on the nature side of the culture/nature dichotomy, and are therefore subject to ecological instead of social rules.

Those dividing lines are, however, increasingly difficult to recognize. As McKibben (1989) has argued, "nature" as we understand the term no longer exists: humans have "ended nature as an independent force" (xix). The changes wrought by global climate change, for instance, have trickled down to affect all species to varying extents. Dizard (1999) disagrees with this assessment and provides a more moderated analysis. He argues that "human control is by no means complete" (15), and whereas there may no longer be true wilderness (humans to some extent have touched it all), there is nonetheless wildness. He goes on to argue that this is where our responsibility to nature originates:

> Once we begin to intervene, we cease to have the moral luxury of refusing responsibility. We have, for better or worse, altered the face of nature – there is simply no place on the globe that remains pristine. Our past intrusions, intentional and unintentional, have bequeathed to us, the living, the imperative of continuing intervention. (Dizard 1999, 145)

For Dizard, this is where pro-hunters and animal advocates part ways. Pro-hunters see themselves as being part of nature (as animals, after all), which translates into an ethic of responsibility for nature. Conversely, animal advocates are arguing for humans to leave nature alone, which Dizard implies leads only to a rights-based discourse on behalf of animals. He states at the end of his book that he is less optimistic about reconciling the animal advocate and pro-hunter positions than he once was because they have these fundamentally differing views of nature.

I am, however, more optimistic than Dizard. An ecofeminist-informed animal advocacy can challenge the overly simplistic culture/nature dichotomy that Dizard and McKibben point to. It may be fair to say that both animal advocates and pro-hunting environmentalists have been guilty of reifying this dichotomy in the past: pro-hunting environmentalists have eschewed ethical duties to animals on the "nature" side of the dichotomy, and animal advocates have perhaps idealized a notion of human-free nature that does not exist. They have both overestimated the theoretical and actual distance between nature and culture today, thereby underestimating the fluidity between the two, arguably to the detriment of animals and the environment. This fluidity is further illustrated in the context of zoos, the focus of the next chapter.

3

Zoos and Aquaria: Species Conservation, Education, or Unethical Imprisonment?

Zoos and aquaria have generally not elicited the same level of vitriolic critique or impassioned support among the public as hunting has. Milstein speculates that this may be because zoos "sit in cultural in-between places of tension" (2009, 42). That is, the animals on display do not fit neatly into the category of culture or of nature, prompting Mullan and Marvin (1987) to suggest that zoo animals are an entirely different class of animals: neither domesticated nor wild. This status may have contributed to the relatively muted opposition to zoos among the public: some may reason that we have done zoo animals a favour by taking them from nature and giving them a place in our culture. Moreover, although sport hunting and zoos are similar in that they are both leisure activities centred on animals, perhaps zoos are viewed more favourably because the animals there have lost their liberty but not their lives, and the loss of liberty may be perceived as being outweighed by an apparent upgrade for individual animals from nature to culture, and as being in the interests of the greater good in the form of conservation and education.

Yet every now and then publicized cases of what zoo life means for individual animals evoke discomfort among the public. For instance, in 2016, staff at the renowned Cincinnati Zoo shot and killed a seventeen-year-old gorilla named Harambe. The shooting occurred after a four-year-old boy climbed into the gorilla's enclosure, and Harambe grabbed and dragged the boy – some witnesses said to protect him, others interpreted it as a sign of aggression

(CNN 2016). There were a variety of responses in the wake of the incident: some cast blame on the boy's mother for allowing him to breach the perimeter, others blamed the zoo for using lethal force, some lamented the loss of a member of a critically endangered species, and still others saw the case as further evidence of the injustice of keeping animals in zoos. The species of the animal involved undoubtedly figured into the significant attention the case received, not only because of his critically endangered status, but because he was a primate, and the video of him attending to the boy reminded viewers of the proximity between our species. In this instance, there were protests outside of the zoo: the divide between culture and nature had been uncomfortably breached, in a literal and figurative sense, and demonstrators were there demanding justice.

This chapter further elucidates the ideological differences between the EM and the AAM by exploring their positions on these places where the coming together of nature and culture is both celebrated and commodified. The focus here is on accredited, more reputable establishments; this is where animal advocates and environmentalists most clearly diverge in their positions, whereas neither side generally argues in favour of the environmental utility of unaccredited, "roadside" zoos (see Laidlaw 2001 for a discussion of unaccredited zoos). This chapter also does not delve into the ethics of keeping wild-caught animals in zoos, as environmentalists and animal advocates are generally in agreement that this is problematic, except under some extenuating circumstances (Callicott 1980). Instead, the focus in this chapter is on the environmental value of accredited zoos and how they stack up against the impacts of captivity on individual animals.

We begin with a brief overview of the history of zoos and the evolution of the modern zoo branded as conservation tool, next turning our attention to the perspectives of environmentalists and animal advocates on modern zoos. The chapter is focused on the two main conservation-minded arguments in favour of zoos. First, that zoos and aquaria are important instruments in protecting and breeding threatened and endangered species, as well as important contributors to conservation efforts in the field. Second, that zoos also have a more indirect effect on conservation: they influence visitors to become more environmentally minded. I assess the research vis-à-vis these specific arguments, weighing the arguments of anti-zoo animal advocates against pro-zoo environmentalists. The chapter ends with an assessment of the environmental and animal advocacy positions in light of what the research demonstrates about the conservation potential of zoos and aquaria, and a discussion of whether or not there might be some common ground to be found between the two positions.

The history of zoos

Wild animals have long been displayed for curious onlookers. By most accounts, the first organized animal collection (the term "zoo" was not yet in use) was held by Queen Hatshepsut of Egypt in about 1500 BC. Contemporary authors speculate that the collection was held to demonstrate the wealth and power of the Queen and the state (Row, McConney, and Mansfield 2014), and that the historic collection and confinement of animals were tied to the more general processes of imperialism, colonization, and slavery (Mullan and Marvin 1987; Malamud 1998) – relationships that continue today.

Centuries later, during the Renaissance period, animal collections came to be referred to as menageries, and were marked by unique architecture (for a discussion of the conceptual and logistical similarities between menageries and the institutionalization of people, see Foucault 1979, 204). By the end of the period, a number of municipally owned public menageries had been constructed (Mullan and Marvin 1987; Roe, McConney, and Mansfield 2014). The term "zoo" came to be used in the nineteenth century, and during this time, the purpose began to shift from pure spectacle and entertainment to include the presentation of some educational and scientific elements (Mullan and Marvin 1987; Roe, McConney, and Mansfield 2014). Today, zoos are generally understood as "collections of captive wild animals that are displayed to the public so that they are easier to observe than in nature" (Tribe and Booth 2003, 66). Aquaria, where fish and water-dwelling animals are kept, are commonly grouped together with zoos, as they serve the same general purpose, but with different species. However, it should be noted that some aquaria, such as SeaWorld, are different from traditional zoos in that their central attraction is captive animals engaged in specific performances to entertain guests, whereas zoos tend to avoid performances involving unnatural animal behaviour (Mullan and Marvin 1987).

During the twentieth century, the stated purpose of zoos expanded to include conservation, facilitated by increasing acknowledgement of environmental deterioration and related species declines, changes in public opinion, improved staff training, and more stringent regulation of wild animal capture (Braverman 2013). With increasing urbanization in the twentieth century, zoos also increasingly served the purpose of putting people in closer contact with nature, from which there was a growing sense of estrangement (Roe, McConney, and Mansfield 2014). This move to bring culture in closer contact with nature coincided with the "illusion of liberty" (Kalof 2007, 155) in zoos, whereby cages gave way to "enclosures" that appeared more natural and less clinical (Mullan and Marvin 1987), and the visitor experience became one of being immersed in nature (Braverman 2013).

As the AAM gained momentum in the second half of the twentieth century, so did the critical attention paid to zoos and aquaria, which Milstein (2009) describes as "constant critique" by the 1970s (29). Segments of the AAM criticized zoos on the grounds that (1) their stated educational and conservation mandates were simply a way of making the real purpose of zoos – making money – more palatable; (2) where educational and conservation efforts were undertaken, there was insufficient evidence to demonstrate that they worked, and even if they did, their value did not outweigh the harm caused to animals by keeping them in captivity; and (3) the objectification of animals through captivity was only reinforcing the subjugation of nature to the whims of humankind.

At about this same time, academics began to turn their attention to zoos and examined not only what the practice of keeping exotic animals for display could tell us about our relationships with animals and nature, but also what it could tell us about our relationships with one another. They wrote about how the human gaze of the animal spectacle results in further objectification and the disappearance of subjectivity (Berger 1980), akin to the effects of the male gaze in patriarchal culture on women (Acampora 2005; Milstein 2009). More recently, Braverman (2013) has written about the gaze vis-à-vis the governance of zoos.

Infrequently told histories of zoos recount how people from marginalized groups (e.g., people with characteristics deemed deformities, the mentally ill, people from colonized locales) were displayed alongside animals (see Braverman 2013; Milstein 2009; Mullan and Marvin 1987), providing evidence to support ecofeminist arguments about the construction of animals and marginalized human groups as existing on the "nature" side of the culture/nature binary, and thus being denied full citizenship in the realm of the cultural. Today messages about race, ethnicity, and gender are still identifiable in zoos, although not as explicitly as in the past. For instance, animal enclosures relay messages about the land that these animals are native to and the peoples who shared the spaces with them (Mullan and Marvin 1987).

The lessons of the zoo – both explicit and implicit – are distributed fairly widely. The World Association of Zoos and Aquariums (WAZA) estimates that over 700 million people visit zoos around the world each year (Gusset and Dick 2011). To put this into perspective, the 150 million people who visit zoos in the US every year exceeds those who attend professional baseball, football, basketball, and hockey games combined (Milstein 2009). According to the European Association of Zoos and Aquaria (EAZA), the equivalent of one-fifth of Europe's population attend EAZA member zoos each year (http://www.eaza.net/), and the Canadian Association of Zoos and Aquariums (CAZA) reports that the equivalent of approximately one-third of the population of Canada attends their accredited venues each year (www.caza.ca). Thus, what is being communicated in these venues and how it is received is important.

WAZA, the overarching global organization, was founded in 1935 and claims 300 member organizations.[8] A review of

WAZA's website, and those of the regional accrediting organizations, indicates how the focus of zoos has changed over the years, and how they continue to reinvent themselves. Education, research, and conservation (both *in situ* and *ex situ*)[9] are currently emphasized. CAZA's website explicitly addresses the changes that have taken place in zoological institutions over time:

> Zoos and aquariums the world over are evolving. Where once many saw their role simply as exhibitors of animals, accredited institutions the world over today share the belief that in addition to a moral and professional responsibility for the welfare of the animals in their care, they also have a responsibility to protect the planet's biodiversity through public engagement, conservation and research. (caza.ca)

WAZA now has an entire section of their website devoted to conservation, wherein they write, "WAZA supports science and research, promotes environmental education, motivates environmental sustainability, combats climate change, advocates for exemplary zoo and aquarium design, encourages animal welfare and participates in international campaigns" (http://www.waza.org/en/site/conservation).

Most recently, these organizations have been emphasizing their roles in *in situ* conservation, or conservation in the animal's natural environment. In their latest conservation strategy (published in 2015), WAZA emphasized that in addition to captive breeding, they are working to strengthen *in situ* conservation efforts, writing, "It is the aim of WAZA to further increase the number of zoos and aquariums involved in the conservation of wild species and habitats and to make zoological institutions the primary non-governmental field conservation organizations" (http://www.waza.org/en/site/conservation). The report introduces their "One Plan Approach," which "mandates that animals maintained in zoological facilities play a conservation role that benefits wild counterparts.... The One Plan Approach links researchers in zoos and aquariums with scientists and conservationists working directly with wild populations" (WAZA 2015, 18). The document also recommends that member organizations contribute 3 percent of their annual budgets to conservation efforts (WAZA 2015), although it does not appear to be a requirement.

The integration of *in situ* conservation efforts appears laudable, as the evidence indicates that those efforts hold more promise than *ex situ* conservation inside zoos (discussed in more detail shortly). However, a close read of WAZA's conservation strategy report reveals another reason for the associations to support *in situ* efforts:

> One key fact we have discovered since 2005, when the last WAZA conservation strategy was published, is that when visitors understand that zoos and aquariums are working to save animals in the wild, their support of us improves dramatically... . Our conservation commitments also help to bolster the perception of zoos and aquariums in the minds of government officials who enact and enforce the laws that affect our operations. It is essential that we gain the trust, confidence and support of the multiple authorities that control and regulate activities that directly impact our future. (WAZA 2015, 12)

In short, supporting *in situ* conservation is good business.

Environmentalist and animal advocate perspectives on zoos

Due to their preference for holism over individual wellbeing, environmentalists are more likely to support captive breeding programmes designed to assist species that are in decline, and education programmes in zoos aimed at fostering pro-environmental values, attitudes, and behaviours. Minteer and Collins (2013) describe the position as follows:

> Most environmental ethicists are sensitive to animal welfare considerations and are certainly aware that many threats to populations, species, and ecosystems impact animal welfare either directly or indirectly. Typically, however, they advocate focusing moral concern and societal action on such ends as the protection of endangered species and the preservation of wilderness rather than reducing the pain and suffering (or promoting the rights and dignity) of wild animals. (p. 43)

Braverman (2013) characterizes the position more bluntly: "zoos more readily sacrifice the individual animal for the benefit of the flock, rather than the other way around" (22).

The animal advocate position on zoos is not as straightforward. Not all animal advocates are opposed to zoos; many adherents of the animal welfare position argue that keeping animals in captivity can be acceptable if done properly. For instance, Warren (2000) asserts that if an animal's zoo enclosure is similar to their natural environment, and if captivity increases his/her life expectancy, then the animal's wellbeing (which she argues hinges less on liberty than human wellbeing does) may not be violated.

While an animal welfare position might not disagree with captivity per se, and would be more concerned with the conditions of confinement, the animal rights and liberation perspectives disagree with the captivity of individual animals in theory, although a utilitarian (Singer 1990) might be convinced that due to the benefits to the entire species or ecosystem that captivity is warranted in specific situations. Of course, actually calculating whether the benefits outweigh the disadvantages would be a difficult task (Regan 1995). The animal rights position on zoos is more clear-cut: absent the need to protect that individual animal, there is no justification for violating an animal's right to freedom (see Regan 1995; Jamieson 2002), thus making zoos morally unacceptable.

Zoo advocates have responded to these arguments in a few different ways. The first is to argue that the characteristics of animals preclude them from having their liberty compromised by zoos. Part of this argument is the assertion that animals are not free in the wild because they are constrained by their environment, illness, predators, and the like; the other aspect is the assertion that animals lack self-consciousness and therefore cannot make meaningful choices and are therefore not free. In short, they are not free in the first place, so zoos are not taking something valuable away from them (Leahy cited by Jamieson 2002). This line of argument seems to have gained little traction because, as Jamieson (2002) points out, it is indisputable that zoos constrain the liberty of animals more than being in the wild, and researchers are increasingly documenting the cognitive complexity of animals.

A second line of argument seeks to undercut the specific critiques made by animal advocates. They dismiss the claims made by animal advocates by asserting that they are focused on problems of the past and not the zoos of today. Additionally, they argue that animal advocates focus on species that do not fare as well in captivity, such as elephants and whales, instead of those that seem to thrive in captivity (Minteer and Collins 2013). It is certainly fair to say that animal advocates tend to focus on the extreme cases, but it is also fair to say that zoo proponents do as well (e.g., successful species reintroductions).

More commonly, proponents argue that zoos serve a greater environmental purpose. This is where the wedge has been placed between animal advocates and environmentalists on this issue. They assert that zoos serve an environmental function by (1) conserving species, and (2) providing attendees with a pro-environment education. The primacy of these two goals has been documented in research analyzing the mission statements of accredited zoos (Patrick et al. 2007).

It is against this backdrop that the following questions are addressed in the remainder of this chapter: Are zoos meaningfully contributing to species conservation? Is this environmental mandate enough to outweigh the harms inflicted by keeping animals in captivity? And does seeing animals in captivity provide enough environmental education to create appreciable differences among visitors, thereby improving the environment? In short, how do the interests of environmentalists and animal advocates compare in the context of zoos? And can their positions be reconciled in any meaningful way?

Zoos as conservationists

Animal rightists have been suspicious of the zoo community's stated shift towards conservation. They wonder if zoos could just be aligning themselves with the growing popularity of environmental concerns in an attempt to make visitors and the public more comfortable with keeping animals in captivity. It is difficult to ascertain what the motivation is, but it is evident that the zoo community has been voicing concerns about species declines, and even mandating participation in conservation efforts among accredited facilities, for several decades now.

The first World Zoo Conservation Strategy released in 1993 urged zoos to turn their attention to conservation efforts in the face of increasing environmental degradation and species declines (Keulartz 2015). Some regional associations have issued specific directives in this regard. For instance, in the EU, the Zoo Directive requires participation by member zoos and aquaria in conservation efforts. Organizations can comply through several methods: conduct conservation research, engage in training programs, exchange information, or undertake captive breeding (Rees 2005). In practice, however, the impacts of zoo conservation programmes appear to be limited. For instance, it is estimated that less than 5 percent of the research conducted is useful for conservation (Rees 2005). Proponents suggest, however, that research in zoos could become more relevant in the field as habitats become increasingly fragmented and wild populations become less diverse, thus becoming more similar to zoo populations and making comparisons more meaningful (Keulartz 2015).

Captive breeding has gained popularity as a conservation strategy since the 1990s, and in 2005 it was formalized in the first iteration of the World Zoo Conservation Strategy (Bowkett 2009; WAZA 2005). In recent years, however, this approach – sometimes referred to as the "Noah's Ark paradigm" because a small number of animals are kept together in confinement instead of in the wild – has come under scrutiny, complete with the use of shipwreck metaphors.

Three main critiques of *ex situ* conservation in zoos (i.e., research and breeding programmes with captive animals) have been articulated in the literature. First, zoos do not have enough physical space to meaningfully conserve species. According to one estimate, the space designated for all zoo animals globally could fit in the city of Brooklyn, NY. This amount of space is reportedly insufficient to keep a large enough number of animals to sustain robust breeding programmes. In addition, it is expected that the space constraints will worsen (somewhat ironically) because of animal welfare gains in demanding expanded enclosures for animals (Keulartz 2015).

Second, the relatively small amount of space available is not allocated to threatened species. Many species in zoos are not actually threatened species due to a preference for large charismatic animals that draw in visitors. It is estimated that zoos house only 15 percent of threatened terrestrial vertebrates (Keulartz 2015).

Finally, the breeding programmes undertaken with threatened species have had low success rates and are quite costly, particularly relative to their success rates (Keulartz 2015; Bowkett 2009). There are two main barriers to success: (1) captivity dulls the skills that animals need to survive and thrive in the wild, and (2) the environment that animals are released into may have changed significantly from when they or their ancestors were wild (Keulartz 2015; Bowkett 2009). According to a recent analysis of the literature, only 16 out of 145 reintroduction programmes have been deemed successful (Keulartz 2015), although these successful cases are certainly rehearsed frequently in the pro-conservation zoo literature, giving the impression that successful introductions are much more common (see Laidlaw 2001).

There is also general agreement that *ex situ* programmes are expensive. It is estimated that it costs 16 times more to care for a black rhino in captivity than to protect the habitat to support him/ her on the outside (Tribe and Booth 2003). These expenditures cannot then be used for other conservation purposes that are most cost-effective, particularly *in situ* efforts (Bowkett 2009). Thus, when WAZA boasts that zoos spend approximately $350 million USD on conservation efforts each year (Gusset and Dick 2011), the statistic obscures the importance of the type of conservation that the money was channelled into: financial contributions do not necessarily equal results.

In light of the limitations of *ex situ* conservation programmes, *in situ* conservation was prioritized at the 1992 Earth Summit in Rio de Janiero (see Chapter 2 of the *Convention on Biological Diversity*). It is clear in the language of Article 9 that in addition to questions about the efficacy of *ex situ* conservation, there was concern that it disadvantages developing countries, which lose "natural resources" in the form of animals in the name of conservation.

An "integrated approach" between *ex situ* and *in situ* conservation is currently being championed in the industry (Keulartz 2015). The second *Zoo Conservation Strategy*, released in 2005, is illustrative of a publicized shift from *ex situ* conservation towards a more integrated approach that combines captivity with research and training, educational programming, and *in situ* conservation efforts (Minteer and Collins 2013; Keulartz 2015). This shift cannot simply be dismissed as window dressing: the number of zoo-supported *in situ* projects has grown rather dramatically in recent years. In the UK, there was a 61 percent increase in *in situ* projects from 1995 to 2000 (Tribe and Booth 2003). In 2010 alone, the AZA reported being involved in 1970 conservation projects (Minteer and Collins 2013). Further, the quality of these projects has reportedly been improved, as has funding; for instance, WAZA was the third most generous conservation funding organization in 2010, behind The Nature Conservancy and the WWF Global Network (Gusset and Dick 2011). The current trajectory of funding provided by zoos and aquaria has led some to speculate that they could become the largest nongovernmental funder of conservation initiatives globally (Tribe and Booth 2003).

Zoo proponents are quick to add, however, that *in situ* conservation is not a replacement for *ex situ*, and that both are necessary. In fact, lately they have argued that *ex situ* conservation efforts are more important now than ever. They point to global environmental threats, such as global climate change (GCC), deforestation, invasive species, and species extinctions, among others, and argue that conserving and studying captive populations of wild animals is a necessary response (Keulartz 2015; Minteer and Collins 2013; Pritchard et al. 2011). Minteer and Collins (2013) raise the spectre of GCC in particular, and argue that *ex situ* populations will be needed to study the impacts, with the hope of protecting wild populations. They also anticipate that the looming GCC crisis will overshadow the critiques of animal advocates: they will become less compelling as the need for captive assurance populations increases (because of the impacts of global change). These ethical objections will also weaken as we see the rise of additional partnerships between *ex situ* and field conservation organizations and facilities and especially as the former become more directly engaged in recovery and reintroduction efforts that benefit animals in the wild. It is one thing to evaluate captive-breeding programs designed to provide a steady supply of charismatic animals for zoo display. These have rightly drawn the ire of animal advocacy organizations... It is another thing to assess those activities with the goal of recovering wildlife populations threatened in the field because of accelerating environmental change. (p. 47)

Nevertheless, zoo proponents (e.g., Keulartz 2015; Minteer and Collins 2013) seem to pin their hopes on ideal zoo scenarios – where small species and those that are threatened are prioritized, and *in situ* conservation projects are well supported – that do not currently apply to many, if any, zoos. Zoo conservation as it currently stands, although improved, is problematic. The conservation mandate is undercut when one looks more closely at the species that are involved. Most of the species currently affected by zoo conservation efforts are mammals, particularly "charismatic primates" (Gussett and Dick 2010, 184). Not coincidentally, these are the animals that most visitors come to see; in other words, they are the most financially lucrative. They are also among those most likely to suffer severe negative impacts from captivity.

Zoo advocates do admit that the emphasis of zoos continues to be on large charismatic animals (Pritchard et al. 2011) and that the majority of species in zoos are not endangered or threatened (Milstein 2009). They also admit that there is a significant disconnect between some zoos' stated conservation mission and what is done in practice. They counter, however, that this disconnect may be a form of self-preservation, as making changes, such as focusing on smaller animals that exhibit fewer negative impacts of captivity, could diminish attendance and thus revenue (Minteer and Collins 2013; Tribe and Booth 2003). Pritchard and colleagues (2011) assert that there are not fiscal incentives for zoos to engage in conservation, noting that the Global Environmental Facility, which is the largest source of funding for biodiversity internationally, does not support *ex situ* conservation. Thus, the *ex situ* conservation practices of zoos are constrained by what visitors will pay to see, because – even though zoos have certainly improved over the years – they have developed around a logic of profits, not conservation (see Laidlaw 2017).

Additionally, the funding of *in situ* conservation efforts by zoos is still minimal, although the aggregated sums reported by industry associations do sound impressive. As it stands, the recommended amount that zoos are expected to contribute to *in situ* conservation is 10 percent of their income; on average, zoos spend less than 5 percent on these programmes (Keulartz 2015). Authors affiliated with WAZA have acknowledged that "for individual zoos and aquariums to fulfill their claim to have conservation of wild species and habitats as the overarching principle of all of their activities, and for WAZA to become a globally recognized conservation organization, current efforts need to be intensified" (Gusset and Dick 2010, 187).

Even if zoos did use conservation and animal welfare considerations to make decisions about what species to keep and breed, and allocated more resources to *in situ* conservation efforts, there are still some less discussed problems with zoos from an animal advocacy perspective. Zoos do not keep all animals from birth through death. Species that are part of a survival breeding programme at an accredited facility have to be sent to another accredited facility if a zoo wants to get rid of them, but other species do not (Braverman 2013). Those surplus or unwanted animals are frequently sold by zoos (another way of generating profits) to other organizations, such as hunting ranches, unaccredited zoos, and individual exotic pet keepers. Estimates of the number of animals involved in these sales are difficult to come by, but according to one report, 19,361 mammals were removed from accredited zoos from 1992 to mid-1998, and 38 percent of these mammals ended up in places with lower animal welfare standards (Milstein 2009).

Other zoo animals are simply euthanized. One such case involving tiger cubs received enough media attention to elicit a response from WAZA. The euthanization took place at Zoo Magdeburg in

Germany in 2008. The zoo had learned after mating two Siberian tigers that the male was not a purebred. The three resultant cubs were euthanized shortly after birth. Zoo Magdeburg, along with other zoos, did not want cubs that were not purebred. The head of the zoo and three other employees were convicted of animal cruelty for the euthanization (Trend News Agency 2010). WAZA issued a statement in support of the zoo staff, stating

> WAZA regards the humane euthanasia of the tiger cubs sired by a known hybrid male by the Zoo Magdeburg authorities as being an entirely reasonable and scientifically-supportable action. WAZA sees the conviction of the three Zoo Magdeburg staff on the premise that humane management euthanasia for conservation purposes is not a "reasonable" course of action to be a repudiation of international consensus on what constitutes best conservation practice. (2010)

In addition to the lethal removal of unwanted animals, animals are killed in zoos to be fed to other animals. These animals and their deaths are generally not viewed by the public, and, indeed, few probably pause to consider the animals that are used as feed in this context (see Mullan and Marvin 1987; Braverman 2013). Some zoos historically allowed visitors behind the scenes to observe the feeding of predator animals, but that was ended due to concern about the gratuitous violence that really served no educational purpose (Mullan and Marvin 1987). There was a notable recent exception that received much attention. Marius, a young giraffe at the Copenhagen Zoo, was killed by staff and his remains were publicly dissected and fed to other zoo animals in front of an audience, including children. WAZA responded, "The massive global attention the fate of the giraffe at Copenhagen Zoo has garnered unfortunately distracts from the very real crisis that the rapidly shrinking numbers of wild giraffes in Africa face" (WAZA 2014). Once again, WAZA's official response sought to detract attention from the specific incident by pointing to the larger environmental picture, undoubtedly expecting that the public would side with environmental holism over the individualism of animal advocacy.

Influencing pro-conservation behaviour through education

In addition to arguments that zoos promote conservation directly through *ex situ* and increasingly *in situ* efforts, zoo proponents argue that they also contribute to conservation indirectly via educating visitors about environmental threats and what can be done about them. There seems to be a sense among researchers in the field that this indirect impact is the most powerful tool zoos have in contributing to conservation (Tribe and Booth 2003). As such, researchers have of late focused on this route to conservation. The research is ongoing, and gaps in the literature remain (Tribe and Booth 2003; Keulartz 2015), but we will focus here on what the literature indicates thus far.

First, studies indicate that zoos are prioritizing the education of visitors, and that visitors consider it a priority as well. Educating visitors is the most commonly listed mandate in zoo mission statements (Tribe and Booth 2003). Further, in a survey of zoo staff, 93 percent of respondents indicated that education was a high or very high priority of their zoo (Roe, McConney, and Mansfield 2014). Visitors also apparently concur: among a sample of 540 visitors, educating children was deemed the most important activity that zoos engage in, and four out of five visitors indicated that teaching visitors what they can do to assist with conservation is also a priority (Roe, McConney, and Mansfield 2014).

Second, there have been a few studies that have documented statistically significant positive impacts of zoos on the environmental education of visitors. Attendance has been associated with a greater sense of connectedness with animals, increased animal and environmental knowledge, and a greater sense of responsibility for animal and environmental wellbeing. Some researchers, however, have noted that the impacts vary depending upon how engaged and knowledgeable the respective visitors are in the first place (Wyles et al. 2013). In their study, Wyles and colleagues (2013) conducted pre- and post-surveys of visitors to an aquarium and found that attendance did improve visitors' environmental attitudes and intentions, but the effect sizes observed were relatively small.

Zoos have also been accused of being "educationally redundant"; that is, people receive quite a bit of information about the environment from other sources, such as the media, television, and films. Smith and Broad (2008) therefore set out to assess if the environmental education impact of zoos extends beyond that of other media. They studied visitors to a zoo who participated in an informative bus tour and found that 40 percent of respondents reported that their knowledge had been enhanced by the experience, whereas 67 percent reported they had been educated by the media. Thus, while the informative bus tour did appear to have a positive impact, it was less than that of the media. The authors also point out that more research is needed to assess if and how this education actually translates into behavioural change.

A third body of literature has demonstrated that visitors are affected by the welfare of the animals in captivity, and that educational potential is negatively affected by poor welfare conditions. Consequently, Keulartz (2015) asserts that for education in zoos to have any hope of success, animals should be in enclosures that are as natural as practicable, which makes sense if zoos are attempting to teach about animals' natural environments. Stereotypic behaviours (e.g., pacing) among animals in zoos poses a particularly significant challenge to making zoos seem as natural as possible (see Miller 2011).

Less commonly discussed in the literature is the possibility that zoos may not be teaching the most uncomfortable lessons about what we are doing to the environment and other species, much less how visitors are implicated in these problems. In fact, one reason why zoos tend not to exhibit local species is that doing so may prompt uncomfortable realizations among visitors about how they themselves are negatively affecting those species. In general, zoos are unlikely to provide information that connects visitors directly to environmental problems and to recommend specific behavioural changes (Milstein 2009). They may also induce environmental complacency because some may assume that the species contained therein are safe (Malamud 1998).

Given the foregoing, the argument can be made that the conservation education provided by zoos does not outweigh the negative impacts experienced by animals in captivity. Recall that the research cited indicates that there is a statistically significant increase in knowledge acquisition from zoo patronage, but the change or effect size is relatively small. Juxtaposed against evidence that participants in other activities, such as backpacking, hunting, and fishing, are more knowledgeable about animals than zoo patrons (Milstein 2009), it is fair to ask if the modest gains in environmental education can outweigh the negative animal welfare impacts. As Milstein (2009) puts it,

> it may not be possible for the zoo visitor, who, according to zoo researchers, spends an average of five seconds at a zoo animal exhibit, to deeply encounter other animals and themselves in ways that influence perceptions or behaviours, or help visitors grapple with or transform the structural eco-social forces in which they play a part. In the end, it is indeed questionable whether the possible payoffs of a three-hour zoo visit outweigh the coercion that keeps animals in captivity for empty, monotonous lifetimes. (pp. 41–42)

Where to from here?

I think that even the most devoted animal rights advocate would admit that in recent years zoos have focused more attention on conservation and environmental education, and the actions of the regional zoo associations and the WAZA indicate that this transition is more than rhetorical: practices, policies, and funding allocations have been modified to support these relatively new missions. This transformation, however, is not a selfless one: it is clearly motivated by self-preservation; the zoo industry is working to keep itself relevant and to keep visitors coming through their gates. It has also been leveraged by the industry to outweigh the critiques of AAM, and some observers have speculated that the environmental turn among zoos will eventually neutralize the critiques of animal advocates (e.g., Keulartz 2015; Minteer and Collins 2013).

I would argue, however, that we are a long way from the critiques of zoos by animal advocates becoming moot. In fact, animal advocates may use continuing declines in some species (such as giraffes) as evidence that the current conservation structure of zoos is not helping. A number of improvements would need to be made to neutralize even some of those critiques, and additionally, evidence of these improvements would need to be documented by independent bodies (those not employed or funded by the zoo industry). Moreover, animal advocates could leverage the zoo industry's conservation mandate to agitate for changes. As Dale Jamieson (2002, 63) points out, "zoos are not going to go away. It is easier to try to change large institutions that are adept at fundraising than it is to abolish them" (Jamieson 2002, 63).

First and foremost, zoos that do not meet the highest standards – which is currently the vast majority of facilities – should be weeded out of existence. In the US alone, 90 percent of the 2,800 licensed facilities that exhibit wildlife do not meet the standards for AZA accreditation (aza.org). Some opponents argue that the differences among zoos are minimal and beside the point. From this perspective, Malamud (1998) writes, "I consider differences among zoos cosmetic, or otherwise insignificant in terms of mitigating their collective implication in a culturally retrograde enterprise" (4). Although all zoos share a reliance on keeping animals in captivity, there are nonetheless animal welfare and environmental differences across facilities that I think warrant attention. If people are going to visit zoos, it is certainly better for them to support those facilities that have the most rigorous standards and are making the most significant environmental contributions. Informing the public about these distinctions is important so that they can make informed decisions.

Yet not all of the responsibility for weeding out the worst zoos should fall upon the shoulders of zoo patrons. The zoo community also needs to openly air their concerns about facilities that do not meet the highest benchmarks. Reflecting on her interviews with zoo professionals and staff, Braverman (2013) remarks that while her participants displayed a willingness to be reflexively critical of zoos, there was a defensiveness against critiques levelled by animal advocates. She writes, "Criticism towards zoos was legitimate, apparently, so long as it did not come from the animal rights front" (24). The zoo community has an obligation to voice their concerns, even if they find themselves in agreement with animal advocates.

Additionally, governments should play a larger role in the regulation of zoos. Governments commonly provide little oversight, and instead zoos have largely policed themselves (Braverman 2013). Instead of fighting what little regulations there are, the zoological associations should welcome them as a way to improve standards at non-accredited facilities or to prompt closures in the absence of improvements. Exerting pressure on governments to better regulate zoos has been a focus of animal advocates in some jurisdictions. However, in the face of neoliberal policies promoting industry self-regulation and a shrinking role of the state, animal advocates are likely in an uphill battle on this front.

Better governance is also needed to make conservation programmes in zoos more successful (see Pritchard et al. 2011). Although regional associations have implemented strategies for conserving and breeding specific species (see Braverman 2013), there is no overarching international strategy in place. Further, experts in the field report that the documents developed by the regional associations and WAZA currently "fall short" (Pritchard et al. 2011, 20). Certainly if preserving species is a goal of zoos, there should be collaboration at the international level to maximize diversity within the respective gene pools. Failure to do so undercuts the argument that conservation is the chief goal of the modern zoo.

Relatedly, which species are kept in zoos should be more carefully thought about. A number of factors ought to be taken into consideration, such as the level of risk faced by the species (i.e., threatened, endangered), success of breeding and reintroduction, and animal welfare considerations. In general, it would be helpful if zoos focused more on smaller species than large charismatic species (such as elephants). Small species have the benefit of requiring less space (making breeding programmes easier to facilitate); generally cost less money, therefore freeing up more resources for other species and *in situ* conservation efforts; and are usually easier to breed and reintroduce (Keulartz 2015; Pritchard et al. 2011).

There are also species that should not be kept in captivity, as the welfare of some species is so severely compromised by doing so. Animals that traverse large geographic areas in the wild, such as migratory birds (Warren 2000), in particular tend not to fare well in captivity. An article published in *Nature* also indicates that carnivores with large territories, such as polar bears, suffer from more health problems, demonstrate stereotypic behaviours, and have difficulty breeding in captivity. The authors conclude, "the keeping of naturally wide-ranging carnivores should be either fundamentally improved or phased out" (Clubb and Mason 2003, 473). In recognition of the significant negative welfare impacts experienced by some species in captivity, a number of zoos, notably due to pressure from animal advocates, have phased out or are currently phasing out their exhibition of some animals, such as elephants at the Detroit Zoo in the US.

Marine mammals are also notorious for not doing well in captivity. Numerous negative consequences have been documented, including higher mortality rates in captivity (Bekoff 2000; 2002). The documentary film *Blackfish* released in 2013 provided viewers with insight into the negative impacts on captivity on killer whales, as well as the health and safety risks posed to trainers working with these animals. There was significant public outcry in the wake of the film, and marine parks such as SeaWorld suffered financial losses due to drops in attendance. SeaWorld has since announced its plan to no longer have killer whale shows and to end its killer whale breeding programme, effectively phasing out its killer whale exhibit. Legislation was also introduced in the US that would ban the keeping of killer whales in captivity across the country. The AZA, not pleased with the proposal, issued the following statement:

> The Association of Zoos and Aquariums strongly believes Congress should not be in the business of deciding which animals that facilities properly licensed by the United States Department of Agriculture should or should not be allowed to publicly display. Aquariums and

zoos accredited by the AZA exceed standards set by the USDA, and provide the best animal care and welfare possible. In addition, they are required to meet ever rising accreditation standards set by AZA.

This statement provides disappointing evidence that the AZA is not prepared to consider the possibility (at least not publicly) that some animals ought not to be in captivity. Therefore, although attending accredited facilities is surely better than frequenting facilities that do not meet the threshold for accreditation, there is certainly much room for improvement among the policies and positions of the accreditation organizations.

Another line of reasoning that I am also sympathetic to argues that the institution of the zoo itself is problematic because – even with the most humane treatment of animals possible – its existence sends the message that keeping animals in captivity is acceptable. This message is irredeemably speciesist because as a society we would not advocate keeping humans in captivity for the stated purposes that zoos serve (i.e., conservation, entertainment; see Regan 1995 on this point). Zoos are therefore a manifestation of the power we wield over other animals (Mullan and Marvin 1987), and their continued existence reaffirms the cultural message that this is not only appropriate but also ought to be celebrated via an outing with one's children. In Jamieson's words, "what zoos teach us is false and dangerous, both humans and other animals will be better off when they are abolished" (2005, 142) (although as noted earlier, he is in favour of incremental improvements in the meantime). Put another way, in reifying the culture/nature binary – a divide that ecofeminists have problematized as undergirding the domination of animals, the environment, women, and all others associated with nature – zoos are perpetuating the problems faced by animals and the environment.

I am sympathetic to that argument, yet I am uncomfortable with sitting on our collective hands waiting for the institution of the zoo to fail. In the meantime, I think it is useful to contextualize the environmental claims of zoos. The environmental argument in favour of zoos hinges on their educational and conservationist functions. However, as demonstrated in the review of various bodies of literature in this chapter, only a minority of zoos can claim to meaningfully address these functions, and the research on their impacts is mixed. The profit motive of zoos constrains what they are able to do to a significant degree; it constrains the types of species they can exhibit and the educational messages they can impart. Simply put, people are not going to pay money to observe small, aesthetically unpleasing species they are not interested in, and to be told that their everyday actions and consumption are responsible for the decline of these and other species, and that they need to make difficult life changes. As Laidlaw (2017, 75) puts it, "when you are out for a nice family day, discomforting, reality-based conservation messaging is a downer." Therefore, a truly environmentally beneficial zoo seems unlikely as well.

In recognition of this quandary, alternatives to the traditional zoo have been proposed. Perhaps most common is the recommendation that zoos only contain animals in need of rescue that cannot survive in the wild (see Milstein 2009). Animal ethicist Tom Regan (1995) has argued that the only acceptable reason for keeping an animal in captivity is if it is necessary to save his/her life, and this model would presumably be consistent with this objective. Such a model could be more successful in environmental education than traditional zoos because patrons would confront the harm endured by these animals as a result of human activities (e.g., being struck by a car). Done well, this model could also draw attention to the economic causes of harms to the environment and animals, such as dwindling habitats and deteriorating environmental conditions due to the ever-expanding treadmill of production and its associated consumption of environmental inputs (such as land) and production of environmental outputs (such as pollution).

It less likely, however, that this sanctuary-style model would be able to contribute more directly to conservation efforts via breeding. Thus it is unlikely that this model would find full support of environmentalist proponents of zoos. Some of the focus on faltering species is certainly grounded in concern for the wellbeing of the animals in that species, but there is also sizable concern for what species loss means for the environment more generally and human wellbeing in particular. Although it is not exactly what Szasz (2007) was referring to with his conceptualization of the Inverted Quarantine (IQ), in that individuals are not trying to reduce their individual environmental risks by altering their consumption, it can be viewed as a commodified and individualized response to environmental risk in the sense that hopes are being pinned on the commodification of individual animals in zoos as a way to mitigate the environmental risks of endangering species while the underlying, systemic causes go unexamined. As argued herein, the zoo as it is currently constituted is particularly ill suited for addressing the underlying causes of species declines.

For some animal advocates, the failure of breeding programmes may not be a problem, as some have argued that saving species through breeding programmes is not advisable. One line of argument is that we have moral obligations to individuals, not species, and therefore concern for species should not trump individual wellbeing (Jamieson 2002). Another line of argument suggests that if the wellbeing of a species is so compromised, perhaps we should let it die out and observe the passing for what it is – the consequence of our harmful environmental behaviour (Malamud 1998). Yet it is hard to envision many animal advocates, particularly the environmentally focused ones, being willing to stand by and watch this happen.

Jamieson (2002) argues that the only way to conserve species is via the *in situ* route of setting land aside for them and changing human behaviour that has pushed so many species to the brink of extinction (and beyond). However, it appears that the time where this would have worked has passed (Keulartz 2015) and that some *ex situ* interventions will be necessary to save some species. A potential compromise between the efforts of environmentalists and animal advocates presents itself here, whereby only those threatened species that tolerate captivity well would be bred and reintroduced. Such breeding programmes could be operated by governmental agencies and/or nongovernmental organizations, but they would not be for profit and ideally would take place away from the objectifying gaze of the public. There are two caveats worth noting here. First, the trend within the zoo industry in North America in particular, consistent with neoliberalism more generally, has been towards privatization of public zoos. So increased government intervention in North America does not look particularly promising at this point in time. In countries such as Germany, however, where the vast majority of zoos are publicly owned (Laidlaw 2017), there may be greater openness to having the government take a greater role in breeding programmes. Second, greater state involvement in breeding programmes would not totally undercut the speciesism that makes keeping animals in captivity possible; it would signal an end to the display of exotic animals for profit and gazing upon captive animals as a source of entertainment, however. For as long as zoos are at the behest of neoliberal consumer culture, their ability to help animals and the environment is fatally flawed, because "no matter how well intentioned zoo staffers may be, inevitably zoos are subject to pressures to increase visitor numbers and attract corporate sponsors" (Milstein 2009, 42). Yet I would not suggest passively waiting for zoos and aquaria as they currently exist to give way to this new form.

Academic observers are divided over the potential of pro-zoo environmentalists and animal advocates seeing eye to eye. Minteer and Collins (2013) are clearly not optimistic, writing:

> Despite attempts by some ethicists and scientists to find common ground between animal- and environmental-centered values at either the philosophic or pragmatic level, many observers believe that the gulf separating ethically individualistic, animal-centered commitments and conservationists' more holistic commitment to promoting the viability of populations and communities is simply too wide to bridge, even in cases where animal-centered and biodiversity-centered advocates have common cause. (p. 43)

On the other hand, Keulartz (2015) believes that both sides of the zoo debate can be integrated. He argues that this can be done through frame restructuring if both sides are willing to modify their positions in response to critiques from the other side. As he puts it, each side "should learn to 'squint' so to speak in order to see things from both angels [sic] simultaneously. Only then will it be possible to find a morally defensible balance between animal welfare concerns on the one hand and species conservation commitments on the other" (339).

If even some of the changes proposed above are made, it is possible to envision the animal advocate and pro-zoo environmental positions coming closer together. On the other hand, if zoos fail to modify their policies and actions to make them more animal- and environmentally friendly, they may inadvertently unify both sides anyway.

4

Fur: "Green" or Irredeemably Cruel Product?

A few years ago, I was driving to work in Windsor, Ontario, Canada when I noticed a new billboard along my route: it proclaimed that "Fur is Green." The billboard was eye-catching, complete with vivid colours and a picture of a female model wearing fur, but what held my attention was the claim that fur is green, presumably meaning that it is environmentally friendly. The Fur Council of Canada had paid for the billboard, and it was the first explicit campaign marketing fur as a green product that I had encountered.

Intrigued, I checked out their website, www.furisgreen.com, for further information once I arrived at my office. The site promised to provide an "informed opinion" and the home page contained the following statement: "At a time when we are all trying to be conscious of how our lifestyles affect nature, fur is an excellent choice. Like leather, suede and shearling, **fur** is a **natural product**, a true gift from nature..." (emphasis in original). The page contained three main sections: "Fur is Eco-Logical," "Animal Welfare," and "People and Cultures."

The "Fur is Eco-Logical" section describes fur as "a natural, renewable, and sustainable" resource. Readers are provided with the following cursory, if not misleading, description of ecological functioning: "In nature, each plant and animal species generally produces more offspring than the land can support to maturity. Like other species, we live by making use of part of this surplus that nature creates." They proceed to juxtapose furs with synthetic

Animal Advocacy and Environmentalism

products, which they describe as being "generally made from petroleum (a non-renewable resource), which is NOT consistent with the sustainable use of our environment." Fur products are further described as being durable, recyclable, and biodegradable, whereas synthetics are depicted as cheap, disposable, landfill fodder. They do acknowledge that "nothing is 100 percent green" and that chemicals do need to be used to process the fur.

They further assure readers that endangered species are not used for fur by the industry, which is governed by "strict government regulations" (http://www.furisgreen.com/renewable.aspx). A photo on the website of a dead coyote laying in the snow is captioned with the statement, "Overpopulated coyotes are more susceptible to disease and parasites including sarcoptic mange" (http://www.furisgreen.com/wildlifemanagement.aspx). They also state that beaver and muskrat populations, which comprise the majority of wild-caught furbearing animals, are thriving. Of note, the "eco-logical" section of the website contains no mention of fur farming or the controversial Canadian seal hunt.

The section on Animal Welfare does contain content specifically about fur farming (http://www.furisgreen.com/animalwelfare. aspx). Here readers are assured that animal welfare laws are followed and that treating the animals in an ethical way is in the best interests of the "farmer" because it results in the best quality fur. As for the welfare of wild-caught fur-bearing animals, readers are advised that being trapped or hunted is a better way to die than the alternative of disease and starvation, and that these deaths are a means to manage wildlife populations and maintain ecological harmony (http://www.furisgreen.com/wildlifemanagement.aspx). This section of the website also contextualizes the proportion of animals killed for fur versus for food (1 percent and 99 percent, respectively), and explains that twice as many pet animals are euthanized in animal shelters each year, and ten times more animals are killed on the roads, than are killed for their fur (http://www.furisgreen.com/peopleandanimals.aspx).

The section of the site devoted to People and Cultures refers to the fur trade as "fair trade" and boasts that 65,000 Canadians work in the fur trade, and that it contributes $800 million to the national economy (http://www.furisgreen.com/fairtrade.aspx). Trappers are described as providing a service as "practicing conservationists" because they have a stake in protecting the land. They reportedly eat what they hunt and then sell the fur. Only one line of text in this section references fur farming, stating, "Fur farming helps to maintain rural communities, at a time when efficient modern agriculture is reducing farming populations in many regions" (http://www.furisgreen.com/traditionallifestyles.aspx), thereby implying that fur farming is a small scale, more traditional, way of farming. Indeed, the entire site provides less information about what fur actually *is* than it does about what it *is not*: it is not produced by "efficient modern agriculture"; it does not claim as many animal lives as roads, shelters, and animal agriculture; being killed for one's fur is not as painful as dying of disease; and fur is not environmentally damaging like its synthetic counterparts.

Interestingly, if one erroneously types in the .ca extension (the common Canadian domain) instead of .com for the furisgreen webpage, a page appears that looks like the furisgreen.com page, complete with the same main sections. However, a closer read makes it apparent that this page is an act of resistance. The introductory text on the main page reads, "Explore the site to find out about the many ways to convince yourself that wearing fur is good for Indigenous communities, the economy, and the environment. Whatever way you want to justify it, we will help you." The text in the "eco-logical section" is particularly scathing. The section provides a description of how wild animal populations have been negatively impacted by trapping, and the green buzzwords used on the authentic page are problematized as follows:

> Whilst it is true that fur is natural, this is only the case if it stays on the animal's back. It's fair to say, therefore, that when we state fur is a "**natural resource**" we are bending the truth. In fact, it isn't even a resource that we have been given any right to tap into BUT it is important that we are using key words such as bf["**natural**", "**renewable**" and "**sustainable**" to lure everyone into a false sense of ecological complacency. (http://www.furisgreen.ca/en/renewable-resource-fur-cruelty.html)

The fact that there are duelling websites devoted to the "green" status of fur is testament to the conflict at hand here. In its Fur is Green marketing campaign, the Fur Council of Canada is rather brilliantly leveraging the current pro-environment sentiment among the general public to stem the tide of anti-fur attitudes, while simultaneously exploiting a relatively recent rift between some (but certainly not all) animal advocates and environmentalists on the issue of fur.

This chapter explores this rift and teases apart the controversy over fur into its two main constituent parts: hunting and trapping wild animals for their fur, and fur farming. Animal advocates have paid a great deal of attention to trapping and hunting (particularly seals) for fur. Although some of this activity has paid off (for instance, the Canadian seal hunt has become a hotly contested practice), it is argued in this chapter that more attention should be paid to fur farming – an area where animal advocacy and environmental concerns more closely align. This chapter further illustrates that the chasm between the environmental movement and the animal advocacy movement varies in size depending upon where the topic is located on the wild-domesticated continuum. The large rifts are apparent closer to the wild end of the continuum (i.e., wild trapped and hunted fur-bearing animals versus fur farming).

The fur trade

The fur trade has a long history and has actually played a fairly significant role in some other historical developments. For instance, it brought different cultures into contact and contributed to the creation of new cultural groups and nation-states (see Sorenson 2010). Furbearing animals were also an important source of clothing as well as food and oil among Indigenous populations and colonizers. In fact, the main historical driver of the seal hunt in Canada was demand for seal oil in the UK.

Today, the global demand for fur is driven rather paradoxically by its status as a luxury item and a potent symbol of conspicuous consumption on the one hand, and its popularity and normalized status on the other. This paradox is illuminated in Magee's (2016) ethnographic descriptions of the ways that wearing fur in Central and Eastern European countries has been normalized as a way to link consumers with their national history and culture, while also being an instrument for displaying one's wealth. She observes that being anti-fur in some of these countries is tantamount to being unpatriotic. Currently, the largest national markets for fur in terms of raw numbers include China, Italy, Germany, Korea, Japan, Russia, the countries of the former USSR, Spain, and the US (Wasley 2009).

This demand is met through the deaths of approximately 40 million fur-bearing animals globally each year (Wasley 2009). Most of the animals killed for the fur industry are located in cold climates, such as Canada and Norway, where animals grow thick fur to protect them from the environment. These countries, however, do not do most of the pelt processing: a great deal of it (approximately two-thirds globally) is done in the EU, followed by the US and China (Zarkadas et al. 2016).

Few people likely realize how internationalized the fur industry is. For many, the mention of fur production instead elicits images of baby seals being clubbed to death in the Canadian seal hunt. Canada certainly has been historically, and continues to be, at the forefront of the war over fur (discussed in detail shortly). Yet the Canadian seal hunt – and hunting or trapping wild animals more generally – constitutes a relatively small segment of the global fur trade. Of animals killed for their fur, 85 percent are from fur farms (Wasley 2009). Approximately 900,000 seals are hunted globally every year (Howse and Langille 2011); between one-quarter and one-third of this total comes from Canada, depending on the quota set that year and the success of the hunt. By way of comparison, mink in Canadian fur farms alone number two million (Nituch et al. 2011).

The AAM has tended to focus on hunting and trapping for fur, even though fur farming costs more animals their lives. This focus made strategic sense, as images of animals suffering in leg-hold traps or being clubbed to death on bloody ice floes could be used to initiate and sustain public support for their cause. Bob Hunter, co-founder of Greenpeace, has referred to such images as "mind-bombs": their strength is that they readily elicit emotion without requiring a detailed explanation (Dauvergne and Neville 2011). In contrast, pictures of animals languishing in fur farms are perhaps not as attention-grabbing as the bloodier images of hunted and trapped animals, and are likely to be more difficult to get.

The focus on fur acquired from wild hunts and trapping has caused more of a tension with environmentalists than might have otherwise been the case. Unlike with sport hunting and zoos (Chapters 2 and 3), where the divide between animal advocates and environmentalists is longstanding, on the issue of fur, many animal advocates and environmentalists were on the same page historically, but a divide between their positions emerged in recent years. This chapter provides insight into that tension and recommendations for how it might be ameliorated moving forward.

Hunting and trapping, and the politics of wild fur

The various positions of the animal advocacy and environmental organizations on the issue of fur, and how they have shifted over time, is perhaps best illustrated via the Canadian seal hunt – the largest hunt of marine mammals in the world (Leaper et al. 2009). The commercial hunt of seals in Canada dates back to the early eighteenth century (Marland 2014). Harp seals and (less commonly) hooded seals are hunted during the spring each year. Born in March, they quickly wean from their mothers and are left to their own devices. The fur they are born with (white for harp seals and bluish for hooded seals) is shed at two weeks of age, at which point they get their adult coat. The young seals do not yet swim and instead stay on the ice. Without their mothers to defend them and the ability to go in the water, they are rather defenceless (Daoust et al., 2002).

After years of intensive hunting, with more than 400,000 (mainly pups) killed each year, the seal population declined precipitously in the latter half of the nineteenth century. The decline evened off when world events in the first half of the twentieth century – two world wars and an economic depression – resulted in fewer human and economic resources being devoted to the hunt. After WWII, the seal hunt regained its previous momentum, and became even more intensive when Norwegian ships also joined in. Once again, hunting caused the seal population to drop (Dauvergne 2010; Dauvergne and Neville 2011; Daust et al. 2002), to the point that it attracted outside attention.

In the 1960s and 1970s, scientists, animal advocacy organizations (such as the International Fund for Animal Welfare, founded in opposition to the seal hunt), and environmental organizations (such as the Canadian Audubon Society and Greenpeace) joined forces against the seal hunt, providing a demonstrative example of how environmental and animal interests intersect. Together, these constituent groups were rather successful in their campaign. One of the creative strategies they employed (mainly undertaken by Greenpeace activists) was spray-painting the white fur on baby seals in a simple yet ingenious way to diminish their economic value (Dauvergne and Neville 2011). Even more significant was the way that the groups, aided by video footage, turned a substantial portion of the public against the seal hunt.

Activists began trying to film the seal hunt. The Canadian government responded by implementing laws criminalizing the actions of hunt observers. The government also tried to gain some of the ground they had lost to anti-seal hunt groups in the now public war over sealing by invoking environmental and cultural defences of the hunt, framing it as a way to ensure balance in the ecosystem and as a traditional activity undertaken by Indigenous groups (Braunsberger and Buckler 2009; Dauvergne and Neville 2011). To be sure, sealing has a long history among some Indigenous groups, one that predates the laws established to regulate the hunt; these groups have advocated on their own behalf to maintain their traditional hunts (see Wenzel 1991).

Another strategy activists employed was to reduce export markets. They were successful in pressuring the US government to ban the importation of seal products, as well as the hunting of seals domestically, in 1972 (Howse and Langille 2011). Then pressure was applied to European markets. In the early 1980s, IFAW took out ads in European newspapers encouraging citizens to write to politicians and demand a ban on the fur acquired from extremely young seals. In response, the European Parliament implemented a temporary ban on these products in 1983. IFAW next worked to implement a boycott of Canadian seafood products to protest the continuation of the hunt. They were able to secure participation from some of the largest European supermarkets (Dauvergne and Neville 2011; Daoust et al. 2002; Braunsberger and Buckler 2009). The threat to the seafood industry pushed Canada in 1987 to stop the hunting of seals under two weeks of age (i.e., those with white and blue fur) and to ban the use of large vessels in the hunt (Dauvergne and Neville 2011).

Throughout this period, the fur industry and the Canadian government periodically tried to frame seals as an environmental threat, specifically as a threat to codfish populations. They argued that the seal hunt was necessary to keep the seal populations in check and, by extension, protect the cod stocks that they fed on. In the late 1970s, bumper stickers that read "Save a cod: eat a seal" began popping up in Newfoundland, the province known as "the front" of the hunt (Marland 2014). Asserting a connection between seal and cod populations became public policy in the mid-1990s when the Canadian Fisheries Minister publicly claimed that the seal population was negatively impacting fish populations. Scientists fought back against this claim; nearly 100 from 15 different countries signed a petition explaining that the science did not support that assessment, and that declining fish populations were due to overfishing (Braunsberger and Buckler 2009).

Even if there was not an ecological connection between the waning seal hunt and crashing cod populations, there was a political-economic association in that the Canadian government sought to make up for the declining revenue and jobs from cod fishing by expanding the seal hunt. To that end, they increased the number of seals that could be killed each year (although now the hunt was limited to seals two weeks and older) and poured millions of dollars in subsidies into the commercial hunt. They were also able to cash in on a demand for fur that was once again growing; in the year 2002, it was up 10 percent globally and 35 percent in the UK alone. That same year, 300,000 seals were killed in the Canadian seal hunt, making it the largest hunt since the 1960s (Dauvergne and Neville 2011).

Opposition by activist organizations to the revived twenty-first century Canadian seal hunt was less strong, for a variety of reasons. Dauvergne and Neville (2011) speculate it was in part because the organizations that had been the most involved – IFAW and Greenpeace – had become more bureaucratic and less confrontational, and had moved on to other causes. For its part, Greenpeace reported it had stepped back from its opposition to the seal hunt due to concern that Indigenous populations were being negatively affected (Burgwald, 2016). Other environmentally focused organizations also backed off from the cause as the anti-seal hunt movement fractured, with animal advocates remaining on the side of opposition and those more concerned with ecological and associated issues taking on a more agnostic position in some cases and a supportive position in others (Dauvergne and Neville 2011; Knezevic 2009).

The timing of the fracturing of the anti-seal hunt into animal advocate and environmentally focused camps coincides with Szasz's (2007) description of a significant segment of the EM turning inward and more towards individual self-preservation (often through consumerism), eventually into what he refers to as Inverted Quarantine (IQ). In short, the spectre of an "out-of-balance" seal population taking an environmental toll that could negatively impact fish stocks and people by extension may have resonated particularly well at this time.

It is not only the specific issue of the Canadian seal hunt that has created a divide between the EM and the AAM vis-à-vis fur. Some environmental/wildlife-focused organizations, such as the National Wildlife Federation, have also voiced their support for trapping animals for their fur. A case in California is illustrative of the tension between the two positions. In the late 1990s, Californians voted in favour of Proposition 4, banning the trapping of animals for fur. The ban was subsequently challenged by the National Audubon society, along with hunters and trappers. They argued that there should be an exemption to make it possible to trap predators of endangered species. Critics of their position pointed out that the predators they were interested in killing also not so coincidentally preyed upon species of animals that hunters like to hunt. One commentator remarked at the time that "The battle over Prop. 4 reflects what appears to be a widening gulf between the 'animal rights' and 'ecological' wings of the animal protection movement" (Dove 2000, 42).

Back in Canada, the government rebuilt the seal hunt around seals older than two weeks, complete with subsidies, to great effect. From 2003 to 2008, nearly 1.8 million seals were killed in the Canadian commercial seal hunt; 98 percent of these seals were just older than the two-week-old minimum age requirement (Leaper et al. 2009). Maintaining the pressure on the hunt was mainly left to animal advocacy organizations, who framed the entire hunt as cruel and immoral. Once again, a Canadian seafood boycott was called for, this time by the Humane Society of the US (HSUS) in 2005. The HSUS estimated that their boycott had pushed export sales of Canadian snow crab down by 36 percent, costing the industry $350 million. It is difficult to ascertain the accuracy of this estimate; however, as Braunsberger and Buckler point out, "even if only 5 percent of the $350 million CAD decline in snow crab exports could be attributed to the boycott, it is much more than the value of sealing, which has been estimated at $12 million CAD in 2007" (2009, 471–472).

Citizens in EU countries were also asked to reinvigorate their efforts to persuade politicians to oppose the hunt. The EU remained perhaps the largest market for seal products from the hunt. The pressure paid off. The European Food Safety Authority undertook an investigation into the hunt. Upon observation, the EU investigators were concerned that the seals experienced significant suffering prior to their death. A blow to the head with a hakapik (a club with a spike on the end) rarely kills the seal immediately. Instead, follow-up is needed to ensure death, but the sealers often move on to striking more seals before ascertaining that the previously struck one is indeed dead. The use of firearms also does not ensure immediate death; a lethal shot is difficult in the context of moving seals and rocking boats. There was also evidence that some seals were skinned alive (Howse and Langille 2011).

A group of members of the Canadian Veterinary Medical Association also observed seal hunts and noted some problems with 2 percent of the kills. (Previous reports had put the proportion of improperly killed seal in the wide range between 0 and 54 percent.) Overall, the group of veterinarians measured an average of 45 seconds between seals being shot and then being killed by a blow to the head. As a result of their observations, they recommended shooting the seals a second time from the boat, while admitting that this may be difficult due to moving seals and boats. They also recommended follow-up, because it could not be concluded from their research that the deaths of the seals were entirely humane (Daoust et al. 2002).

In the absence of reassurance that the hunt was entirely humane, in 2009, the EU approved a ban on seal product imports from Canada, specifically citing moral concerns about the welfare of the seals. Nonetheless, there are a number of exemptions under the ban: Canadian seal products can enter the EU as long as they are exported and do not enter the EU market; seal products from traditional hunts conducted by Indigenous communities can enter the EU market, as can seal products from hunts conducted on the grounds of "sustainable management," as long as they are sold on a not-for-profit basis; and EU citizens can bring products home with them that were purchased abroad for their own use (Howse and Langille 2011).

The ban, coupled with the global recession and poor ice conditions, have resulted in recent seal hunts below the allowable quota (Dauvergne and Neville 2011). Based on data collected by the Canadian government, approximately 218,000 seals were killed in 2008 (the year before the EU ban). In the years since, the numbers have varied from a low of approximately 38,000 to a high of 98,000 (Fisheries and Oceans Canada 2016a).

The governments of Canada and Norway, along with Indigenous groups and industry stakeholders, challenged the EU ban at the World Trade Organization. In short, they argued that the ban imposed an unfair trade restriction, and that it unduly affected

Indigenous communities (for more information on the challenge, see Dauvergne and Neville 2011; Howse and Langille 2011). It was the first test of the invocation of trade restrictions for moral reasons. In defence of the ban, comparisons between moral concerns about animals and religious beliefs were invoked, and the ability of countries to ban the importation of animal-derived food products that are in conflict with dominant religious beliefs were cited (see Howse and Langille 2011).

The challenge was ultimately unsuccessful and the EU's ban on the specified seal products was upheld. However, the Government of Canada has not given up on the commercial seal hunt. Fisheries and Oceans Canada (2016b) states on their website that

> The Government of Canada is committed to maintaining existing markets for Canadian seal products and supporting the development of potential new markets .... To meet the requirements set by the European Union, the Government of Canada has established a program to invest $5.7 million over five years to support the development of systems to certify seal products resulting from hunts traditionally conducted by Indigenous communities, and to produce business advice and training to help Indigenous communities develop effective business practices. Additionally, this investment will support the efforts of the broader sealing industry to increase market access opportunities.

Thus, the Canadian seal hunt will continue into the foreseeable future, but it will likely look different than it did in the past. Animal advocates will need to give very careful consideration to how they address it going forward, and distinguish between the Indigenous hunt and the commercial hunt for furs sold domestically or to markets outside the EU.

Fur farming: the borderland between wild and domesticated

Although the issue of fur historically brought environmentalists and animal advocates together, the history of the Canadian seal hunt demonstrates that it has more recently become a wedge issue. Fur industry stakeholders have been quick to try to exploit this divide by framing fur as being a sustainable, green product. Magee sums up this somewhat surprising turn of events as follows: "Until quite recently, it would have been difficult to imagine fur's promotion as an ethical product, an emergence that seems to be the result of a growing concern with sustainability" (2016, 290). Ecofeminists such as Gaard (2017) have argued that notions of sustainability have been anthropocentric and need to be reevaluated using a nonspeciesist ecofeminist lens. I whole-heartedly agree with that as a longer-term project; however, in the shorter term, I would emphasize that the framing of fur as sustainable has been so successful because attention has been focused on the killing of wild animals for their coats. Fur farming deserves more attention, for reasons detailed below. Here animal and environmental activists are not as easily pitted against each other.

The vast majority (85 percent) of animals killed for their fur are bred, raised, and killed on fur farms (Wasley 2009). As far as geographic distribution goes, approximately two-thirds of fur farms are located in Northern Europe, and approximately one-tenth in North America (Wasley 2009). The leaders in fur farming are Denmark, China, Finland, and Russia (Bonesi and Palazon 2007; Wasley 2009). It has been banned elsewhere, such as in Austria and the UK (Bonesi and Palazon 2007). In the UK, the ban has explicitly been framed as being in the interests of "public morality."

The fact that there are a large number of animals being raised for fur globally (exact estimates are hard to come by) is evidenced by the fact that research into how to use their waste as an energy source has been deemed a valuable use of time (see Zarkadas et al. 2016). Like farms raising animals for human consumption, discussed in the next chapter, fur farms house a great many animals, some upward of 75,000 animals, and generate *a lot* of manure as a result. As with animal agriculture for human consumption, fur farm manure is high in specific nutrients (such as nitrogen) that can contaminate groundwater. This can run into bodies of water where algae overgrows (due to the high nitrate content) and the result is eutrophication (Goodwin 1997; Zarkadas et al. 2016). Water and air quality problems associated with fur farms have been reported in some locations, such as the Great Lakes region of the US and in Finland (Goodwin 1997).

The environmental problems associated with farming animals for their fur, as with farming animals for food (detailed in the next chapter), can be explicated via the treadmill of production concept, which highlights the expansion imperative of capitalism as problematic. The investment in technologies to keep accelerating the treadmill contributes to the problem (see Schnaiberg 1980; Gould, Pellow, and Schnaiberg 2008). The expansion imperative vis-à-vis fur has been witnessed in the increased use of fur as trim on garments (e.g., the use of coyote fur on Canada Goose brand coats) as the popularity of garments made entirely out of fur has waned in recent years. Moreover, in the face of environmental challenges, technology is being mobilized by the industry to monetize waste (such as fecal matter). And the use of animals as inputs is rendered unproblematic by an industry that uses reproductive science and technologies to create a constant stream of high-value fur-bearing animals.

Even if one accepts the conceptualization of these animals as a "renewable resource," the animal welfare challenges on these farms are difficult to deny. Animals in fur farms are kept in close quarters, as doing so reduces costs and therefore increases profits. As a result, they are susceptible to physical and psychological problems. Psychological problems may be particularly endemic to fur farms because animals kept for fur (such as mink and fox) have not been thoroughly domesticated, as animals kept for food have been, and may therefore suffer even more from extreme confinement, as the cages they are kept in do not come close to replicating their natural environment. For instance, mink are not given access to water to swim in, which is an activity that occupies a significant amount of their time in the wild. Using an experimental design, a study on farmed mink published in the journal *Nature* found that not having access to water to swim in induces distress levels (measured by cortisol levels) akin to that produced by being deprived of food (Mason et al. 2001). More generally, research across species farmed for their fur indicates that they often suffer from self-mutilation and reproductive problems (Linzey 2006).

The conditions on fur farms are conducive to the rapid spread of disease. Nituch and colleagues (2011, 5) explain, "Commercial farms are potential sources for the maintenance and spread of infectious disease because animals are often kept at continuously high population densities (for example, some mink farms house >10,000 mink), and new animals are regularly imported from other sources, increasing the potential for infectious diseases to flourish." These diseases can spread to proximal wildlife populations in two key ways. First, diseases can spread from fur farms to wild populations via contact with fur farm animal manure and other byproducts. Viruses can survive in manure, soil, and animal carcasses, some for as long as two years (Nituch et al. 2011). Second, disease can spread through animal-to-animal contact when animals escape from farms, are released from farms, or, less commonly, if wild animals enter fur farms.

Once again, mink provide an illustrative example of the problem. Observers have noted that wild populations of American mink have been declining in Canada over the past several years. Factors identified to date, such as habitat destruction and over-hunting, cannot entirely explain the observed declines. Nituch and colleagues (2011) theorize that the transmission of Aleutian Disease (AD) from farmed mink to wild populations could be part of the problem. The disease compromises the immune system and negatively impacts reproduction. It is a significant problem, to the degree that researchers have noted that it "may become a limiting factor in the industry's ability to produce mink" (Nituch et al. 2011, 2). A study of samples from mink farms in Canada found that approximately one-third of the mink were positive for the AD antibodies, indicating that they had indeed been exposed to the disease. In the sample of wild mink tested by the Nituch team, AD antibodies were found in nearly one-third of the samples. Further, the incidence was greatest in areas with high fur farm densities. As a result, they recommend improved biosecurity measures on fur farms to prevent wild and domesticated animals from coming into contact with one another (Nituch et al. 2011).

Another negative impact that fur farms can have on surrounding wildlife also stems from the escape/release of farmed animals. Released/escaped farmed animals can interbreed with wild populations. Nituch et al. (2011) cite one study that found that 64 percent of wild mink tested in Southern Ontario were hybrids of wild-fur farmed mink. This can affect the wild population in two different problematic ways. The interbreeding could negatively impact the population and cause declines, or the opposite could occur: the hybrid animals could overbreed and outcompete other species. They can also become invasive species in locations where they did not previously exist. This scenario has played out across Europe, where the non-native American mink was imported to populate fur farms. They have since established thriving feral populations in some regions, and as a result have negatively affected native populations (Bonesi and Palazon 2007). One study quantified the impact of the mink on ground-nesting birds in Finland (cited by Bonesi and Palazon, 2007); they found that when mink were removed from one region, fifteen of twenty-two species of ground-nesting birds increased, including two species that had been extinct in that region. As a result of their own research and that of others, Bonesi and Palazon (2007) recommend not establishing mink farms in countries where feral populations have not yet been established.

There are many potentially significant impacts that fur farming can have on the environment. Yet these impacts have not received much attention from the media and advocacy groups – certainly considerably less than has the killing of wild animals for their fur. The remainder of the chapter details recommendations for refocusing critiques of fur, and delineates spaces where common ground can once again be reached between the AAM and the EM on this specific issue.

The argument in favour of fur

There are two main environmental arguments in favour of commercially killing animals for their fur. The first is that killing animals for their fur, specifically through trapping and hunting, can be a valuable wildlife management tool to control disease and populations. This argument was foregrounded in the "Fur is Green" campaign described at the opening of the chapter. In their defence of the seal hunt, the Government of Canada also popularized this assertion, arguing that the codfish stocks had declined because of seal populations that were presumably increasing due to a declining seal hunt. They backed away from this assertion after virulent opposition from scientists, but an examination of the Government of Canada's Fisheries and Oceans website indicates that they are back at it, this time suggesting that grey seals are responsible for half of the natural mortality of large cod (Fisheries and Oceans Canada 2016c). A review of Fisheries and Oceans' own statistics on the seal hunt (see Fisheries and Oceans Canada 2016a) indicates, however, that the number of grey seals killed in the seal hunt has increased dramatically in the past several years. Linking the importance of the grey seal hunt with fostering an improved cod population appears rather disingenuous.

Canadian stakeholders are not the only ones drawing a link between seal populations and ecological sustainability. The British Fur Trade Association has been quoted as stating, "There is no conservation reason to ban the trade in seals. The Canadian seal hunt is well regulated and monitored by scientists. **Victims of this ban will be the growing seal populations** and the communities, including the Inuit, that depend on them" (cited by Wasley 2009, 33; emphasis mine). The warning implies that seal populations will overshoot their carrying capacity and collapse, causing individual seals to suffer.

Environmentalists and even some animal welfarists may find this concern compelling, whereas animal rightists/abolitionists would have serious problems with killing animals as an environmental strategy, as discussed in the previous chapters. This tension is evident among some of the large wildlife-focused charitable organizations. The World Wildlife Fund supports "sustainable" hunts of seals and other animals, whereas the Sea Shepherd Conservation Society (2003) has been critical of the WWF for taking this position. Regardless, even if one accepts the claim that killing animals for their fur can be justified on the grounds of wildlife management, given that 85 percent of animals killed for their fur are on fur farms, the justification would only apply in a minority of cases.

The second main environmental argument in favour of fur applies to all fur products and not just those from wild populations. It is argued that fur is more environmentally friendly than synthetics, which are produced from petrochemicals. The fur industry argues that fur garments last longer than other fabrics and therefore they are more environmentally friendly than synthetic products; they biodegrade once disposed of whereas synthetic materials do not; and fur farms engage in recycling by feeding the animals the waste products from the meat, fish, and dairy industries (International Fur Federation n.d.).

There has not yet been a great deal of research conducted to assess those claims. One of the few extant studies compared the impacts of full-length mink coats and mink-trimmed coats with their faux fur analogues. The study found that the environmental impacts of fur coats are greater, and the only way that the impacts would come close to being comparable is if the fur coat had a lifespan four times longer than the faux coat (Bijleveld, 2013). The International Fur Federation hired a consulting agency to undertake its own analysis. Their report concludes that while faux fur performs well, respectively, on respiratory organics emissions, ozone layer depletion, and terrestrial acidification, natural fur consumes less non-renewable energy, poses fewer global warming impacts, fewer impacts from ionizing radiation, and produces fewer emissions. They do note, however, that a definitive conclusion cannot be reached because of data limitations and assumptions that had to be made as part of their analysis (DSS Management Consultants 2012). Further research is certainly required to draw more robust conclusions.

Some environmentalists and environmental organizations have also been moved by cultural arguments in favour of fur. As mentioned earlier, Greenpeace abandoned its campaign against the Canadian seal hunt out of concern that it was negatively affecting Indigenous populations. While they are against commercial seal hunting, they support the right of Indigenous populations to hunt and fish. A statement on their website reads, "when Greenpeace and others campaigned against the seal hunt in the 1970s and 1980s, we didn't adequately distinguish between the inhumane and cruel industrial hunt and the traditional one. The results were devastating to many Arctic Indigenous communities. Hunting and fishing in this harsh landscape is, for many, their only means of survival" (Burgwald 2016). They have also issued an apology and developed a policy in support of Indigenous rights in collaboration with First Nations (Kerr 2014). As noted earlier, the EU also recognized this distinction in its ban on seal products from Canada and provides exemptions for products from traditional, Indigenous hunts. This distinction between the (larger scale) commercial hunt and that undertaken by Indigenous groups that have been doing so for generations is certainly an important one. Nonetheless, it should not be assumed that all Indigenous peoples are supportive of the fur industry; some have voiced opposition to the use of dozens of animals to create one article of clothing that could otherwise be produced with the pelt of one large animal (Sorenson 2010).

The seal hunt is also part of the culture and economy of the province of Newfoundland and Labrador. On the economic side, it makes up from 0.06 to 0.12 percent of the province's Gross Domestic Product and employs 5,000–6,000 people (Marland 2014). It is not a large industry, but nonetheless cannot be disregarded, as it is important to those who work in it. Consequently, many Newfoundlanders are particularly incredulous of attacks on the industry from those perceived as outsiders. For instance, in 2006 the Premier of the province appeared on CNN's *Larry King Live* show virulently defending the seal hunt against Paul McCartney and his then-partner Heather Mills. The province even turned against Canadian hockey icon Don Cherry when he made negative comments about his co-host eating a seal burger while in Newfoundland (CBC News 2015).

The cultural arguments and the need to be culturally sensitive are compelling, particularly from an ecofeminist perspective attentive to power imbalances. However, it should be noted that just as the argument (detailed above) that fur is an environmentally friendly product because it is essentially a by-product of wildlife management applies to killing wild furbearing animals instead of fur farming, so does this concern about the impacts of the fur trade on Indigenous populations and the people of Newfoundland and Labrador more generally. Thus, the most convincing environmental and cultural justifications for the killing of fur-bearing animals really only apply to a minority (15 percent) of cases.

The position against fur

Concern for animal welfare applies to both wild-caught and farmed fur animals, although the focus of the concern varies. For wild-caught and killed furbearing animals, the primary animal welfare concern is with the death. There are concerns about trapped animals being injured and suffering in traps until they die or are found and killed, and with hunted animals, such as seals, suffering from injuries prior to death. Conversely, the animal welfare concern about farmed furbearing animals is primarily with the way their lives are lived in cramped captivity with thousands of other animals, where illness can and does easily spread. Research documenting that the inability to access water to swim in among farmed mink is as distressing as not being fed, discussed earlier, puts the deprivations of captivity into context.

Although concern for the animals themselves is the focus of animal advocates (welfarists and abolitionists alike), there are also environmental considerations relevant to wild-caught and fur-farmed furbearing animals that could be leveraged against the claim that "fur is green." First, wild fur-bearing animals, notably seals, are already under significant pressure given the environmental changes wrought by global climage change (GCC). These pressures include diminishing ice quality, which has contributed to lower kill ("harvest") numbers. Further, the fish that seals consume are reportedly becoming increasingly more difficult to come by. A study published in the journal *Nature* reports that the number of Antarctic seals is dropping, and that it is most clearly related to an associated decline in the availability of krill, their food of choice, which is in turn related to changing weather patterns (Coulson and Clegg 2014).

Second, although the industry as well as national and subnational governments emphasize the fact that there is science behind their determination of quotas for hunts, that science is not uncontested. Leaper and colleagues (2009) argue that the current method used to determine quotas in the Canadian seal hunt is not precautionary (counter to the claims of scientists and politicians), as it has not been fully tested through simulation, and its ability to account for uncertainties is unknown. Further, they point to the following aspects of the calculations as being particularly problematic: the reference points used in the models are from gross population estimates instead of estimates of carrying capacity; the population surveys are not conducted in years where the weather and ice conditions are poor; and there is a five- to seven-year lag between overharvesting and when it would show up in population changes, so it could be too late by the time a problem is detected. Hammill and Stenson (2010), who work for the Department of Fisheries and Oceans, write in response that more conservative strategies, such as that proposed by Leaper and colleagues, "may never be accepted by managers and industry" (1). One is left to wonder, then, what level of risk has been accepted here?

Where to now?

One environmental argument in favour of fur that cuts across production methods is that it is less environmentally damaging than synthetics. The research commissioned by the fur industry has concluded that the impacts of synthetic furs are significantly greater, whereas the research sponsored by a group of nongovernmental organizations has found that the impacts of real fur are more significant. Moreover, there are potential ecological impacts that have not been accounted for in their calculations. The risks of fur farming, detailed herein, include escaped/released non-native animals becoming invasive species and forever altering local wildlife populations, the potential infection of local wildlife populations with diseases endemic to concentrated animal operations, environmental impacts of producing feed for all of these animals, and risks of environmental contamination via the tonnes of manure created. With hunting and trapping, there are uncertainties about how GCC will affect fur-bearing animal populations and if the current methods used to determine quotas are sensitive enough to these changes. It will be important for animal advocates to communicate these risks when confronted with claims about fur being "green."

In addition to questions about the environmental impacts of real versus faux fur, some people have been uncomfortable with a strong anti-fur position that vilifies the wearing of fur by all and fails to attend to the important differences between commercial and Indigenous hunting and trapping of fur-bearing animals. Fur tends to be critiqued as a luxury item, yet as Magee (2016) found in her ethnographic research in Poland, designating fur as a luxury item can be overly simplistic and problematic. Animal advocates would do well to use caution when tempted to make these generalizations. A more nuanced approach would no doubt focus energy where it is better spent, and be more likely to attract public support.

I would recommend focusing attention on fur farming instead of wild hunting and trapping. This may strike some animal advocates as counterintuitive, as the focus on the hunting of baby seals has been a cornerstone of the movement. That focus made sense at the time. It united ecologically minded and animal-minded individuals in a common cause. There were also powerful images of baby seals being clubbed to death that could be used to elicit sympathy and support from the public – the so-called mindbomb strategy.

The social environment has changed since that strategy was effective. The public has gotten used to, perhaps even become desensitized to, animal advocates employing certain images. Further, with the popularity of social media, people are often bombarded with messages and images. Dauvergne and Neville (2011, 205) explain, "the use of mindbombs tends to diminish their effectiveness over time, creating a cycle of ever-more startling images

with ever-decreasing effectiveness. More activists are also compet-
ing for each minute-or-so of daily protest-fame." They continue,
"Audiences for these campaigns, who were previously swayed by
emotional appeals, are developing a fatigue of perceived moral
superiority and an immunity to the images from traditional activist mindbombs" (Dauvergne and Neville 2011, 207).

Admittedly, it is perhaps more difficult for animal advocates
to gather images of the realities in fur farms, and the images of
their deaths might not be as ghastly as blood-splattered ice floes.
What fur farming does have going for it as a target is that it makes
some of the arguments in favour of fur moot (e.g., that killing
fur-bearing animals is part of cultural traditions that ought to
be respected, and that not killing animals will lead to ecological
imbalances). Focusing critical attention on fur farms makes practical and strategic sense. It is practical because the vast majority
of fur that is produced (85 percent) is produced on fur farms,
and therefore improving the lives of animals in this context, and
ideally abolishing the practice, would have a huge impact. Such a
focus is also strategic in that animal advocates could once again
win environmentalists over on the topic of fur, thus making it
more difficult for the fur industry to cash in on the schism between
animal advocates and environmentalists on this issue.

Fur farming has many potentially significant environmental
impacts that have not received much social movement or public
attention, and they are the types of environmental impacts that the
current EM tends to be focused on: those that put people at risk
(Szasz 2007), such as contamination of ground water and unleashing invasive species. This focus would also be consistent with the
perspective of some animal advocates, such as Linzey (2006), that
fur farms are particularly problematic. He writes, "some systems
of abuse cannot be reformed, because, although their worst
aspects may be ameliorated through regulation, they constitute a
moral offense that is so grave and so ingrained that abolition is the
only proper course of action" (164).

The Canadian seal hunt is a fraction of the size it used to be, as
demonstrated earlier. The ban on commercial seal product imports
into the EU, now upheld by the WTO, will no doubt continue to

take a significant toll. It is time to focus on fur farms. Moreover, campaigns specifically against fur farming can draw on the work being done in opposition to farming animals more generally – the topic of the next chapter. The massive scale of farming animals for food makes the intersecting impacts (on animals, the environment, and marginalized groups of people) of neoliberal free market capitalism, and the applicability of the treadmill of production and Inverted Quarantine concepts even more apparent. These insights are valuable for critically evaluating farming animals for food and fur, and for animal and environmental reasons, alike.

5

Industrial Animal Agriculture: Injustice Writ Large?

In 2006 the film *An Inconvenient Truth* was released. It was the creation of former US Vice President and Presidential nominee Al Gore, and detailed in a way accessible to a general audience what global climate change (GCC) is, what science indicates is causing it, what the impacts will be, and what can be done to mitigate them. Yet one particularly inconvenient truth was left out of the film: the impact that industrial animal agriculture (IAA) is having on GCC. A lot has changed in the past ten-plus years since that film was released: there is growing consensus around the anthropogenic causes of climate change, the public is more aware of GCC as a serious problem, and the role that animal agriculture plays in it is increasingly being acknowledged.

That same year the Food and Agriculture Organization of the United Nations published a groundbreaking report. *Livestock's Long Shadow* was the outcome of years of work by the Livestock, Environment and Development Initiative (LEAD), and it was supported by several supra-national and national governmental organizations. It detailed the results of analyses aggregating emissions along the livestock commodity chain. Based on the analyses, the researchers concluded that the livestock sector is "one of the top two or three most significant contributors to the most serious environmental problems, at every scale from local to global" (Steinfeld et al. 2006, xx). For instance, their findings indicate that animal agriculture produces 18 percent of the total global greenhouse gas emissions that contribute to GCC. This is more than is produced by the transportation sector. Researchers with the World Bank subsequently suggested that the 18 percent estimate was too conservative. Their analyses instead indicated that animal agriculture is responsible for just over half of greenhouse gas emissions globally (Goodland and Anhang 2009).

A few years after the report was released, one of my graduate students and I undertook a study to see if the growing empirical literature documenting a connection between animal agriculture and GCC was being reflected in the materials published by environmental and animal advocacy organizations internationally, meat industry stakeholder groups, governmental regulators, and the media (Bristow and Fitzgerald 2011). We found three of the six animal advocacy organizations examined cited the *Livestock's Long Shadow* report specifically, and four of the six cited animal agriculture's contribution to GCC more generally as a reason to abstain from consuming animal products. Notably, all except one of the animal advocacy organizations accused environmental groups of not paying enough attention to the environmental impacts of animal agriculture. Five of the six environmental organizations analyzed drew a link between animal agriculture and GCC, but none of them explicitly cited *Livestock's Long Shadow*, and the attention paid to the issue did not notably increase after the publication of the report. Further, none of the environmentally focused organizations recommended adopting a vegetarian or vegan diet as a way to reduce one's contribution to GCC. Our analysis of large daily print newspapers in Canada (the *Globe and Mail*) and the US (*USA Today*) for two years prior and after the release of the *Livestock's Long Shadow* report found that while the number of articles addressing the connection between animal agriculture and GCC increased slightly after the release of the FAO's report, the number of articles that addressed it was quite small. Further, only one article in *USA Today* and five in the *Globe and Mail* mentioned dietary changes as a way to combat GCC (Bristow and Fitzgerald 2011).

Although I have not conducted a formal follow-up analysis, based on my observations, the connection between animal agriculture and GCC (and environmental problems more generally) is more frequently and widely acknowledged today than it was even just a few years ago. This chapter details the research documenting these connections and explores how the environmental impact of IAA – particularly vis-à-vis GCC – has brought environmental and animal advocates into closer theoretical and applied positions over the past several years. I argue in this chapter that the issue of GCC in particular and the immense amount of attention it has garnered from the general public, from various governments, and from supranational organizations has given the EM and AAM unprecedented opportunity to work together. Although there has been limited cross-pollination and communication in the past (Bristow and Fitzgerald 2011), on this one issue the main interests of the contemporary EM and AAM – GCC and the mass production of animals for human consumption, respectively – are coalescing, creating fertile ground for academic and activist coalition-building.

The topic of IAA also has immense potential to garner support for the environmental and animal advocate causes particularly because it appeals to the Inverted Quarantine (IQ) impulse. There is growing awareness among the public that IAA can have harmful environmental and human health consequences. For instance, environmental justice groups are standing up against the siting of concentrated animal feeding operations (CAFOs) and slaughter-houses in their communities, as concerns mount about localized environmental degradation (Ladd and Edwards 2002) and the social impacts in communities (Fitzgerald, Kalof and Dietz 2009).

To further develop these connections, this chapter begins with a brief overview of IAA.[10] Next, the impacts of the industry are examined, with a focus on the environmental consequences and the animal welfare concerns. The chapter concludes with a discussion of how animal advocates and environmentalists may be drawn closer together around this specific issue.

Industrial animal agriculture: how we got here

Our current ways of raising and slaughtering animals for human consumption are relatively new, historically speaking.[11] For much of our animal-keeping history, animals were raised, killed, and consumed by those who owned them (subsistence farming). Historians estimate that during the sixteenth century there was a shift in focus from this subsistence farming to farming with the intent of selling the products. The amount of excess food produced increased with the passage of time as more animals were kept on less land, breeding became more efficient, and artificial animal feed was introduced to promote faster and more sustained animal growth (Thompson 1968).

Animal agriculture morphed dramatically with the application of industrial logic in the second half of the nineteenth century. During this period, human labour was increasingly replaced through mechanization. This mechanization, along with other scientific and technological applications, made it possible to satisfy the increasing demand for animal products that had been stoked by industrialization and urbanization. The scale of livestock production increased dramatically, although the production of livestock animals became concentrated on fewer and fewer farms as the twentieth century wore on (Fitzgerald 2003; Hardeman and Jochemsen 2012).

Early impacts of the industrialization of animal agriculture became apparent in mid-nineteenth-century Western Europe, where the increasing supply of animal products contributed to declining economic value per animal. The response there and elsewhere was not to slow down production; instead, farmers pursued increased industrialization, which eventually resulted in overproduction,[12] and the increasing detachment of food production from the natural limits of the environment and animal bodies (Hardeman and Jochemsen 2012). The impacts were apparent in North America by the turn of the twentieth century, with overgrazing and decimated pastureland (Franklin 1999). One "solution" was the creation of feedlots, where instead of grazing, many animals were confined to relatively small areas of land and fed grains, which had the effect of fattening them up more quickly for slaughter (Skaggs 1986).

In the US, the combination of scientific and technological developments, along with Depression-era policies, combined to create significant grain surpluses. For a period after World War II, much of these surpluses were shipped to Europe in support of the reconstruction effort. As agriculture in Europe increasingly recovered and industrialized, however, this market for US surpluses disappeared. The next solution that industry stakeholders and government officials arrived at was to increase the domestic demand for grains. This would be accomplished by feeding livestock animals more grains (e.g., corn) and increasing the number of livestock animals (Winders and Nibert 2004). At the time, "it seemed like a win/win solution for grain and livestock farmers, who were already concentrating the production of animals in feedlots and massive barns" (Fitzgerald 2015, 13).

The US government promoted livestock production via policies such as price supports and research funding. The research they supported pointed to the creation of CAFOs as the path forward to increasing livestock production.[13] In this form of production, there is a high concentration of animals in relatively small spaces. This method simultaneously increases the number of animals produced while reducing costs in the form of land, labour, and feed expenditures (Ibrahim 2007). This concentration is made possible through the prolific use of antibiotics (Ibrahim 2007; Wilkie 2005) and by mutilating the animals – including debeaking chickens and removing pigs' tails – to reduce the amount of injuries they inflict upon one another, and increase profits, by extension.

This increasingly industrialized and integrated form of production had the intended effect of increasing production and reducing production costs. The case of chickens in the US is illustrative in this regard. The cost of producing chickens dropped by nearly 90 percent from 1947 to the close of the twentieth century. Production simultaneously increased, for individual birds on average and in the aggregate. There was a two-thirds increase in the weight of chickens from 1940 to 2001, and they took half as long to reach their full weight as they had in the past. The industry also produced more of these larger chickens overall: the four largest chicken companies produced five times more chickens in 2002 than they did only twenty years earlier (Starmer et al. 2006).

Industrialized animal agriculture and its CAFOs are now

ascendant in the US and in many other developed countries, although some countries, notably member countries of the EU, have banned some of the worst practices (Rollin 2006). In the US, 97 percent of the livestock produced comes from this mode of production (Ibrahim 2007). This has been spreading in recent decades, as the technologies from developed countries and capital from multinational companies are being invested in meat production in developing countries. It is estimated that approximately half of livestock production globally is being done using the industrialized CAFO method, and this proportion is increasing quickly (Matheny and Leahy 2007). Production in South and East Asia in particular is rapidly industrializing (Heinrich Boll Foundation and Friends of the Earth Europe 2014). According to recent estimates, growth in industrialized methods of producing livestock is twice that of more traditional farming methods, and more than six times that of grazing-based systems (Verge et al. 2007).

The increasing production in developing countries, however, is not simply the result of increasing demand within their own borders. As developed countries increasingly degraded their own lands and companies sought new ways to cut costs, livestock production has been outsourced to developing countries with more land, and weaker environmental and animal welfare regulations (Nierenberg 2003). Nibert (2002; 2013) characterizes this process as a form of neocolonialism, and argues that the consequences have been immense, including the dislocation of Indigenous human and animal populations, often by force; upending subsistence agriculture; and significant environmental damage, particularly deforestation. Mexico is currently quite attractive to such development because it does not restrict the size, number, or location of CAFOs (Ponette-Gonzáleza and Fry 2010). To be sure, however, the movement of livestock production has not only been from developed to developing countries. In recent years, some companies have relocated their livestock production from Western Europe to the US to exploit weaker regulations there (Nierenberg 2003; Zande 2008).

Although it might appear counterintuitive, the industrialization of the production of animals for food can imperil food security in locations where it is undertaken, as it tends to displace subsistence agriculture. Additionally, non-native livestock populations can negatively impact native animal populations, akin to the problem with fur farms discussed in the previous chapter. This can further negatively affect subsistence farming (Nierenberg 2005).

Industrializing animal agriculture is also not the win for farmers that many assume it will be. They are required to make substantial financial investments (e.g., for new infrastructure, drugs, feed) to buy into this new mode of production. Some find it necessary to enter into contracts with large agri-food companies that come with strict conditions that restrict their autonomy. For many, these contracts commence a vicious cycle of having to invest more capital to meet contractual obligations, and then being so in debt that they cannot afford to leave the contractual relationship (Horowitz 2006; Starmer et al. 2006). Additionally, this type of production requires less labour and therefore has cost farming jobs in developed and developing countries alike (Food and Agriculture Organization 2017a).

But surely there are regulations in place to protect people, animals, and the environment from this type of production...

The regulations that are in place vary across nations and even subnationally in some cases (leading to geographic shifts in production, discussed above). Within the US, much of the regulation of CAFOs has been downloaded to the state or municipal level, and these regulations have been largely reactionary responses to the spread of neoliberal policies that have facilitated the negative impacts of industrialized animal agriculture on communities (Burmeister 2002). This has resulted in the concentration of livestock production in regions and, by extension, the concentration of localized environmental impacts (detailed shortly).

Some jurisdictions further protect the industry by prohibiting disparaging speech about it. Eleven states in the US have food disparagement laws on the books that regulate speech vis-à-vis food and how it is produced; these laws famously landed celebrity Oprah Winfrey in legal hot water years ago when she commented on air that she would not eat beef again due to the "mad cow" outbreak. Criminal laws were invoked against lawyer-activist Robert F. Kennedy Jr. in Poland for making negative comments about animal agriculture there (Kennedy 2009). In addition to laws limiting speech, there are laws in some jurisdictions criminalizing taking photos and videos inside livestock production facilities. These efforts have been quite pronounced in the US, where some states, such as Iowa, have passed laws that essentially criminalize documenting evidence in these ways by whistleblowers. Similar legislation was recently passed in New South Wales, Australia (Farrell 2016).

Animal welfare concerns

One notable aim of these food disparagement and so-called ag-gag laws is to keep the treatment of animals out of the view and discursive space of the public. Just a few decades ago, this would have seemed ridiculous, as the public had much more access to how animals were raised for food. Today, however, much of the public in Western developed countries is out of touch with how animal-derived products are produced (see Fitzgerald 2015).

Entire volumes have been written on the welfare of livestock animals. Due to space constraints, we cannot delve into great detail here, and instead the focus will be on the most pressing areas of concern. These concerns include physical space constraints, medical procedures undertaken without anaesthetic, and premature illness and death. The particularities of these concerns are often species-specific, but the general issues they raise all apply across species.

Within IAA, chickens are largely kept in large barns and do not have access to the outdoors. They are kept in two different ways, depending upon their purpose: those used for meat are generally uncaged and live on the floor of the building with hundreds if not thousands of others, and those kept for eggs are kept in extremely small cages with other chickens. Each method of confinement has its own associated problems. Those kept for meat have to fight their way past others to access food and water. Those kept for their eggs often develop problems from standing on the wire of the cages. This extreme confinement is quite stressful, and cutting off their beaks (without anaesthetic) is standard practice so that the stress of confinement does not cause them to injure or kill one another. Even if they do not injure one another, many succumb to illnesses caused by this method of production. Those bred for meat grow very large very quickly, which contributes to physical ailments and even "Acute Death Syndrome," characterized by a dramatic and immediate death. Those kept for egg production are susceptible to "caged layer fatigue" as their bodies succumb to the demands of constant egg production (Mason and Finelli 2005).

Pigs also spend their lives in industrialized production confined indoors, and female pigs spend much of their lives reproducing. Once their piglets are weaned they are promptly removed to be fattened for slaughter or put into breeding themselves. Like chickens, their bodies are also altered without anaesthesia to reduce the harm they inflict on one another: their tails are cut off, their teeth are clipped, and the males are castrated shortly after they are born. The way they are reared also takes a toll: their rapid growth makes them susceptible to Porcine Stress Syndrome, which causes sudden death (Mason and Finelli 2005), and the ammonia in their waste makes them susceptible to pneumonia (Dunayer 2001).

Veal calves and dairy cows are often kept in extreme confinement, as are cows raised for beef, although the latter generally have access to the outdoors on feedlots, where they are fattened for slaughter. Mench (2010) and colleagues have speculated, however, that this may soon change as cattle production marches down the same path towards intensive indoor confinement that chicken and pig production has followed. Cows are generally dehorned and castrated without anaesthetic. Like chickens and pigs, they are vulnerable to illnesses caused by the way they are kept, such as infections and abscesses (Dunayer 2001; Mason and Finelli 2005). These are just the animal welfare issues with being raised in a CAFO environment; there are other welfare concerns with the transportation and slaughter segments of the IAA commodity chain (see, for instance, Fitzgerald 2015; Fitzgerald and Tourangeau 2018; Eisnitz 1997; Pachirat 2011).

Thanks to ongoing campaigns by animal welfare advocates, some jurisdictions have recently banned some of the worst ways that animals are treated within IAA. In 2012, the EU banned the very small cages that confine chickens used for egg production and set required minimum amounts of space (750cm) per chicken (Council of the European Union DIRECTIVE 1999/74/EC), and, in 2013, banned the use of gestation crates for pigs (Council of the European Union COUNCIL DIRECTIVE 2008/120/EC). This is a good start, but a great deal of work remains to be done in the EU and elsewhere to improve the lives of animals used in animal agriculture.

Animal welfare advocates continue to apply pressure on the industry. Their strategies to date have included educational initiatives aimed at consumers and shareholders, boycotts of specific companies to induce change, and ballot initiatives where voters vote on specific production techniques. The strategies and their efficacy have varied by jurisdiction. Abolitionists, on the other hand, have put their energy into advocating for alternatives to IAA entirely, such as by promoting veganism. The work of both of these threads within the AAM on behalf of animals used as food have long and rich histories. More recently, some environmental organizations have begun to turn a critical eye towards animal agriculture as the negative environmental impacts of the hyper-industrialized form have become increasingly evident.

Industrialized animal agriculture and the environment

The current IAA system has been touted as having several benefits, including the ability to produce more animal-derived food products than ever before, produce a greater variety of products, and to do so with less space and human labour than in the past (Fitzgerald 2003). In short, it appears to be an efficient, productive, and profitable system. Yet academics are increasingly pointing out the ways that the benefits of the industry have been overestimated because a great deal of the associated costs have been externalized (see Weis 2010; Imhoff 2010); that is, the system itself is not held responsible for certain costs, and those costs are absorbed in other ways. The environment has been absorbing a great deal of these costs, in the form of deforestation, biodiversity loss, pollution, water use, and emissions that contribute to GCC. Evidence of these impacts are discussed in turn below.

Deforestation

Despite its efficiencies, animal agriculture takes a lot of space: more than a third of land globally is used by animal agriculture, and when the land that is used to produce animal feed is taken into consideration, it uses more than two-thirds of agricultural land globally (Koneswaran and Nierenberg 2008). Given how much space it takes up, animal agriculture necessarily has a large impact on land use. It contributes to deforestation in two main ways: through making space for CAFOs and pastureland, and to produce the crops that are converted to feed. This deforestation not only clears land of trees that people and animals rely upon, it also disrupts the carbon cycle; it is responsible for producing approximately 2.4 billion metric tons of carbon dioxide per year. This impact is exacerbated by the additional loss of carbon sink capacity (Steinfeld et al. 2006).

Deforestation due to animal agriculture is particularly endemic to some regions. The FAO (2005) has identified it as one of the main causes of deforestation in Latin America (see also Nibert 2002), and the Amazon has been hit particularly hard (see Mahar 1989; Faminow 1998). In an assessment using satellite imagery and economic and demographic data in forty-one tropical countries, the impacts of agriculture on deforestation were second only to urbanization. In order to stem the impacts, the researchers recommend using incentives to increase production on land that has already been deforested, as well as initiatives to minimize new clearing (DeFries et al. 2010).

Biodiversity loss

One particularly significant environmental consequence of defor-estation is that it results in habitat and associated biodiversity loss. A recent paper titled "Biodiversity conservation: The key is reducing meat consumption" published in *Science of the Total Environment* describes animal agriculture as "the predominant driver of natural habitat loss worldwide" (Machovina et al. 2015, 420). Globally almost one-half of grassland loss and one-third of forest loss can be directly attributed to conversion of land for food production, and approximately three-quarters of land used to produce food is used to produce animal products. The authors assert that although it is "difficult to quantify, animal product con-sumption by humans (human carnivory) is likely the leading cause of modern species extinctions, since it is not only the major driver of deforestation but also a principle driver of land degradation, pollution, climate change, overfishing, sedimentation of coastal areas, facilitation of alien species, and loss of wild carnivores and wild herbivores" (Machovina et al. 2015, 420). Therefore, if zoos (discussed in Chapter 3) are truly concerned about species extinc-tions, they ought to be directing attention to the role of animal product production and consumption.

Moreover, there are reasons to think that the problem will only get worse. Among the seventeen countries that have been identi-fied as being "megadiverse," meaning that they house significant numbers of species and collectively house the majority of species on the planet, eleven are witnessing increasing per capita meat consumption. Further, several of these countries (e.g., China) will need to increase their animal agriculture land use by more than 30 percent in order to keep up with demand. This does not bode well for species that rely on the land that will be expropriated or those likely to be seen as a threat to livestock animals (Machovina et al. 2015).

Animal agriculture also contributes to biodiversity loss in more indirect ways, notably through climate change. It is a primary anthropogenic driver of GCC (discussed in more detail shortly), and GCC is expected to have devastating impacts on biodiversity. There are various estimates of how significantly the climate could change globally. Researchers estimate that if the midrange estimates come to fruition, then 15 to 37 percent of species will be driven extinct by 2050 (Thomas et al. 2004).

Pollution

Greenhouse gases are not the only by-product of the industry that has negative environmental impacts. The industry also releases pollutants into the environment. In fact, it is claimed that animal agriculture is second only to the coal industry in the amount of systemic pollution it is permitted to get away with (Hahn Niman 2009), mainly in the form of air and water pollution. In 2005, the Environmental Protection Agency in the US excused the excessive emissions of 6,700 CAFOs. The regulatory penalties of some of these facilities would have been an estimated $27,000USD per day (Zande 2008). No doubt, there are many others whose illegal pollution goes undetected, and there are some levels and types of pollution that are permissible.

The levels of bioaerosols and endotoxins in CAFOs and in surrounding areas are particularly problematic (Donham et al. 2007; Mirabelli et al. 2006). Animal bodies naturally contain bacteria that are sloughed off and enter the air. The sloughing off of these bacteria would not necessarily pose a problem if it were only a few animals; however, because CAFOs contain thousands of animals, they release a lot of bacteria. These thousands of animals also produce a great deal of manure, and the application of the manure to land can spread the bacteria further afield. Green and colleagues (2006) tested for these bacteria in air samples and found the highest concentrations were found in CAFOs. They also found high concentrations downwind of CAFOs. The concentrations inside and downwind of CAFOs were so high that they reached the threshold to be classified as a human health hazard. As a result of their findings, the authors recommend locating CAFOs a distance of at least 200 metres away from residential areas.

This diminished air quality has been associated with significant human health consequences, particularly respiratory ailments. CAFO workers are most at risk, although the air quality also poses a threat to those who live near CAFOs (Mirabelli et al. 2006). Research indicates that this threat is as significant as other more commonly discussed respiratory threats, such as second-hand cigarette smoke. A study of asthma symptoms among a sample of 60,000 12- to 14-year-olds in North Carolina found that wheezing in the past year was 5 percent more likely if their school was located within three miles of a CAFO and 24 percent more likely if odours from the CAFO were appreciable at least twice a month. The effect of proximity to a CAFO on asthma symptoms was akin to the effects of sociodemographic factors, use of a gas stove, and exposure to second-hand smoke (Mirabelli et al. 2006). Other studies have linked proximity to CAFOs to other health consequences, such as digestive problems, mood, and sleep disorders (Donham et al. 2007).

Water pollution can also extend well beyond the confines of CAFOs. Agriculture is generally the largest contributing factor to pollution of rivers, streams, reservoirs, and lakes (Centner 2006). Much of the risk to water stems from manure. It is no secret that animals produce waste; they actually produce more waste than people do (Stathopoulos 2010), which is compounded by the fact that there are more livestock animals alive at any point in time than there are people. In the US alone, approximately five tonnes of animal waste is produced for every person, and overall there is 130 times more animal than human waste produced (US General Accounting Office 1999), for a total of 500 million tonnes of manure that needs to be dealt with every year (Centner 2006). Whereas human waste must be treated, animal manure does not have to be treated before being spread on cropland (Hahn Niman 2009; Zande 2008), as doing so would be a huge expense for the industry (Tietz 2010). Analyses of manure from CAFOs commonly find potentially dangerous contents, such as bacteria, ammonia, methane, hydrogen sulfide, carbon monoxide, disinfectants, cyanide, phosphorous, nitrates, heavy metals, drugs administered to the animals, and over 100 types of pathogens (Stathopoulos 2010; see also Hahn Niman 2009; Tietz 2010).

The industry is therefore faced with the problem of what to do with the immense amount of manure produced that may contain noxious elements. Large CAFOs commonly store the manure they produce in massive lagoons. These lagoons are lined so that the contents do not leak out; however, the contents can and have escaped when liners tear or when rain causes them to overflow (Tietz 2010). One such incident caused the release of 120,000,000 gallons of manure (Hahn Niman 2009; Tietz 2010). When manure is released like this, the contents can enter the water system. The contents can also enter the water system when rain falls on manure that has been spread on fields and runs off into bodies of water (West et al. 2011).

Even when manure is not contaminated with noxious elements, it is high in nitrogen and phosphorus. The addition of these nutrients to water can cause eutrophication, which starts a process where plants overgrow and deplete the oxygen, which kills fish, and, by extension, the animals that consume them (Centner 2006; West et al. 2011). The bacteria in the manure can also enter waterways. One governmental assessment of water around a CAFO in the state of Michigan in the US found that 98 percent of their weekly samples had *E coli* levels in excess of the water quality standards (Zande 2008). In their research, West and colleagues (2011) found that water quality downstream from wastewater treatment plants was significantly better than that around CAFOs. The water around CAFOs suffered from elevated levels of phosphorus and antibiotic-resistant bacteria. All of the CAFO sample sites had unacceptable levels of phosphorus and approximately 42 percent tested positive for bacteria that were resistant to multiple antibiotics.

Water use

In addition to potentially compromising water quality, IAA is also responsible for a tremendous amount of water use. Mekonnen and Hoekstra (2012) conducted an exhaustive analysis of the global water footprint of animal agriculture, leaving out only some difficult to quantify indirect impacts. The worst offenders are cows raised to produce beef (accounting for 33 percent of water used by farm animals), followed by dairy cattle and pigs (responsible for 19 percent each), and broiler chickens (responsible for 11 percent). The majority of the water used by the industry is used in the production of feed crops.

When the water use of animal agriculture is compared with the production of crops for human consumption, the inefficiencies of animal production become increasingly apparent. Mekonnen and Hoekstra's (2012) analysis documents an average water footprint per calorie of beef twenty times greater than for cereal and starchy root products. The researchers conducted a case study of dietary impacts on water use in the US and found that 37 percent of the water footprint of an average US citizen was due to meat consumption, and they estimate a vegetarian diet is associated with a 30 percent reduction in the water footprint. They do not provide information about the impact of a vegan diet. They conclude,

> because of the larger dependence on concentrate feed in industrial systems, this intensification of animal production systems will result in increasing ... water footprints per unit of animal product. The pressure on the global freshwater resources will thus increase both because of the increasing meat consumption and the increasing ... water footprint per unit of meat consumed. (Mekonnen and Hoekstra 2012, 413)

What are the implications? Well, according to Mekonnen and Hoekstra, "managing the demand for animal products by promoting a dietary shift away from a meat-rich diet will be an inevitable component in the environmental policy of governments" (2012, 413). It should be noted that this recommendation does not appear to be shaped by a particular concern for animals as sentient beings, as the title of their article is "A global assessment of the water footprint of farm animal *products*" (emphasis mine).

Global climate change (GCC)

As discussed at the opening of this chapter, a decade ago the Food and Agriculture Organization of the UN released a groundbreaking report (Steinfeld et al. 2006) summarizing the results of years of research. The main conclusions were that animal agriculture is one of the top contributors to the most serious environmental problems we currently face, notably global climate change (GCC). The industry actually emits more of the greenhouse gas emissions that contribute to GCC than the transportation sector. Take the average consumer in the US, for example: a one-fifth reduction in his/her meat consumption would reduce their contribution to GCC via greenhouse gas emissions the same amount as if they had switched to driving a hybrid vehicle (Lappe 2010).

IAA contributes to GCC in a number of ways. The production of methane, which is a particularly potent greenhouse gas, has been flagged as problematic. The industry also uses a lot of fertilizers to grow feed crops, and the processing of feed also contributes to greenhouse gases. The transportation of feed and animals also contributes mightily to the production of greenhouse gases (Steinfeld et al. 2006; Lappe 2010). Overall, it is estimated that if global dietary trends follow along their projected path, by 2050 there will be an 80 percent increase in greenhouse gas emissions associated with food production and deforestation for said production (Tilman and Clark 2014). As discussed above, if even the midrange predictions of climate change come to fruition, the environmental impacts will be profound.

The "sustainability time bomb"

Richard Twine has described the combination of an increasing demand for meat and an exponentially increasing human population as a "sustainability time bomb" (2010, 129). It is an apt description. All of the environmental impacts of IAA discussed in this chapter are positioned to worsen as globally people consume more animal products, the industrial method of production spreads around the world, and the population of people continues to increase.

Although the per-capita meat consumption in some developed countries has started to level off, the demand among the large population in developing countries is quickly expanding. A snapshot of the ten years from 2000 to 2010 is illustrative: during that period, the global demand for meat increased 25 percent, milk 47 percent, and eggs 24 percent (FAO 2012). This high and increasing demand means that at any point in time there are an awful lot of animals being raised globally for consumption: approximately 56 billion land animals killed around the world each year (Twine 2012). To put this into perspective, the human population currently sits at approximately 7.5 billion.

Animal advocates have been sounding the alarm about the environmental impacts of animal agriculture for years, which admittedly coincided nicely with their own interests. As recently as 2011, research examining a sample of environmental organizations, governmental agencies, and newspapers found that discussions explicitly linking IAA and environmental degradation were few and far between (Bristow and Fitzgerald 2011). It would appear that this has started to change over the past few years.

The World Bank is reportedly being more cautious about funding IAA initiatives in developing countries due to growing acknowledgement of the impacts of such production on the environment, noting on their website that

> agriculture, forestry and land use change are responsible for 25% of greenhouse gas emissions. Mitigation in the agricultural sector is part of the solution to climate change. The current global food system also threatens the health of people and planet: agriculture accounts for about 70 percent of water use and generates unsustainable levels of pollution and waste. (World Bank 2017)

The FAO is also now recommending reducing the demand for animal-derived food products, particularly among the affluent, and has even started to frame animal agriculture as a threat to food security: "livestock may compromise food stability in the long term through their contribution to climate change via greenhouse gas emissions (the amount of which is debatable), environmental degradation, biodiversity loss and water scarcity" (FAO 2017b, 7).

This threat to food security is partially due to the caloric inefficiencies of animal-based food products. The production of one calorie of beef requires 11 to 17 calories of feed to produce (Dauvergne 2010). In general, one acre of cereal crops produces five times the amount of protein than an acre used for meat production does (Imhoff 2010). It will not be possible to produce enough grain to produce enough meat to satisfy the demands of an increasing human population that consumes more meat. Attempting to do so will exacerbate hunger and starvation among some populations (Mallon 2005; Winders and Nibert 2004).

In sum, if significant changes are not made, the negative environmental impacts of IAA, as well as the food insecurity it generates, will worsen with time due to changing dietary habits in developing countries and an increasing human population globally. These trends will continue to bring the concerns of animal advocates and environmentalists into closer alignment.

The way forward: challenging the Treadmill of Production (ToP) and the Inverted Quarantine (IQ)

Jasper and Nelkin predicted in the early 1990s that the attention paid to animals in research would be eclipsed by that paid to the IAA behemoth, writing that "factory farming may well be the central animal rights issue of the 1990s. It will test the honesty of the fundamentalists, who have often gone after easy targets that help them raise funds, rather than after the practice that consumes – by far – the most animals" (1992, 174). Their rather disparaging reference to "fundamentalists" notwithstanding, it is a thought-provoking point: would a movement that had historically focused on grisly uses of animals engaged in by relatively small segments of the population (e.g., scientists, hunters, trappers) be able to raise the requisite funds to sustain itself by mounting a more broad-based cultural critique that would necessarily point a finger at those who consume animal products (nearly the entire population)? In this way, the political would become uncomfortably personal for many people.

As discussed earlier, there has been an appreciable shift within the AAM towards a sustained critical focus on IAA and away from the focus on vivisection. This shift could have actually ended up alienating people that animal advocates aimed to recruit, and even some of those already in the ranks of the movement (e.g., animal welfarists).[14] However, the change in focus did not occur in a vacuum: it has been supported in several ways by the larger social context. The increasing focus on the actions of individuals (vis-à-vis meat consumption) instead of groups of actors (e.g., scientists, hunters, well-off people wearing fur) coincided with what Szasz (2007) has diagnosed as a trend towards Inverted Quarantine within the environmental movement. That impulse has certainly not been confined to environmentalists. In the latter decades of the twentieth century, the healthfulness of meat (particularly red meat) was increasingly questioned. It was the dawn of concerns about cholesterol levels and food-borne illnesses (e.g, "mad cow" disease, *E. coli* contamination). Even as the industry channelled more money into marketing (Fitzgerald 2015), it could not stave off a shift in perceptions that was taking place. Refraining from consuming animal products was no longer simply a radical, anti-establishment act; for some people, it was (also) an act of self-preservation (personal quarantine, or as Szasz terms it, "inverted quarantine").

Szasz (2007) argues that the problem with Inverted Quarantine for the environmental movement is that it has made the movement less political. Certainly there are animal activists who bemoan the fact that some people who abstain from eating animal products do not adopt the politics of veganism. Rather than being motivated by ending the oppression of animals, they are driven by their own health concerns; they are better understood as being plant-based eaters instead of vegans. However, I would argue – and this is where I may surprise and even upset some folks in the movement – that the manifestation of the Inverted Quarantine impulse in the AAM in the form of adherence to a plant-based diet instead of vegan politics is not a bad thing. It may not cause political anaesthesia for animal advocates, as Szasz argues it has done for the EM.

Regardless of its motivation, the Inverted-Quarantine impulse has increased the amount of critical attention paid to IAA. It is perhaps *the* exception to the rule that no publicity is bad publicity. This impulse is making people more conscious consumers, just not in the way that would be most clearly ideal for animal advocates. Nonetheless, in doing so it has helped to make refraining from consuming animal products more palatable, and by extension has made alternatives more palatable due to increasing innovation caused by increasing demand. The boom in milk alternatives is illustrative here.

Plant-based eating without the vegan politics will not be a replacement for the AAM, but it may be viewed as external complementary support. Increasing focus on IAA can only be positive for the AAM, for a number of reasons. First, the majority of the harms perpetrated against animals globally are committed in the name of food production. If the goal of the AAM in general is to minimize animal suffering, then this is the place to act.

Second, the focus on animal agriculture can help to bridge the divide between camps within the movement. As Peter Singer has remarked, "ending factory farming should be the priority issue for all concerned with either the welfare, the preference satisfaction, or the capabilities of nonhuman animals" (Singer 2002, 1). Even those committed to animal welfare but not animal liberation or rights (e.g., Grandin 2007) have acknowledged that there are systemic problems within IAA. Nonetheless, I do not want to oversell the unifying potential of the issue of IAA; there are still differences within the movement as far as the recommended best strategies for changing practices within the industry and outright abolishing it. A focus on IAA within the movement has certainly not eliminated internal divisions, but I think it is safe to say that it has given the movement a common cause, and even driven productive debates over strategy.

Third, the focus on industrial animal agriculture (IAA) has made coalition-building between the AAM and the EM more feasible, which I argue will ultimately strengthen both. Just as IAA became the most common focus of the animal advocacy movement, global climate change became the central focus of the mainstream environmental movement. The recent research, described earlier, identifying industrialized animal agriculture as one of the top contributors to global climate change provides empirical evidence that environmentalists and animal advocates can make common cause in challenging the industry's practices. Further, it is not just at the global level that overlapping concerns are found: common cause between the two movements is also evidenced at the local level where environmental justice protests regarding the impacts of CAFOs are taking place. Just as the environmental movement has gained widespread support, at least partially because of the Inverted Quarantine impulse and the mounting evidence that harms against the environment also harm people, the animal advocacy movement is poised to gain growing support as it becomes increasingly apparent that many harms against animals are also associated with negative impacts on the environment and people. In this way, some animal issues can be usefully refracted through environmental issues. This way of thinking about the movements together provides concrete grounding for ecofeminist arguments about how the interests of those grouped together on the nature side of the constructed culture/nature dichotomy are intricately connected.

Szasz (2007) is correct to be concerned about the long-term impacts of the Inverted Quarantine (IQ). People have become so concerned about their individual wellbeing in relation to environmental issues in particular that they can lose sight of the larger structural political issues, inducing a "political anaesthesia." I think, however, that there is less reason to be pessimistic regarding this potential outcome for the animal advocacy movement. Szasz (2007) notes that the IQ can create teachable moments where people can be exposed to larger, more systemic issues, even while their initial driver may have been self-oriented concern. While he is not particularly optimistic about the potential of these teachable moments to ignite more political fervour in the environmental movement, the animal advocacy movement may be different.

As detailed herein, research indicates that the AAM is unusual because many of the issues it problematizes have a deeply emotional element, and people are most commonly recruited into the movement through being exposed to these affective aspects. Further, unlike other movements that rely heavily on recruiting through established social networks, the AAM recruits heavily through materials people see or read, with 58 percent in one sample of activists indicating that that is how they were recruited (Lowe and Ginsberg 2002). The "teachable moment" opportunities might therefore be particularly productive for the AAM due to the relatively quick and straightforward way that pro-animal messages can be conveyed, such as through a poster of a pig in a gestation crate at an organic grocery store – the observer needs little information to make the connection. It is about affective connection, not scientific explanation. Similarly, a number of documentaries released in recent years (*Food Inc.*, *Forks over Knives*, *What the Health*) have raised questions about the individual health consequences of the consumption of animal products; they also expose viewers to snippets of the realities of animal lives within the industry. Animal images are, in the words of Jasper and Poulsen (1995, 495), good "condensing symbols," and people are increasingly being exposed to them even via the small spaces "teachable moments" provide.

Finally, I think that the focus on industrialized animal agriculture that the Inverted Quarantine impulse has facilitated has been a gateway to more explicit political economic analysis of animal issues. The political economic factors that enable other uses of animals that the movement has focused on have not been as obvious, and were perhaps not as easily diagnosed. I think it fair to say that political economic factors are apparent once one scrapes the surface of IAA (see Nibert 2002, 2013; Fitzgerald 2015). A more thoroughgoing political economic analysis can help to counter-balance the individualized level of concern endemic to the IQ, and it could also bring the animal advocacy movement into closer alignment with the political economic arguments driving the environmental movement.

The treadmill of production (ToP) perspective has been used by scholars to see the current environmental predicament in the context of broader structural political economic influences. This perspective is beginning to be applied to the harms perpetrated against animals (e.g., Nibert 2013; Novek 2003; Stretesky et al. 2014). These analyses substantiate that the worst and most pervasive abuses of animals are perpetrated due to the profit motive. Because animals are a "renewable resource," however, in that they are bred to replace those that are killed before them, the ToP. will not be threatened as much by the loss of animal inputs as it is by the potential loss of environmental inputs, unless the environmental inputs are traced back to their origin as animal issues (e.g., the use of water by industrial agriculture). It is on the output side of the treadmill that animals pose the clearest threat to the political economic order, particularly in the context of IAA via the immense and growing amount of manure and methane that pose significant environmental and human health risks.

The IQ impulse that Szasz (2007) argues has served to depoliticize the environmental movement may actually benefit animal activism: the shift to a focus on industrial animal agriculture seems less radical as people become increasingly concerned about individual-level risks posed by the products of the industry. The focus on industrial animal agriculture has several associated benefits for the movement, including targeting the sector where the greatest absolute number of animals are harmed, serving as a unifying cause across most factions within the movement, solidifying connections between animal advocacy and environmentalism, and making the political economic forces related to animal oppression increasingly clear. While I understand Szasz's concerns about the impacts of the IQ on environmentalism, there are reasons to think that it is having significant positive direct and indirect impacts on concerns over industrial animal agriculture and animal advocacy more generally. Increasingly, IAA has become a common cause for animal advocates and environmentalists alike, whereas other animal issues (such as hunting, fur, and zoos) have become veritable wedge issues that those with an interest in perpetuating uses of animals can exploit. The next chapter weaves together how the historic rifts between the movements might be transcended, how common sources of resistance can be challenged, and how social forces, including those shaping concern about industrialized animal agriculture, may bring the movements together.

6

Reconciliation and the Way Forward

Earlier I described how in 1980 philosopher J. Baird Callicott wrote an article wherein he argued that the differences between the environmental movement and animal activism were irreconcilable. One of the many critiques he levelled against the animal advocacy movement (AAM) was that widespread adoption of a vegetarian diet would result in ecological disaster. The divorce between the two movements that the article incited stuck, even though eight years later Callicott published another article attempting to qualify what he had said. Nearly forty years later, I think the time is ripe for true reconciliation.

Today, widespread vegetarianism (and even veganism) is being held up as one of the best strategies for addressing *the* problem that the environmental movement (EM) has come to focus on: global climate change (GCC). The AAM and the EM have been coming into closer alignment on the issue of industrial animal agriculture (IAA), and there are practical and theoretical reasons to facilitate this partnership. Some critics, however, have argued against the environmental and animal advocacy movements forming coalitions around single issues, specifically on the issue of IAA (for example, see Holt 2008). What I am arguing for is not coalition-building around this one specific issue, but instead a more thoroughgoing partnership between the two movements that, among other things, will make it easier to resist attempts by interest groups to leverage the divide between the two for their own benefit. To this end, this book has examined three specific topics – sport hunting, fur, and zoos – over which the movements have faced off over the years, to demonstrate that even on these issues there is productive space where the movements could come together.

This final chapter further develops and synthesizes these points. It begins by highlighting the social forces that I argue can facilitate partnership between the two movements, reiterating where the movements might be able to work together on specific issues of concern. After laying this groundwork, the chapter moves to a discussion of the common targets of the movements and points of resistance they both face. After discussing these very practical points of convergence, we explore the more theoretical reasons in favour of partnership between the two movements.

From divisions to alliances

In the Introduction, I detailed four factors that I think have served to distance the environmental movement and the animal advocacy movement from each other: differences in their respective gender compositions, relations to science, levels of analysis, and (per-ceived) associations with radicalism. In recent years, there have been changes in several of these areas that could alter the relations between the movements. With regard to gender, I have argued that the preponderance of men in the environmental sciences and in elements of the EM, coupled with the gendering of concern for animals as feminine, may have facilitated the denigration of concern for animals as irrational and overly sentimental, while environmental concern has become rationalized and normalized. While the construction of concern for animal wellbeing in stereo-typed and devalued ways ought to be problematized (see Donovan 1990; Donovan and Adams 2007), it may be further undercut as more women enter the environmental sciences and more men enter animal advocacy, which is currently the trend, although to be sure, gender disparities still remain (Herzog 2007; McGurie et al. 2012).

Another change that may serve to bring the movements closer together is the changing relations between the AAM and science.

As detailed in Chapter 1, one of the main issues that spurred the formation of the early modern AAM was a critique of scientific experimentation on animals and a more generalized distrust of science. Beers (2006) notes in her history of the anti-cruelty movement that resistance grew as the movement began to enjoy some success in the nineteenth century. One primary form of resistance was to frame the animal advocates as anti-science misanthropes. Some in the medical field even constructed caring for animals as "zoophil-psychosis." Beers writes, "With so many women in the movement, the doctors further concluded that the weaker sex was particularly susceptible to the malady. Coming from men who were increasingly viewed as sociocultural role models, such charges undermined antivivisection's credibility" (Beers 2006, 16). Being cast as anti-science was, and continues to be, particularly damaging.

The AAM's perspective on science has become more nuanced as the movement has matured, and, in recent years, it has increasingly drawn on scientific developments to support its campaigns. These areas include using biomedical research to challenge the applicability of animal models to human health and to champion the creation of centres for Alternatives to Animal Models internationally; drawing on nutrition science and health research to support claims that people need not consume animal products and that doing so can cause serious health problems (e.g., Campbell 2006); invoking cognitive ethology to demonstrate the rich mental and emotional lives of animals (e.g., Bekoff 2000); and drawing from climate science to document the significant contributions of IAA to GCC (Steinfeld et al. 2006). Recently the movement has set its sights on tissue engineering as a way to produce meat without killing animals, with the goal of ending IAA as we know it (Roberts 2017). I am not suggesting that animal advocates have fully and uncritically embraced scientific and technological developments, nor am I suggesting that they should, but their positioning vis-à-vis science has shifted in a way that can bring it into closer alignment with the environmental movement.

Any changes in the levels of analysis that the movements engage in and ways that the movements have been associated with radicalism have admittedly been less significant to date than those observed vis-à-vis gender composition and the relation to science. Nonetheless, some modest shifts are worth pointing to here. As illustrated throughout this book, environmentalism is grounded in a concern for ecosystems. The AAM, by contrast, grew out of a concern for the wellbeing of animals and has advocated for appreciating animals as individuals instead of as a deindividuated mass. This is perhaps best illustrated by the concept of animal rights; animal rightists seek to grant individual animals inviolable rights (although proponents of this perspective do differ on which rights would be most appropriate). I think it is fair to say that the AAM has been popularly associated with this specific approach (as evidenced by the fact that the movement is commonly referred to as the "animal rights" movement). Nonetheless, there have been notable critiques of the individualistic rights-based perspective from within the movement (e.g., Singer 1987; Donovan 1990). Further, an examination of specific issues of concern to animal advocates, such as those detailed in this book, provides insight into various perspectives within the movement that do not necessarily cohere with a rights-based perspective. In short, associating the entire movement with one perspective within it has undercut the ability to appreciate its nuances and recognize important commonalities with other movements. The previous chapters have demonstrated how on specific issues (hunting, zoos, fur, and animal agriculture), these different levels of analysis need not be incommensurable.

Finally, the spectre of radicalism remains. I think it fair to say that the AAM continues to be more widely perceived as being associated with the radical flank within the movement than is the EM, although they have been linked together in recent years by some security agencies, such as the FBI in the US, which has identified radical environmental and animal advocacy groups (specifically mentioning the Animal Liberation Front and the Earth Liberation Front) as a "serious terrorist threat" that has eclipsed right-wing extremism (Jarboe 2002).

Nevertheless, some issues of concern to animal advocates are marching towards the mainstream, owing in part to broader social forces. As already discussed, the inverted quarantine (IQ) impulse that Szasz (2007) diagnosed as being endemic to the modern EM may also bring members of the public into closer contact with the AAM on issues that also threaten human wellbeing (e.g., IAA), thereby disabusing many of the notion that the demands of animal activists are all that radical. Moreover, as increasing numbers of homes in developed countries include companion animals, and affective ties with these animals are strengthened, issues facing companion animal species – such as animal abuse and euthanasia due to overpopulation – have become more mainstream concerns.

Caring for companion animals may now be mainstream, but the eventual impacts could be radical. Historian Richard Bulliet (2005) has charted a shift in developed countries from what he labels as the domestic to the postdomestic era. In the domestic era, people came into regular contact with animals who had been domesticated for human consumption. He points to a shift that became apparent in the 1970s, in which people became more removed from the animals they consumed while at the same time increasingly sharing their homes with companion animals with whom they developed strong affective ties. Others have framed pet keeping as part of a trend towards commodifying and accumulating nature under neoliberalism (e.g., Bakker 2010), and as symptomatic of other related social changes, such as declining family size, alienation, ageing populations, (sub)urbanization, and a need for mobility that can preclude having children (Nast 2006).

Regardless of the specific factors associated with increasing pet-keeping, it has given rise to a building tension between the affection people feel for their pets and their consumption of other animals that science (such as cognitive ethology) increasingly indicates are socially and cognitively complex (Bulliet 2005). James Serpell (2009) accordingly speculates that pet keeping could lead to a revolution, of sorts. He writes:

> when we elevate companion animals to the status of persons; when we empathize with them and acknowledge their resemblance to ourselves, it becomes obvious that the notion of human moral superiority is a phantom: a dangerous, egotistical myth that currently threatens our

survival. Ironically, as the forerunners of animal domestication, pet-keeping led us into our present, destructive phase in history. Perhaps, by making us more aware of our biological affinities with animals and the natural world, it will help to lead us out again.

The consequences of the shift to the postdomestic era, as Bulliet describes it – and encroaching neoliberalism more generally – for the AAM and its relation to the EM remain undertheorized, but I have suggested here that they could be significant. The growing affinity for companion animals may make at least some people, including environmental activists, supporters, and academics, more sympathetic to at least some causes championed by the AAM. Bulliet (2005) points to the AAM's campaign against IAA as one that might particularly benefit from the growing sentiments for pets. I concur, and for that and other reasons, have argued herein that the AAM would do well to focus its finite resources on IAA, as the payoffs could be significant.

I acknowledge that my advice runs counter to that provided by Jasper and Nelkin (1992) twenty-five years ago in their now classic book on the AAM, as well as Einwohner's (1996) study of four animal advocacy campaigns. Among other things, they recommended not targeting uses of animals that are popular, con-sidered necessary, and have long traditions. Certainly, consuming animal products would fit into these categories. They caution that targeting these types of uses would reduce public support for the movement. Their advice then would seem to be for the AAM not to target the consumption of animal products and the animal agriculture industry. In response, I would invoke the title of Naomi Klein's title of her recent book on climate change: *This Changes Everything*. Global climate change and the current socio-political context also changes the wisdom of applying the advice provided by Jasper, Nelkin, and Einwohner today. This specific issue perhaps more than any other has the potential to bring the AAM and the EM into closer alignment, which I argue would benefit both movements, and joint messaging on the topic of IAA just might gain and hold the public's attention. Additionally, the number of animals killed in this one industry vastly outnumbers all others; even modest changes here can have significant payoffs in terms of animal lives.

Any negative repercussions of focusing on an activity that the vast majority of the population is highly invested in might be mitigated by the IQ impulse. The AAM's shifting focus to IAA has coalesced with increasing health concerns about animal products and awareness of the environmental impacts of IAA. Thus, as the AAM has concentrated on getting the public to consider alternatives to consuming animal products, the public is also being primed by more mainstream messaging about personal health and environmental wellbeing (and human wellbeing by extension), augmented by messaging about individual resposibilization under neoliberalism. The movement's challenge in the past has been getting people thinking about the very topics that they do not want to think about. For all of its faults, the IQ has facilitated exactly this process, which we cannot expect social movement scholars writing years ago to have foreseen.

In sum, the AAM and the EM may be brought into closer alignment due to demographic shifts in membership and a shift in priorities within the AAM from the use of animals in science to the use of animals in IAA. This shift may contribute to challenging the perception that the AAM is anti-science. It may further bring the EM and the AAM into closer alignment via the increasingly documented connection between industrialized agriculture and climate change, against the backdrop of a shift in the environmental movement to a focus on global climate change and away from conservation, which is exactly where many of the tensions between the two movements (e.g., hunting, trapping, zoo conservation) were grounded. This shift may be further facilitated by broader cultural shifts that are strengthening affective relations between many people and their companion animals, and by extension to some (although limited) degree, the questioning among people who do not have a previous affinity with animal advocacy of rather arbitrary species lines drawn to delimit which animals are to be cared for and which ones are to be used for pleasure and profit. This movement forward, however, may be stalled if historic acrimony between the two movements around issues such as sport hunting, fur, and zoos go unchallenged.

Challenging historic divides

In writing about a controversial coyote hunt in the Northeastern US, Boglioli (2009) highlights the value of controversies in generating better cultural understandings. He recounts how a colleague had used a NASCAR metaphor to illustrate the value as follows:

> What do NASCAR mechanics do to test a new engine? Do they let it idle in the garage for a little while? No, they red-line it, let it run until it's about to blow, and then they take it apart and see how the different parts held up to the demands of extreme pressure. Under pressure, then, we can often learn things about the workings of a system that may not be apparent under normal circumstances. That's exactly why public controversies can be so interesting and valuable to study. (p. 204)

It is in this spirit that I turn to an analysis of what can be learned from the controversies surrounding sport hunting, fur, and zoos vis-à-vis potential collaborations between the AAM and the EM.

Sport hunting

As described in Chapter 2, there is a longstanding philosophical and political rift between some environmentalists and animal advocates on the issue of hunting. To complicate matters further, as the EM gained mainstream support, individual hunters and hunting interest groups increasingly justified their pursuit by drawing on environmental arguments (Fischer et al. 2013; Kheel 1995; Einwohner 1999b). Thus, it is sometimes difficult to see where justifications for sport hunting end and environmental concern begins.

Nonetheless, there are some arguments in favour of hunting for environmental reasons that cannot be summarily dismissed, three of which I consider to be fairly strong. The first, and likely most popular, is that hunting is a necessary tool for managing wildlife populations and supporting ecosystems by extension. A number of scenarios are said to call for wildlife management, such as over-population, controlling disease, and controlling invasive species. Second, hunting results in less pain and suffering and environmental degradation than IAA does, as hunted animals enjoy freedom before being killed, whereas farmed animals spend their lives in intensive confinement. Finally, significant conservation efforts are funded via revenue generated from hunters, in the forms of licenses and taxes.

There are some weaknesses in these arguments (detailed in Chapter 2) that animal advocates would do well to focus their attention on, and in doing so demonstrate that the interests of environmentalists and animal advocates are not that far apart. In the first instance, some studies indicate that killing significant numbers of certain species can create a vacuum that may be filled by more members of the unwanted species (McCallum and Hocking 2005). There is also evidence that sport hunting targeting individuals with certain characteristics (e.g., big antlers) can have negative impacts on some species and contribute to what some have referred to as *evolution in reverse* (e.g., Coltman et al. 2003). Even when hunting appears beneficial from an ecosystem stand-point, it is not a panacea for wildlife problems. Treating it as such serves to limit the amount of attention devoted to understanding and addressing the causes of the underlying problems, such as the population imbalances caused by the decimation of predator species. Strategic attention by animal advocates could be focused on drawing attention to the broader causes of these environmental problems and to the research demonstrating that hunts and culls are not always the most effective method to use. A great deal of the environmentalist support of sport hunting is grounded in the notion that it is necessary to promote ecological wellbeing, and it is often assumed this assertion is grounded in scientific research, whereas opposition by animal advocates is grounded in senti-mental concern for individual animals. Animal advocates would do well to focus on instances where research demonstrates that hunting is not resulting in improved ecosystems, and to advocate for further much-needed research not funded by and geared towards the interests of hunters.

The second assertion – that sport hunting results in less pain and suffering and environmental degradation than industrialized agriculture – is not easily refuted if one accepts the underlying premise that meat consumption is necessary. If meat is going to be consumed, then procuring it through hunting is arguably preferable. I do not think that it can be disputed that by and large hunted animals have a greater quality of life than those animals housed within IAA. The time of death is likely a different story, as in theory at least, there are measures in place to minimize the suffering of farm animals at slaughter, whereas the deaths of hunted animals vary from the ideal of the "clean kill" to slow painful bleeding out from injuries. On the environmental side, however, it is surely the case that the environmental damage wrought by industrialized agriculture (detailed in Chapter 5) outweighs that produced by current levels of hunting in most regions. Many animal advocates would certainly challenge the necessity of meat consumption; however, given the current and increasing global demand for it, responsible hunting is likely preferable to industrial production. Yet it is unclear what proportion of the population could sustainably satisfy their demand for meat via hunting.

Finally, the claim that sport hunting generates significant revenue that is channelled back into conservation efforts cannot be refuted. A few points of qualification, however, are warranted. There has been little empirical research on the environmental costs of hunting. Such work would be useful to weigh against the monies generated by hunting. There is a growing literature, however, that points to some negative impacts on communities in developing countries, where people have been removed from their lands and have lost access to natural resources (Benjaminsen et al. 2013). Further, funding conservation efforts through the proceeds of hunting licenses and fees has had the effect of making conservation professionals somewhat beholden to hunting interests (see Muth and Jamison 2000), and has given the state leeway to step back from being responsible for some conservation efforts. Thus, in the absence of sport hunting, conservation efforts, at least in the short term, would likely falter in many countries. Animal advocates will need to be prepared to recommend and advocate for alternatives both in order to win over environmentalists and to prevent doing greater damage to animal populations and ecosystems in the long term.

I understand that sport hunting has been an appealing target for animal advocates, likely because it involves a direct harm that is inflicted upon animals by identifiable actors. However, as delineated above, I think there is reason to be more nuanced and strategic about how the movement addresses the topic of sport hunting, which would have longer-term payoffs. More specifically, focusing on cases that are tied to environmental harms, particularly with supportive empirical evidence, would be prudent. The successful campaign against duck hunting in Australia described by Munro (1997) is illustrative: instead of making ethical arguments, the animal advocacy group focused on the environmental impacts of the hunt and were thereby able to convince a larger segment of the population that the hunt was problematic.

Although the population of sport hunters is declining in many regions, I do not think that this specific issue is going to fade into the background of environmental–animal advocacy relations. It will likely continue to be a persistent wedge issue as culls are increasingly called for due to declining predator populations causing ecosystem imbalances, to control the spread of disease, and to control invasive species. This is one area where the AAM is going to have to seriously reflect on how it wants to position itself in relation to the EM.

In his work on sport hunting and its animal advocate critics, Jan Dizard (1999) argues that what divides pro-hunters and animal advocates is that pro-hunters see themselves as being part of nature – as predators that naturally strike down prey – whereas animal advocates seek to convince people to leave nature alone. I think this is an overly simplistic view of the AAM. There are varying perspectives on hunting within the movement, as detailed in Chapter 2, with some, such as Peter Singer (1993), suggesting that hunting could be justified if a population has outstripped its ability to feed itself. My take is that the movement does not seek to convince people to leave nature alone as much as it seeks to argue that culture should not be privileged over nature (an argument that ecofeminists have been making for years); in other words, it problematizes anthropocentrism. Challenging anthropocentrism will best serve the long-term goals of both the AAM and the EM, as will guarding against the reification of the culture/ nature binary.

Zoos and aquaria

Zoos and aquaria are an interesting case because they occupy a liminal space between nature and culture. Focusing attention here on the divide between the animal advocacy movement and the environmental movement can be quite productive. Like the topic of sport hunting, an examination of zoos and aquaria brings the tension between the holism of environmentalism and the individualism of animal advocacy to the fore, although the debate between the two on the topic of zoos is relatively new. As the stated purpose of zoos and aquaria shifted towards conservation in the twentieth and twenty-first centuries, they gained support from environmentalists, particularly conservationists. In recent years the regional and international zoo associations have been highlighting the ways that zoo and aquaria facilitate conservation both directly through *ex situ*, and increasingly *in situ*, efforts, and indirectly through educating visitors about the environmental challenges we face and encouraging attitudinal and behavioural change.

For their part, animal advocates have argued that zoos are just engaging in greenwashing as a way to divert attention from the treatment of the animals they keep so that they can continue to make money, which is the *raison d'être* of the institution. They further argue that there is insufficient evidence that the stated goals of zoos and aquaria – conservation and education – are being met; moreover, even if this evidence did exist, it would not outweigh the harms that individual animals endure as a result of being kept in captivity. Finally, they argue that zoos and aquaria reinforce the cultural message that the subjugation of nature is acceptable.

A review of the empirical literature does indicate that the ability of zoos and aquaria to meet the goal of meaningful conservation is currently limited. More specifically, they do not have the space necessary to enact significant breeding programmes; they prioritize keeping "charismatic megafauna" instead of threatened and endangered species; and breeding and reintroduction programmes have had very limited success. In the face of these limitations, zoo associations have been pointing to their increasing emphasis on *in situ*, or field, conservation to substantiate their positive environmental impacts. Such efforts are promising, and would certainly be more acceptable to animal advocates than removing animals from their natural environments and keeping them in captivity; however, the review of zoo association documents provided in Chapter 3 indicates that only a small proportion of zoo funds are being allocated to such efforts.

The second environmental contribution that zoos are said to make is through educating visitors about current environmental threats and what can be done to mitigate them. Although this contribution may not receive as much attention from the public as the entertainment value of zoos, the sense in the zoological literature is that it is via this indirect impact that zoos can most significantly contribute to conservation. Indeed, an analysis of zoo mission statements (Tribe and Booth 2003) indicates that educating visitors is the most commonly included mandate.

Research does indicate that zoos are having an educational impact on visitors. However, several caveats are worth reiterating here. First, active learning, such as through guided tours, appears to be the most beneficial, and certainly not all visitors take advantage of these opportunities (Smith and Broad 2008). Second, the effect sizes of the educational initiatives documented in studies are relatively small; even the environmental education provided via active learning opportunities is not more significant than the environmental education provided through other means, notably the media (Milstein 2009). Third, the quality of the animal enclosures (i.e., how natural they appear) and the welfare of the animals therein impacts the educational efficacy of the facility, so the educational messages transmitted by some zoos may be undercut by the physical state of the zoo (Keulartz 2015). Finally, the educational messages transmitted are rather general, and do not often help visitors make connections between their own actions and environmental harms, much less recommend specific behavioural changes (Milstein 2009).

Many animal advocates would no doubt argue that the current educational and conservation benefits of attending zoos do not outweigh the impacts on the individual animals kept there. Further, some might argue that not only do zoos and aquaria not have appreciable environmental benefits, they teach visitors – particularly children – that subjugating animals for amusement is acceptable, and further that they might actually induce environmental complacency through giving the impression that species of animals harmed by human actions will be saved and repopulated through these efforts (for example, see Malamud 1998).

There is an expectation by at least some in the zoological literature that these and other critiques levelled by animal advocates will be trumped by pending environmental crises, such as GCC, species extinctions, and habitat loss, which will lead to greater acceptance of zoos and aquaria among the general public (see, for instance, Minteer and Collins 2013). It is a valid point. It also serves to indicate where animal advocates should strategically focus their attention and research: on the degree to which zoos and aquaria actually benefit the environment. In the face of impending environmental doom, animal advocates may not be able gain traction on the issue of animal welfare and the ethics of keeping animals in captivity if there is a perception that zoos and aquaria are useful conservation tools, and therefore benefit humans by extension. Focusing on the shortfalls of zoos and aquaria in this respect may weaken public support for them, but what the ultimate consequences of weakened public support would be is a matter of speculation. Could zoos and aquaria fade from the landscape? Perhaps, but like Dale Jamieson (2002), I think it is unlikely; however, I think that it may be possible to dramatically alter their current form. What will be most productive, at least in the medium range, is for the AAM to use any weakened public support as leverage to get zoos and aquaria to make meaningful changes – changes that could also help to bridge the divide between animal advocates and environmentalists.

The goals of environmentalists and animal advocates could best be met if zoos and aquaria were pressured to make the following changes, detailed in Chapter 3. First, dedicate more resources to *in situ* conservation efforts. Second, prioritize the keeping of threatened and endangered species, and facilitate breeding and release where possible. Third, make enclosures as natural as possible in order to maximize animal welfare and improve visitor education concerning animal behaviours and their environment. Fourth, facilitate the closure of facilities that do not meet the highest standards. This will require zoos and aquaria and their associations to be vocal about the shortcomings of facilities instead of attempting to obscure problems. Fifth, cooperate internationally with one another to facilitate more robust breeding programmes and improve conservation by extension. Sixth, devote more resources to caring for animals that have been injured or for other reasons cannot live in the wild. This would benefit those animals while also helping to educate visitors about the ways that animals are harmed by humans. Seventh, acknowledge that some species (such as wide-ranging carnivores) ought not to be kept in captivity because there is no way to do so while ensuring sufficient animal welfare. Finally, zoos need to better demonstrate the continuity between nature and culture, instead of reifying the nature/culture binary. Otherwise, zoos and aquaria are simply buying into and perpetuating the very origins of the problems faced by animals and the environment that they allegedly seek to address.

Improved enforcement of animal welfare laws in these facilities would facilitate some of these changes; in particular, it would likely accelerate changes at unaccredited facilities; this should be supported by zoological associations. An even more expansive role of the state could entail operating zoos and aquaria as centres for breeding and reintroducing species of animals that are threatened and tolerate captivity well. These facilities could be operated as not-for-profit organizations, and therefore conservation instead of profit maximization would guide decision-making. Admittedly, this would not end the speciesist logic of keeping animals in captivity; however, it would help to usher in the end of keeping animals in captivity for entertainment, which is certainly more problematic than keeping animals to protect and strengthen populations. I recognize that this is an ideal, and that in the current neoliberal context of downloading state responsibilities this would take significant pressure; however, limited conservation successes among zoos and aquaria and accelerating species losses might be expected to apply more pressure to states and even supranational bodies.

To give credit where credit is due, the dedication of the regional zoological associations to conservation has been more than rhetorical in recent years. They have made progressive modifications to their policies and practices vis-à-vis conservation, as evidenced by increased *in situ* efforts, and have mandated greater resource allocations to it. Yet there is significant room for improvement on the conservation and animal welfare fronts, as detailed in Chapter 3. In the absence of meaningful state action, environmentalists and animal advocates could work to apply pressure to the zoological associations for better outcomes. Productive changes could bring animal advocates and environmentalists closer together on the issue of zoos, although, with time, failure by zoos and aquaria to change may also bring both sides together as the limitations of the current model become increasingly apparent.

Fur

The issue of fur is distinct, compared to sport hunting and zoos, in that historically the animal advocacy movement and a fairly large portion of the environmental movement were actually united in opposition to one aspect of the industry: the commercial seal hunt. The divide between the two movements on the issue of fur has been more recent. As detailed in Chapter 4, opposition to the Canadian seal hunt by environmental organizations weakened in the twenty-first century as the organizations became more institutionalized, focused on other causes, and became concerned about the impacts of anti-fur activities on Indigenous human populations (see Burgwald 2016).

The divide between the two movements on this issue has been leveraged in recent years by the fur industry and some governments. The industry has used "fur is green" campaigns as a way to win support for its products from the large population of those concerned about the environment. The industry, in conjunction with the Canadian government, has also claimed a connection between the decline in the seal hunt and declining cod fish populations. Scientists have challenged these claims. Yet the timing of the fracturing of the anti-seal hunt into animal- and environment-focused camps coincides with the increasing momentum of the Inverted Quarantine. At this moment in time, the notion that declining seal hunts would result in declining fish population for human consumption and that alternatives to fur products were causing environmental harms that would harm people by extension, could have resonated particularly strongly.

Within this broader social context, there are two complementary strategies that I propose for the AAM. First, I would suggest emphasizing the negative environmental impacts of hunting and trapping furbearing animals. Traps can capture and kill many animals other than those targeted, including animals from populations that are currently in decline or threatened; trapping and hunting can alter the prey/predator ratios within ecosystems and have negative long-term consequences (see Goodwin 1997), particularly in a time of rapid climate changes. Hunting and trapping proponents will no doubt argue that this is not a problem because restrictions are placed around the killing of animals by species, such as in the form of quotas. However, the science behind these regulations has been contested. In short, there is concern that the measures may not be sufficiently precautionary (see Chapter 4). These potential environmental impacts are worth emphasizing.

A second strategy that may prove useful is to focus anti-fur activism on farmed fur instead of that procured through hunting/trapping. This would make practical and strategic sense for a number of reasons. First, this is where the vast majority of animals (85 percent) killed for fur originate. Second, there are significant welfare concerns associated with high-concentration captivity, such as that practiced on fur farms, particularly with species that are not thoroughly domesticated. Third, the interests of animal and environmental advocates are not as easily framed by opponents as being at odds around the issue of fur farming due to its potentially significant negative environmental impacts, such as on water and air quality, transfer of illnesses to wild animal populations, risks of compromising wild populations through cross-breeding, and the risk that farmed species will escape and/or be released and establish themselves as an invasive species.

A focus on farmed fur also undercuts the two most significant arguments in favour of fur: that it is a byproduct of wildlife management strategies for controlling disease and population levels, and that it is a traditional cultural practice that should be respected. Even if the premise that hunting/trapping furbearing animals is good wildlife management is accepted, it is worth emphasizing that it does not apply to the vast majority of fur products on the market, considering that so many are produced via fur farming. In addition, the cultural concerns that many environmentalists (and others) have had about anti-fur activism are not as salient when it comes to the issue of fur farming. Declines in fur farming would not disproportionately impact a specific cultural group or region (such as Indigenous groups in Canada) like declines in some hunting and trapping activities would.

In sum, the most compelling environmental and cultural arguments in favour of fur really only apply to less than one-fifth of the industry. Fur farming is most vulnerable, and it is an area where the concerns of animal and environmental advocates come together most closely. I am aware that my assertion that fur farming should be prioritized over hunting and trapping furbearing animals may not sit well with some, as eliciting sympathy for seals being clubbed to death is akin to tradition within the movement. However, the social and environmental context has changed. The EU's ban on commercial products from the Canadian seal hunt (the largest hunt of marine mammals globally) and the WTO's ruling in favour of the ban has significantly, and likely irrevocably, damaged the Canadian seal hunt. Further, although the hunting and trapping of animals for their fur served as a strategic focus because images could be captured of them suffering and meeting a bloody demise, these images (or "mindbombs") may not resonate as well today given the barrage of images via (social) media that people are exposed to. In contrast, the potential environmental impacts of fur farming may resonate quite well in cultures focused on how environmental degradation will ultimately affect them as individuals.

Confronting similar targets and points of resistance

There may, therefore, be ways for the AAM and the EM to come together even on the issues that have divided them in the past. Moreover, as previously discussed, there are broader trends – such as changing demographics in the movements and changes in their relations to science – that can be expected to bring the movements closer together. The movements may also be drawn together by the common forms of resistance they are encountering. For instance, the lumping together of the movements by external forces, such as via state repression under the banner of crackdowns against terrorism (Best and Nocella 2004; Liddick 2006), may forge alliances.

Moreover, there are two concepts that scholars have formulated to describe some of the most challenging aspects of our time, specifically with regard to the environment, that hold within them insight into the future of the relationship between the AAM and the EM: the *Inverted Quarantine* and the *Treadmill of Production*. Each concept, and how it might be applied to better understand the relationship between the two movements, is revisited below.

The Inverted Quarantine (IQ)

The IQ concept was developed by Andrew Szasz (2007) to capture a trend observed in the EM in recent years: a shift away from environmentalism grounded in altruism to an environmentalism grounded in a concern to protect one's self and loved ones from environmental harms, often through specific consumer choices. The purchase of organic foods is an illustrative example: Szasz argues that the demand for these products has been caused more by a desire to stave off potential negative health consequences from consuming food treated with chemicals than an interest in protecting other species and the environment more generally from the negative impacts of these products. He cites considerable evidence in his book indicating that this indeed has been the case, although the absolute impacts on the movement cannot easily be quantified. On the one hand, the IQ could be at least partially responsible for the widespread popularity of environmentalism in many Western countries, as people may feel more inclined to become involved with and identify with a movement that they see as being in their own self-interest to some degree. On the other hand, Szasz (2007) argues that the IQ impulse will ultimately prove problematic for the EM, as people become so involved in their own individual consumerist actions that they fail to attend to the broader political economic factors involved in generating the very problems they seek to insulate themselves from, marking a "political anesthesia," in his terms.

I have argued that just as the EM has gained so much support because people increasingly seek to protect themselves in the face of growing evidence that harms against the environment also harm all people, the AAM is poised to gain growing support as it becomes increasingly apparent that many harms against animals are also associated with negative impacts on the environment and people (the impact of IAA on GCC is but one example). In this way, some animal issues will be refracted through environmental issues, and the IQ impulse may bring the movements closer together in relation to the concern most people have in common: themselves. Stated differently, animal issues may become third-order concerns, with the environment as the second order and human wellbeing the primary concern.

I am not as pessimistic about the impact of the IQ on the animal advocacy movement as Szasz (2007) is about its impact on the environmental movement. Increasing concern for animal issues, even if it comes by way of environmental issues, is an improvement. Further, as noted, Szasz speaks to the potential of teachable moments while in the IQ. These teachable moments might be particularly productive for animal advocacy. Those recruited into the movement tend to be drawn in not by networks but by educational material they read or saw that evokes an emotional response, instead of by being won over by science, for instance. In that sense, the IQ may give the movement a captive audience, figuratively speaking. The IQ can also benefit the AAM in another way. As I argued earlier, the IQ impulse may be partially responsible for the increasing shift to plant-based diets. At least one study (Lowe and Ginsberg 2002) has found that eating a plant-based diet served as an entry point to the AAM (64 percent of their sample indicated that being vegetarian/vegan made the AAM more attractive to them. Also of note, companion animal issues attracted 29 percent of them). Despite its faults (e.g., continued consumerism), the IQ phenomenon could bring the AAM and the EM closer together at the micro level and positively affect the AAM in particular.

The risk is that all of this could ultimately backfire by inducing a more individualistic, self-interested, and anthropocentric perspective. This is where I think the EM can particularly benefit from a closer relationship with the AAM because it challenges the anthropocentric notion that humans are the centre of the universe, and might be particularly well suited for reminding people (even environmentalists) of the problems associated with anthropocentrism. In his book, McKibben declares that the death of nature has occurred – that we have "ended nature as an independent force" (1989, xix). He diagnoses the following message that Western societies send as the primary driver of environmental problems: "you are the center of the world, the most important item in all creation" (1999, xxiv). He notes that environmentalists have not been immune to this messaging. Later in his book, he writes, "The idea that the rest of creation might count for as much as we do is spectacularly foreign, even to most environmentalists" (174). This belief is particularly problematic for environmentalism because it detracts from feeling a part of something larger. McKibben laments, "What would it mean to our ways of life, our demographics, our economics, our output of carbon dioxide and methane if we began to truly and viscerally think of ourselves as just one species among many?" (172). In short, the spectre of nature can humble people and make them feel smaller; therefore, the death of nature marks a risky turning point for humanity. Yet it is particularly at this moment that the AAM can help in reminding people that they are but one of many species of animals, and that there is much we share in common with those other species.

The treadmill of production (ToP)

In making the case for academic work and activism addressing the ToP, Gould and colleagues write that

> Treadmill theory encourages scholars, activists, and others to explore deeply, rather than to gloss over, the contradictions in social responses to environmental disorganization. These paradoxical institutional and individual responses illustrate most clearly the dynamics of social system–ecosystem relations. Ultimately, it is in the resolution of such paradoxes that ecologically sustainable and socially just solutions may be found. (2008, 16–17)

I would suggest that the divide between the EM and the AAM has been one such paradox, and resolving this specific paradox could be particularly beneficial. I made the case throughout this book that bridging the divide between these two movements is not only practicable, it would be to the advantage of both. Of note, it would assist in demonstrating the fallout from the ToP.

Animals have not been given much attention within treadmill theory, perhaps because they are considered a renewable resource: when they killed to fulfil human ends they are simply replaced by the next batch of animals bred to replace them or those that move into an area to fill an ecological vacuum. The treadmill is not, therefore, much threatened by the loss of animal inputs, except perhaps in the context of threatened and endangered species. At the output side of the treadmill, however, animals pose a significant threat to the political economic order, particularly in the context of IAA. Most notably, as detailed earlier, the immense and growing amount of manure produced poses environmental and human health risks, and the methane produced is a significant contributor to GCC. The global expansion of IAA described in the last chapter is a perfect illustration of the treadmill phenomenon.

As the concept of the IQ can be utilized to highlight the intersections between environmental and animal concerns, so too can the treadmill of production. As discussed herein, it can be applied to examine the continuing expansion of IAA (for fur and food) and the environmental impacts of the inputs and outputs. Increasing inputs of land are required, which drives deforestation and habitat loss (see Chapter 5), among other problems. Then when species suffer due to habitat loss, it is used as justification for placing them in captivity (Chapter 3) and using lethal means to "restore ecological balance" (Chapters 2 and 4), all the while securing additional profits. On the output side, the industrial animal agriculture treadmill spews manure and greenhouse gases that result in pollution and exacerbated GCC. The treadmill will only continue to accelerate as the industry looks to expand its markets in developing countries. Moreover, instead of confronting the inherent unsustainability of this model, technological "fixes" are increasingly turned to, such as producing energy from manure and engineering livestock animals that produce less methane (Chapter 5). All the while, the neoliberal state embraces the use of private interests to promote conservation (i.e., hunters, trappers, zoos). The interests of animal advocates and environmentalists are inextricably linked in this political economic system, and increased attention by the EM and the AAM to IAA will continue to bring these intersections into sharper focus.

Environmentalists might respond that they need not attend to animal welfare/liberation/rights in order to secure better environmental conditions, and, moreover, doing so could be risky because it may undercut the legitimacy they have gained. I offer up the following three responses. First, the AAM (particularly utilizing an ecofeminist lens) can provide a powerful critique of simplistic and divisive binary ways of thinking (e.g., humans versus animals), as well as anthropocentrism (and speciesism) that some (e.g., McKibben 1989) have noted continue within the EM. Even the field of green criminology, which holds so much promise for uniting academic concern for and analyses of harms and crimes against animals and the environment, has been critiqued for adhering to anthropocentric and speciesist assumptions, and dualistic ways of thinking more generally (Halsey 2004), although recent developments in specific areas of the literature hold promise (Taylor and Fitzgerald forthcoming). Without at least challenging anthropocentrism, it is unclear how it would be possible to move beyond simple reform to redress the actual underlying causes of environmental degradation. Gould and colleagues have lamented this reformist orientation among the mainstream EM, arguing that the strategy of cooperating with those in power (i.e., policy-makers, industry) will not result in the necessary challenge to the treadmill of production. The critique of anthropocentrism and speciesism articulated by the AAM would be particularly helpful in challenging the treadmill of production. The AAM could also provide additional support for critiquing consumption, although it should be noted that just as the EM is vulnerable to "environmentally friendly" consumerism, particularly in the context of the IQ (Gould et al., 2008; Szasz 2007), animal advocacy is vulnerable to "animal friendly" consumerism (see, for example, Stanescu 2013). It would be mutually beneficial for the EM and the AAM to work together to address this more specific challenge.

Second, the EM and the AAM are up against powerful interests, including embedded cultural values and an entire political economic system. Those interested in systemic change suggest that subnational and national movements aimed at policy change will be insufficient, and instead international movements and changes will be required (Gould et al. 2008; Fitzgerald 2015) – a resource-intensive endeavour. Even those interested in more modest environmental reforms would likely admit that significant resources are necessary to effect change. Forming coalitions can be a valuable means for maximizing resources and expanding networks (see, for instance, Van Dyke and McCommon 2010). Accordingly, Gould and colleagues recommend that the EM cultivate coalitions; they particularly recommend working with organized labour and anti-racist organizations, and mention more generally the organizational capacity of the educated middle class as well as the need to address issues of social inequality (Gould et al. 2008). Although they do not specifically mention the AAM, this is an area that animal advocates could contribute to, particularly those employing an intersectional perspective grounded in critical ecofeminism. In the very least, collaboration between the movements would undercut the ability of interest groups (i.e., the commercial hunting industry, the zoo industry, and the fur industry) to leverage current divisions between the movements to their own advantage and to the detriment of both environmental and animal wellbeing.

Finally, if I am correct that changing conditions internal and external to the AAM are increasing public support for it, and that the AAM and EM will be brought closer together on a number of issues, it may soon be in the best interests of the EM and its constituent organizations to consider animal welfare/rights issues as concern for them begins to filter up from their activists and supporters. For years now individual animal advocates have viewed the EM favourably and have also considered themselves environmentalists (see, for instance, Jamison and Lunch 1992). The reverse – environmentalists looking favourably upon the AAM – is currently less common; however, as discussed herein, there are social changes afoot that are likely to have a positive impact, such as the changing gender composition of the AAM. Although I disagree with the stereotyping of animal advocates as being overly sentimental because the majority are women, and with the implication that sentimentality is bad thing, a changing gender composition will nonetheless likely undercut this perception, as will the changing circumstances that are challenging the contention that the AAM is anti-science. As this takes place, it will be worthwhile to update Kruse's (1999) study: he found in a nationally representative sample in the US that although a relationship exists between support for environmentalism and animal advocacy, once gender was statistically controlled for, the relationship was insignificant for men. Until a relationship between support for environmentalism and animal advocacy develops for men, if indeed it still has not, we may expect women to be at the forefront of pushing for greater collaboration between the two movements.

Collaboration between the EM and the AAM is already taking

place at the grassroots level. Groups have developed in opposition to the opening of CAFOs in their communities. They are primarily focused on environmental contamination and the health consequences thereof, but they are also challenging the actual economic model that requires stockpiling animals as though they are inanimate objects (Ladd and Edwards 2002; see Kemmerer 2015a for additional illustrative examples). There is also notable affinity between the radical flanks of both social movements (see Scarce 1990). Cianchi even suggests that concern for animals is often a gateway to radical environmentalism, writing, "I am struck reading accounts of radical environmentalism how often witnessing animal pain and responding empathetically seems to serve as a trigger" (2015, 20). This more grassroots momentum could significantly influence the broader movement.

Admittedly, there is less evidence of coalition-building between the large, bureaucratized animal and environmental organizations. Due to their dependence on donations, however, it is in the best interests of these large organizations to be responsive to the concerns of their donors and to address emerging issues of concern. If their bases are increasingly interested in issues that cross the constructed boundary between the two movements, it will be in their own best interests to respond. Future research will be needed to assess where and how this takes place. I suspect that as the environmental impacts of IAA in particular become increasingly apparent, in order to be conceptually consistent and to be responsive to evolving concerns among their constituency, the large environmental organizations will need to address the proverbial elephant – or the cows, pigs, and chickens – in the room.

Theoretical (in)consistencies

The EM and the AAM are both concerned with the impacts of culture on nature. Nonetheless, they generally have different conceptualizations of the relationship between nature and culture. The relationship between the movements as it has developed around specific issues varies, depending upon where the specific issue is located on the culture–nature or domesticated–wild continuum. The large rifts are apparent closer to the wild end of the continuum (e.g., hunting and trapping), whereas there is greater agreement regarding issues situated at the domesticated end of the continuum. This is an additional reason why it is strategic for the AAM to focus on IAA: the animals involved in the industry are situated on the domesticated side of the continuum, and the industry has demonstrated significant negative effects on the conservation-type concerns that have divided the movements for so long. We might perhaps expect that the rift between the two movements at the wild/nature side of the continuum will narrow with time; that pole on the continuum is becoming increasingly difficult to locate, as nature is socialized. According to McKibben's arguments, the nature pole has vanished. Either way, the boundaries between culture/nature and domesticated/wild are becoming increasingly blurred, which may further serve to bring the EM and the AAM into closer collaboration.

A truly intersectional approach, such as that advocated by ecofeminists (e.g., Adams 1990; Gaard 2017), assists with better understanding the harms inflicted upon those situated on the nature side of the continuum (against the environment, animals, and denigrated social groups). It is also essential for better understanding and challenging the cultural sources of these harms (e.g., patriarchy, colonialism, anthropocentrism, speciesism) and resistance to efforts to effect change. In attempting to deconstruct the culture/nature binary, instead of following in the tradition of attempting to elevate certain groups to the side of culture, ecofeminists point to the value of nature and those associated with it, and cultivate affinities where once there were perceived barriers.

With this goal in mind, ecofeminists have been less focused on which specific ethical approach to the environment or other animals is best than they have been on better understanding the interconnected harms perpetrated against those situated at the nature side of the continuum and strategizing for change (see Kheel 1993). This book has been intended as a modest contribution to demonstrating that many of the most pressing harms against the environment and animals are very clearly interconnected, and that ameliorating and putting an end to these harms will be expedited by the movements working together on shared interests and against mutual points of resistance.

As explained in earlier chapters, providing a sustained analysis of how the movements are situated vis-à-vis each other has required to some extent having to gloss over the diverse positions and interests *within* each of the movements. I have focused mostly on the movements within the national contexts of Canada and the US. While I wish that space constraints did not prohibit a more expansive treatment here, I am confident that with time and greater cross-pollination between the movements and their respective areas of academic study, there will be ample opportunities for more nuanced analyses of where and how points of convergence are emerging, and the challenges encountered along the way.

Sources of resistance or challenges common to both movements will undoubtedly need to be confronted. I have demonstrated how the shrinking role of the state under neoliberalism has negatively (although not uniformly) affected animals and the environment (through, for instance, allowing commercial interests such as sport hunters and zoos to play such a significant role in decision-making vis-à-vis conservation), and how responsibility for mitigating environmental risks has been increasingly downloaded to individual consumers, who according to Szasz (2007) and his conceptualization of the IQ, are responding through individualized consumer-based actions, which he fears will ultimately depoliticize the EM. I have explained how the IQ phenomenon might actually bring the two movements closer together and increase interest in and support for the AAM, at least in the near term. Moreover, I have utilized the treadmill of production concept, as articulated by Schnaiberg (1980), and Gould, Pellow, and Schnaiberg (2008), to gain a foothold in understanding current expansion of IAA in particular, how this accelerating treadmill simultaneously degrades the environment and animal and human lives, continuing the legacy of the historically grounded entanglements of oppression that David Nibert (2002; 2013) has so clearly documented. Theorists of the treadmill of production have hypothesized that it is encroaching upon the biophysical limits of the environment, and that breaching these limits will ultimately cause a crisis in the political economic system. I have argued that although animals tend to be an overlooked part of the ToP, they could figure prominently in the looming crisis, particularly vis-à-vis IAA.

Numerous authors before me have been able to articulate more thoroughly and persuasively the intricacies and value of the ecofeminist perspective (see, for instance, Eckersley 1992; Gaard, 2017; Warren 1997; Adams 1994; Noske 1989) than I have been able to undertake here. However, I hope the value of this book can be found in demonstrating how an ecofeminist perspective that foregrounds the intersections of harms perpetrated against those constructed as part of the nature side of the culture/nature dichotomy is key to demonstrating the ways that the AAM and the EM can move beyond the historic tensions that have divided them, even on the three most contentious issues between the two: sport hunting, zoos and aquaria, and fur. As social changes (such as increasing affection for companion animals), and changes within the movements (shifting demographics, relations to science, and a focus on the connection between IAA and GCC) bring the movements into closer alignment, the truly intersectional perspective provided by critical ecofeminism will be invaluable for grounding and guiding this collaborative project.

I have to admit that more than once while writing this book I lamented to a few close colleagues that perhaps it was a mistake, because in challenging long-held disagreements and dogma, along with recommending compromises and concessions between two social movements and areas of academic study that I care so much about, I may have alienated myself from both of them. Yet as this book draws to a close I find myself hopeful. I am hopeful that the most significant rifts between the EM and the AAM will be overcome by shifts in conceptualizations, by strategizing a little differently, and by some give-and-take on both sides. I am hopeful that my projection that the AAM is poised to make significant strides in the not-too-distant future will come to fruition. Finally, I am hopeful that the potential of unifying against the sources of challenges and resistance that I have traced out in this book will be helpful for others who are also thinking through these issues. I hope they may be able to build upon and refine what has been sketched out here. I want to underscore, however, that even if the political anaesthesia that the Inverted Quarantine threatens us with is overcome, and the treadmill of production is fundamentally altered in the face of crisis, unless we heed the ecofeminist call to disrupt the constructed culture/nature dichotomy and cultivate respect and caring for those situated along the culture–nature continuum, we will simply be replacing one problematic system with another.

Notes

1 The term "animal" is used as shorthand throughout to refer to nonhuman animals.
2 There are significant literatures examining the social construction of perceived differences on the basis of race and sex, and problematizing biological essentialism (see, for instance, Butler 2007; Hill Collins 1998; Lorber 1995). Moreover, some have problematized the notion of distinct categories of species (see Dawkins 1993; Kim 2015).
3 Although the term "neoliberalism" is frequently used, it is rarely explained. I prefer Harvey's definition, as it is both descriptive and concise. He explains, "Neoliberalism is in the first instance a theory of political economic practices that proposes that human well-being can best be advanced by liberating individuals' entrepreneurial freedoms and skills within an institutional framework characterized by strong private property rights, free markets, and free trade" (2005, 2). In short, the process promotes individualism, self-responsibility, the commodification of aspects of the world that in the past were considered necessities (e.g., water), and the externalization of social and environmental costs.
4 I generally prefer the terms "welfarists," "liberationists," and "rightist/abolitionists" to refer to the three perspectives and use them throughout the book because they are descriptive and not value judgments, unlike some of the terms Jasper and Nelkin (1992) use (e.g., pragmatists, fundamentalists).
5 For a notable exception, see Atran (2003).
6 For a discussion of non-environmentally focused arguments in favour of hunting, see Vitali (1990), Peterson (2004), and Pardo and Prato (2005).
7 Even more controversially, some jurisdictions introduce infectious diseases to wildlife in an attempt to control the populations of some animals, such as rabbit populations in Australia, New Zealand, and Europe (McCallum and Hocking 2005).

8 These are vastly outnumbered by unaccredited zoos. In the US, for instance, in the year 2011 there were 214 accredited and 800 nonaccredited zoos (Braverman 2013).

9 *Ex situ* conservation takes place outside of the animal's natural environment (i.e., in a zoo), whereas *in situ* activities take place in the field and can include habitat remediation, species reintroduction, and supplementation (Tribe and Booth 2003). Pritchard and colleagues (2011) have suggested, however, that the distinction between the two may be rendered moot by the continued loss of truly wild places and animals.

10 Due to space constraints, fishing and fisheries are not covered in this chapter. For a thorough analysis of this topic, please see Kemmerer (2015b).

11 A discussion of the origins of meat consumption and the domestication of animals as livestock to be used for food is beyond the scope of this chapter; for specific information on these topics, see Fitzgerald (2015), Chiles and Fitzgerald (2017), Mithen (1999), and Kalof (2007).

12 This overproduction was further facilitated by governmental policies, particularly in the US. For further details, see Rifkin (1992), Striffler (2005), Horowitz (2006), Winders and Nibert (2004), and Fitzgerald (2003).

13 Due to space constraints, a more detailed description of the factors that contributed to the industrialization of animal production cannot be provided here. For further information about the various contributing factors, see Fitzgerald (2016), Winders and Nibert (2004), Starmer et al. (2006), Twine (2010), Gunderson (2011a; 2011b), Novek (2003), Hardeman and Jochemsem (2012), Noske (1989), and Weis (2010).

14 Without a doubt, there are likely some people who have been turned off by a critique of individual consumption behaviours; however, there are no indications that it has damaged the movement.

References

Acampora, Ralph. (2005) Zoos and eyes: contesting captivity and seeking successor practices. *Society and Animals* 13(1): 68–88.

Adams, Carol J. (1990) *The Sexual Politics of Meat: A Feminist–Vegetarian Critical Theory*. New York: Continuum Press.

Adams, Carol. (1994) *Neither Man Nor Beast: Feminism and the Defense of Animals*. New York: Continuum Press.

Adams, Carol and Josephine Donovan. (1995) *Animals and Women: Feminist Theoretical Explorations*. Durham, NC: Duke University Press.

Agyeman, Julian, David Schlosberg, Luke Craven, and Caitlin Matthews. (2016) Environmental justice: from inequity to everyday life, community, and just sustainabilities. *Annual Review of Environment and Resources* 41: 321–340.

Anderson, Elizabeth. (2004) Animal rights and the value of non-human life. In Cass Sunstein and Martha Nussbaum (eds.) *Animal Rights: Current Debates and New Directions*. Oxford: Oxford University Press, pp. 277–289.

Arluke, Arnold, Jack Levin, Luke C. Jack, and Ascione, Frank. (1999) The relationship of animal abuse to violence and other forms of antisocial behavior. *Journal of Interpersonal Violence* 14: 963–975.

Arluke, Arnold, and Clinton Sanders. (eds.) (2008) *Between the Species: A Reader in Human–Animal Relationships*. New York: Allyn and Bacon.

Ascione, Frank. (1998) Battered women's reports of their partner's and their children's cruelty to animals. *Journal of Emotional Health* 1: 119–133.

Ascione, Frank, and Ken Shapiro. (2009) People and animals, kindness and cruelty: research directions and policy implications. *Journal of Social Issues* 65: 569–587.

Ascione, Frank, C. Weber, T. Thompson, J. Heath, M. Maruyama, and K. Hayashi. (2007) Battered pets and domestic violence: animal abuse reported by women experiencing intimate violence and by nonabused women. *Violence against Women* 13: 354–373.

Atran, Scott. (2003) Genesis of suicide terrorism. *Science* 299: 1534–1539.

Australian Broadcasting Corporation. (2011) The people who would spare the cane toad. Article by Sara Phillips, January 11.

References

Baker, R. (1985) *The American Hunting Myth*. New York: Vantage Press.

Bakker, Karen. (2010) The limits of "neoliberal natures": debating green neoliberalism. *Progress in Human Geography* 34(6): 718–735.

Barker, Colin and Gareth Dale. (1998) Protest waves in Western Europe: a critique of "New Social Movement" theory. *Critical Sociology* 24(1/2): 65–104.

Barrett, Betty, Amy Fitzgerald, Rochelle Stevenson, and Chi Ho Cheung. (2017) Animal maltreatment as a risk marker of more frequent and severe forms of intimate partner violence. *Journal of Interpersonal Violence*. Advance online publication: https://doi.org/10.1177/0886260517719542

Beers, Diane. (2006) *For the Prevention of Cruelty*. Athens: Ohio University Press.

Beck, Ulrich. ([1992] 2007) *Risk Society: Towards a New Modernity*. Los Angeles: Sage.

Beirne, Piers. (1999) For a non-speciesist criminology: animal abuse as an object of study. *Criminology* 37(1): 117–148.

——. (2011) Animal abuse and criminology: introduction to a special issue. *Crime, Law, and Social Change* 55: 349–357.

Beirne, Piers and Nigel South. (2007) Introduction: Approaching green criminology. In Piers Beirne and Nigel South (eds.) *Issues in Green Criminology: Confronting Harms against Environments, Humanity, and Other Animals*. New York: Routledge, pp. xiii–xxii.

Bekoff, Marc. (2000) Animal emotions: exploring passionate natures: current interdisciplinary research provides compelling evidence that many animals experience such emotions as joy, fear, love, despair, and grief – we are not alone. *BioScience* 50(10): 861–870.

——. (2002) Ethics and marine mammals. In W. Perrin, B. Würsig, and H. Thewissen (eds.), *Encyclopedia of Marine Mammals*. San Diego: Academic Press, pp. 398–404.

Benjaminsen, T.A., Mary J. Goldman, Maya Minwary, and Faustin Maganga. (2013) Wildlife management in Tanzania: state control, rent seeking and community resistance. *Development and Change* 44(5): 1087–1109.

Bennett, Jeff and Stuart Whitten. (2003) Duck hunting and wetland conservation: compromise or synergy? *Canadian Journal of Agricultural Economics* 51: 161–173.

Bentham, Jeremy. (1789) *An Introduction to the Principles of Morals and Legislation*.

Benton, Ted. (1993) *Natural Relations: Ecology, Animal Rights and Social Justice*. New York: Verso.

Berger, John. (1980) *About Looking*. New York: Pantheon Books.

Best, Steven and Anthony Nocella. (2004) *Terrorists or Freedom Fighters? Reflections on the Liberation of Animals*. New York: Lantern Books.

Bijileveld, Marijn. (2013) *Natural Mink Fur and Faux Fur Products: An Environmental Comparison*. Delft: CE Delft.

Boglioli, Marc. (2009) Illegitimate killers: the symbolic ecology and cultural politics of coyote-hunting tournaments in Addison County, Vermont. *Anthropology and Humanism* 34(2): 203–218.

References

Bonesi, Laura and Santiago Palazon. (2007) The American mink in Europe: status, impacts, and control. *Biological Conservation* 134: 470–483.

Bowkett, Andrew. (2009) Recent captive-breeding proposals and the return of the ark concept to global species conservation. *Conservation Biology* 23(3): 773–776.

Boycott. *Business and Society Review* 114(4): 457–489.

Boyle, Alan and Michael Anderson (eds.). (1998) *Human Rights Approaches to Environmental Protection*. Oxford: Clarendon Paperbacks.

Braunsberger, Karin and Brian Buckler (2009) Consumers on a mission to force a change in public policy: a qualitative study of the ongoing Canadian Seafood

Braverman, Irus. (2013) *Zooland: The Institution of Captivity*. Stanford: Stanford Law Books.

Brennan, A. (2003) Humanism, racism and speciesism. *Worldviews* 7: 274–302.

Bristow, Elizabeth and Amy Fitzgerald. (2011) Global climate change and the industrial animal agriculture link: the construction of risk. *Society & Animals* 19: 205–224.

Broida, J., L. Tingley, R. Kimball, J. Miele, and H. Dahles. (1993) Personality differences between pro- and anti-vivisectionists. *Society & Animals* 1: 129–144.

Brulle, R. J. (2000) *Agency, Democracy, and Nature: The U.S. Environmental Movement from a Critical Theory Perspective*. Cambridge, MA: MIT Press.

Bullard, Robert. (2000) *Dumping in Dixie: Race, Class, and Environmental Quality*. 3rd ed. Boulder, CO: Westview Press.

Bulliet, R. (2005) *Hunters, Herders and Hamburgers: The Past and Future of Human–Animal Relationships*. New York: Columbia University Press.

Burgwald, Jon. (2016) Where does Greenpeace stand on seal hunting? http://www.greenpeace.org/canada/en/blog/Blogentry/where-does-greenpeace-stand-on-seal-hunting/blog/55360/ Accessed June 2, 2017.

Burmeister, L. (2002) Lagoons, litter and the law: CAFO regulations as social risk politics. *Southern Rural Sociology* 18(2): 56–87.

Butler, Judith. ([1990] 2007) *Gender Trouble: Feminism and the Subversion of Identity*. New York: Routledge.

Cahoone, Lawrence. (2009) Hunting as a moral good. *Environmental Values* 18: 67–89.

Calhoun, Craig. (1993) "New Social Movements" of the early nineteenth century. *Social Science History* 17(3): 385–427.

Callicott, J. Baird. (1980) Animal liberation: a triangular affair. *Environmental Ethics* 2(4): 311–338.

——. (1988) Animal liberation and environmental ethics: back together again. *Between the Species* 4(3): 163–169.

——. (1989) *In Defense of the Land Ethic: Essays in Environmental Philosophy*. Albany: State University of New York Press.

Campbell, T. Colin and Thomas Campbell. (2006) *The China Study: Startling Implications for Diet, Weight Loss and Long-Term Health*. Dallas: Benbella Books.

References

Card, James. (2012) Hunt, fish… and save the planet. *Earth Island Journal* (Autumn): 49–53.

Carson, Rachel. (1962) *Silent Spring*. Boston, MA: Houghton Mifflin.

Cartmill, Matt. (1993) *A View to a Death in the Morning*. Cambridge, MA: Harvard University Press.

Castree, Noel. (2010) Neoliberalism and the biophysical environment 1: what "neoliberalism" is, and what difference nature makes to it. *Geography Compass* 4(12): 1725–1733.

_____. (2010) Neoliberalism and the biophysical environment 2: theorising the neoliberalisation of nature. *Geography Compass* 4(12): 1734–1746.

_____. (2011) Neoliberalism and the biophysical environment 3: putting theory into practice. *Geography Compass* 5(1): 35–49.

Catton, W. R. J. (1980) *Overshoot: The Ecological Basis of Revolutionary Change*. Urbana: University of Illinois Press.

CBC News. (2015) February 8. Don Cherry explains "barbarian" comment, has "no problem" with seal meat. http://www.cbc.ca/news/canada/newfoundland-labrador/don-cherry-explains-barbarian-comment-has-no-problem-with-seal-meat-1.2949490 Accessed June 1, 2017.

Centner, T. J. (2006) Governmental oversight of discharges from concentrated animal feeding operations. *Environmental Management* 37: 745–752.

Cherry, Elizabeth. (2016) *Culture and Activism: Animal Rights in France and the United States*. London: Routledge.

Chiles, Robert M. and Amy Fitzgerald. (2017) Why is meat so important in Western history and culture? A genealogical critique of biophysical and political-economic explanations. *Agriculture and Human Values*: 1–17.

Cianchi, John. (2015) *Radical Environmentalism: Nature, Identity and More-Than-Human Agency*. New York: Palgrave McMillan.

Clay, J. W. (2004) *World Agriculture and the Environment: A Commodity-by-Commodity Guide to Impacts and Practices*. Washington, D.C.: Island Press.

Clubb, R. and G. Mason. (2003) Animal welfare: captivity effects on wide-ranging carnivores. *Nature* 425: 473–474.

CNN (2016) In gorilla's death, critics blame mother, Cincinnati Zoo. http://www.cnn.com/2016/05/29/us/cincinnati-zoo-gorilla-shot/

Coltman, David, Paul O'Donoghue, Jon T. Jorgenson, John T. Hogg, Curtis Strobeck, and Marco Festa-Blanchet. (2003) Undesirable evolutionary consequences of trophy hunting. *Nature* 426: 655–658.

Convention on Biological Diversity. Available at https://www.cbd.int/gbo1/chap-02.shtml

Coulson, Tim and Sonya Clegg. (2014) Fur seals signal their own decline. *Nature* 511: 414–415.

Council of the European Union. (1999) Council Directive 1999/74/EC of 19 July 1999 "Laying down minimum standards for the protection of laying hens."

_____. (2008) Council Directive 2008/120/EC of 18 December 2008. Laying down minimum standards for the protection of pigs.

References

Currie, C. L. (2006) Animal cruelty by children exposed to domestic violence. *Child Abuse and Neglect* 30: 425–435.

Curtin, D. (1996) Toward an ecological ethic of care. In K. J. Warren (ed.), *Ecological Feminist Philosophies*. Bloomington, IN: Indiana University Press.

Cushing, S. (2003) Against "Humanism": speciesism, personhood, and preference. *Journal of Social Philosophy* 34: 556–571.

Daoust, Pierre-Yves, Alice Crook, Trent Bollinger, Keith Campbell, and James Wong. (2002) Animal welfare and the harp seal hunt in Atlantic Canada. *Canadian Veterinary Journal* 43: 687–694.

Dauvergne, P. (2010) *The Shadows of Consumption: Consequences for the Global Environment*. Cambridge, MA: MIT Press.

Dauvergne, Peter and Kate Neville. (2011) Mindbombs of right and wrong: cycles of contention in the activist campaign to stop Canada's seal hunt. *Environmental Politics* 20(2): 192–209.

Dawkins, Richard. (1993) Gaps in the mind. In Paola Cavalieri and Peter Singer (eds.), *The Great Ape Project*. New York: St. Martin's Griffin, pp. 81–87.

DeFries, Ruth, Thomas Rudel, Maria Uriarte, and Matthew Hansen. (2010) Deforestation driven by urban population growth and agricultural trade in the twenty-first century. *Nature Geoscience* 3: 178–181.

Dietz, T., L. Kalof, and P. Stern. (2002) Gender, values and environmentalism. *Social Science Quarterly* 83: 351–364.

Dizard, Jan. (1999) *Going Wild: Hunting, Animal Rights, and the Contested Meaning of Nature*. Boston: University of Massachusetts Press.

Donham, K. J., S. Wing, D. Osterberg, J. L. Flora, C. Hodne, K. M. Thu, and P. S. Thorne. (2007) Community health and socioeconomic issues surrounding concentrated animal feeding operations. *Environmental Health Perspectives* 115: 317–320.

Donovan, Josephine. (1990) Animal rights and feminist theory. *Signs* 15: 350–375.

Donovan, Josephine and C. Adams. (2007) *The Feminist Care Tradition in Animal Ethics: A Reader*. Chichester, West Sussex: Columbia University Press.

Dove, Jackie. (2000) Caught between a trap and a lawsuit. *The Animals' Agenda* 20(1): 42–45.

Dowie, M. (1995) *Losing Ground: American Environmentalism at the Close of the Twentieth Century*. Cambridge, MA: MIT Press.

Dryzek, John. (2005) *The Politics of the Earth: Environmental Discourses*. Oxford: Oxford University Press.

DSS Management Consultants. (2012) A comparative life cycle analysis: natural fur and faux fur. Public Summary. http://www.fureurope.eu/wp-content/uploads/2015/02/LCA_-final-report.pdf Accessed June 2, 2017.

Dubois, Sara and H. W. Harshaw. (2013) Exploring "humane" dimensions of wildlife. *Human Dimensions of Wildlife* 18: 1–19.

Duffy, Rosaleen. (2014) Interactive elephants: nature, tourism and neoliberalism. *Annals of Tourism Research* 44: 88–101.

Dunayer, J. (2001) *Animal Equality: Language and Liberation*. Derwood: Ryce Publishing.

References

Dunk, Thomas. (2002) Hunting and the politics of identity in Ontario. *CNS* 13(1): 36–66.

Dunlap, Riley and Angela Mertig (Eds.). (2014) *American Environmentalism: The U.S. Environmental Movement, 1970–1990.* London: Taylor and Francis.

Dunlap, Thomas. (1988) Sport hunting and conservation, 1880–1920. *Environmental Review* 12(1): 51–60.

Dzirutwe, MacDonald. (2015) Zimbabwe will not charge U.S. dentist for killing Cecil the lion. Yahoo News, October 12 https://www.yahoo.com/news/zim babwe-says-not-charge-u-dentist-killing-cecil-133842381.html?ref=gs

Eckersley, R. (1992) *Environmentalism and Political Theory: Toward an Ecocentric Approach.* Albany: SUNY Press.

Edwards, B. and A. Ladd. (2000) Environmental justice, swine production and farm loss in North Carolina. *Sociological Spectrum* 20: 263–290.

Einwohner, Rachel. (1999a) Gender, class, and social movement outcomes: identity and effectiveness in two animal rights campaigns. *Gender and Society* 13(1): 56–76.

_____. (1999b) Practices, opportunity, and protest effectiveness. *Social Problems* 46(2): 169–186.

_____. (2002) Motivational framing and efficacy maintenance: Animal rights activists' use of four fortifying strategies. *The Sociological Quarterly* 43(4): 509–526.

Eisnitz, Gail. (1997) *Slaughterhouse: The Shocking Story of Greed, Neglect, and Inhumane Treatment inside the US Meat Industry.* Amherst, NY: Prometheus Books.

Everett, Jennifer. (2001) Environmental ethics, animal welfarism, and the problem of predation: A Bambi lover's respect for nature. *Ethics and the Environment* 6(1): 42–67.

Faminow, M. (1998) *Cattle, Deforestation and Development in the Amazon: An Economic, Agronomic and Environmental Perspective.* Wallingford: CAB international.

Farrell, Paul. (2016) Barnaby Joyce and NSW ministers target charity status of animal rights groups. *The Guardian.* December 8. https://www.theguardian. com/australia-news/2016/dec/08/barnaby-joyce-and-nsw-ministers-target-charity-status-of-animal-rights-groups. Accessed May 5, 2017.

Favre, David. (2004) A new property status for animals: equitable self-ownership. In Cass Sunstein and Martha Nussbaum (eds.), *Animal Rights: Current Debates and New Directions.* New York: Oxford University Press, pp. 234–250.

Fellenz, M. R. (2007) *The Moral Menagerie: Philosophy and Animal Rights.* Champaign: University of Illinois Press.

Fischer, Anke, Vesna Kerezi, Beatriz Arroyo, Miguel Mateos-Delibes, Degu Tadie, Asanterabi Lowassa, Olive Krange, and Ketil Skogen. (2013) (De)legitimizing hunting: discourses over the morality of hunting in Europe and Eastern Africa. *Land Use Policy* 32: 261–270.

References

Fisheries and Oceans Canada. (2016a) Statistics on the seal harvest. http://www. dfo-mpo.gc.ca/fm-gp/seal-phoque/seal-stats-phoques-eng.htm Accessed June 13, 2017.

____. (2016b) Seal market. http://www.dfo-mpo.gc.ca/fm-gp/seal-phoque/ market-marche-eng.htm Accessed June 13, 2017.

____. (2016c) Grey seals and cod. http://www.dfo-mpo.gc.ca/fm-gp/seal-phoque/ cod-morue-eng.htm Accessed June 14, 2017.

Fitzgerald, Amy J. (2005a) The emergence of the figure of "Woman-the-hunter": gender equality or complicity in oppression? *Women's Studies Quarterly* 33(1&2): 86–104.

____. (2005b) *Animal Abuse and Family Violence: Researching the Interrelationships of Abusive Power.* Lewiston: Mellen.

____. (2015). *Animals as food: (Re)connecting production, processing, consumption, and impacts.* East Lansing: Michigan State University Press.

Fitzgerald, Amy, Linda Kalof, and Thomas Dietz. (2009) Spillover from "The Jungle" into the larger community: slaughterhouses and increased crime rates. *Organization and Environment* 22: 158–184.

Fitzgerald, Amy and David Pellow (2014) Ecological defense for animal liberation: a holistic understanding of the world. In A. Nocella, J. Sorenson, K. Socha, and A. Matsuoka. (eds.) *Defining Critical Animal Studies: An Intersectional Social Justice Approach for Liberation.* New York: Peter Lang Publishers, pp. 28–50.

Fitzgerald, Amy and Wesley Tourangeau. (2018) Crime versus harm in the transportation of animals: a closer look at Ontario's "pig trial." In Allison Gray and Ronald Hinch (eds.), *A Handbook of Food Crime: Immoral and Illegal Practices in the Food Industry and What to Do about Them.* Bristol: Policy Press, pp. 213–228.

Fitzgerald, Deborah. (2003) *Every Farm a Factory: The Industrial Ideal in American Agriculture.* New Haven, CT: Yale University Press.

Fjellstrom, R. (2002) Specifying speciesism. *Environmental Values* 11: 63–74.

Flynn, C. P. (2011) Examining the links between animal abuse and human violence. *Crime, Law, and Social Change* 55, 453–468.

Food and Agriculture Organization of the UN. (2005) *Cattle Ranching Is Encroaching on Forests in Latin America.* FAO, Rome.

____. (2012) *World Agriculture towards 2030/2050 – The 2012 Revision. ESA Working Paper 23–03.* FAO, Rome.

____. (2017a) *The future of food and agriculture: trends and challenges.* http:// www.fao.org/3/a-i6583e.pdf

____. (2017b) *Strengthening Sector Policies for Better Food Security and Nutrition Results: Livestock.* Rome: FAO.

Foucault, Michel. (1979) *Discipline and Punish.* London: Penguin Books.

Francione, Gary. (1996) *Rain without Thunder: The Ideology of the Animal Rights Movement.* Philadelphia: Temple University Press.

____. (2010) *The Animal Rights Debate: Abolition or Regulation.* New York: Columbia University Press.

References

Franklin, Adrian. (1998) Naturalizing sports: hunting and angling in modern environments. *International Review for the Sociology of Sport* 33/4: 355–366.

____. (1999) *Animals and Modern Cultures: A Sociology of Human–Animal Relations in Modernity*. Thousand Oaks, CA: Sage.

Franklin, A., B. Tranter, and R. White. (2001) Explaining support for animal rights: a comparison of two recent approaches to humans, nonhuman animals, and post-modernity. *Society & Animals* 9(2): 127–114.

Franklin, Julian H. (2005) *Animal Rights and Moral Philosophy*. New York: Columbia University Press.

Fraser, H. M. and N. J. Taylor. (2016) *Neoliberalization, Universities and the Public Intellectual: Species, Gender and Class and the Production of Knowledge*. London: Palgrave Macmillan UK.

Freeman, M. and G. Wenzel. (2006) The nature and significance of Polar Bear conservation hunting in the Canadian Arctic. *Arctic* 59(1): 21–30.

Gaard, Greta. (1993) Living interconnections with animals and nature. In Gaard (ed.), *Ecofeminism: Women, Animals, Nature*. Philadelphia: Temple, pp. 1–12.

____. (2001). Tools for a cross-cultural feminist ethics: exploring ethical contexts and contents in the Makah Whale Hunt. *Hypatia* 16(1): 1–26.

____. (2017) *Critical Ecofeminism*. New York: Lexington Books.

Gavin, Shelley and Harold Herzog. (1998) "Attitudes and dispositional optimism of animal rights demonstrators." *Society and Animals* 6(1): 1–11.

Globe and Mail Editorial, Sunday, September 20, 2015. http://www.theglobe-andmail.com/opinion/editorials/in-quebec-a-step-forward-for-animal-rights/article26430969/

Goode, Erica. (2015) After Cecil furor, US aims to protect lions through Endangered Species Act. *The New York Times*, December 20. http://www.nytimes.com/2015/12/21/science/us-to-protect-african-lions-under-endan-gered-species-act.html?_r=0).

Goodland, R., and J. Anhang. (2009) Livestock and climate change: what if the key actors are… cows, pigs, and chickens? *World Watch Magazine* 22(6): 10–19.

Goodwin, J. P. (1997) The ecological costs of fur farming. *Earth First* 17(4): 27.

Gottlieb, R. (1993) *Forcing the Spring: The Transformation of the American Environmental Movement*. Washington, D.C.: Island Press.

Gould, K. A., A. Schnaiberg, and A. S. Weinberg (1996) *Local Environmental Struggles*. New York: Cambridge University Press.

Gould, Kenneth, David Pellow, and Allan Schnaiberg. (2008) *The Treadmill of Production: Injustice and Unsustainability in the Global Economy*. Boulder; London: Paradigm Publishers.

Grandin, Temple (Ed.). (2007) *Livestock Handling and Transport*. 3rd edition. Cambridge: CABI.

Green, C. F. et al. (2006) Bacterial plume emanating from the air surrounding swine confinement operations. *Journal of Occupational and Environmental Hygiene*, 3(1): 9–15.

Gunderson, R. (2011a) From cattle to capital: exchange value, animal commodi-fication, and barbarism. *Critical Sociology* 39(2): 1–17.

References

_____. (2011b) The metabolic rifts of livestock agribusiness. *Organization and Environment* 24(4): 1–19.

Gunn, Alastair. (2001) Environmental ethics and trophy hunting. *Ethics & the Environment* 6(1): 68–95.

Gusset, M. and G. Dick. (2010) "Building a Future for Wildlife"? Evaluating the contribution of the world zoo and aquarium community to in situ conservation. *International Zoo Yearbook* 44: 183–191.

——. (2011) The global reach of zoos and aquariums in visitor numbers and conservation expenditures. *Zoo Biology* 30: 566–569.

Haggerty, Julia, Hugh Campbell, and Carolyn Morris. (2009) Keeping the stress off the sheep? Agricultural intensification, neoliberalism, and "good" farming in New Zealand. *Geoforum* 40: 767–777.

Hahn Niman, N. (2009). *Righteous Porkchop: Finding a Life and Good Food Beyond Factory Farms.* New York: HarperCollins.

Haines, Herbert H. (1984). Black radicalization and the funding of civil rights: 1957–1970. *Social Problems* 32 (1): 31–43.

Halsey, Mark. (2004) Against "green" criminology. *British Journal of Criminology* 44: 833–853.

Halsey, Mark and Rob White. (1998). Crime, ecophilosophy and environmental harm. *Theoretical Criminology* 2(3): 345–371.

Hammill, Michael and Garry Stenson. (2010) Comment on "Towards a precautionary approach to managing Canada's commercial harp seal hunt" by Leaper et al. *ICES Journal of Marine Science* 67(2): 321–322.

Hardeman, E. and H. Jochemsen. (2012) Are there ideological aspects to the modernization of agriculture? *Journal of Agriculture and Environmental Ethics* 25(5): 657–674.

Hargrove, E. C. (1992) *The Animal Rights / Environmental Ethics Debate: The Environmental Perspective.* Albany: SUNY Press.

Harper, Breeze. (2012) Going beyond the normative white "post-racial" vegan epistemology. In Psyche Williams-Forson and Carole Counihan (eds.), *Taking Food Public: Redefining Foodways in a Changing World.* New York: Routledge, pp. 155–174.

Harrison, Annabel, Scott Newey, Lucy Gilbert, and Daniel Haydon. (2010) Culling wildlife hosts to control disease: mountain hares, red grouse and louping ill virus. *Journal of Applied Ecology* 47: 926–930.

Hawkins, R. Z. (1998) Ecofeminism and nonhumans: continuity, difference, dualism and domination. *Hypatia* 13: 158–197.

Hayward, Tim. (2004) *Constitutional Environmental Rights.* Oxford: Oxford University Press.

Heffelfinger, James, Valerius Geist, and W. Wishart. (2013) The role of hunting in North American wildlife conservation. *International Journal of Environmental Studies* 70(3): 399–413.

Heinrich Boll Foundation and Friends of the Earth Europe. (2014) Meat Atlas: Facts and figures about the animals we eat. https://www.foeeurope.org/sites/default/files/publications/foee_hbf_meatatlas_jan2014.pdf

References

Herzog, Harold. (2007) Gender differences in human–animal interactions: A review. *Anthrozoos* 20(1): 7–21

Hill Collins, Patricia. (1998) It's all in the family: intersections of gender, race, and nation. *Hypatia* 13(3): 62–82.

Holt, David M. (2008) Unlikely allies against factory farms: 'Animal rights advocates and environmentalists. *Agriculture and Human Values* 25: 169–171.

Horowitz, R. (2006) *Putting Meat on the American Table*. Baltimore: The Johns Hopkins University Press.

Horrigan, L., R. S. Lawrence, and P. Walker. (2002) How sustainable agriculture can address the environmental and health harms of industrial agriculture. *Environmental Health Perspectives* 110(5): 445–456.

Howse, Robert and Joanna Langille. (2011) *Permitting pluralism: The seal products dispute and why the WTO should accept trade restrictions justified by noninstrumental moral values*. New York University School of Law: Public Law and Legal Theory Research Paper Series, Working paper No. 11–82.

Ibrahim, D. M. (2007) A return to Descartes: property, profit, and the corporate ownership of animals. *Law and Contemporary Problems* 70: 87.

Imhoff, D. (Ed.). (2010) *The CAFO Reader: The Tragedy of Industrial Animal Factories*. Berkeley: University of California Press.

International Fur Federation. (n.d.) Fur is green and sustainable in the environment. https://www.wearefur.com/responsible-fur/environment/ Accessed June 1, 2017.

Jabour, Julia. (2008) Successful conservation – then what? The de-listing of *Arctocephalus* Fur Seal species in Antarctica. *Journal of International Wildlife Law and Policy* 11: 1–29.

Jackson, C. (1993) Doing what comes naturally? Women and environment in development. *World Development* 21(12): 1947–1963.

Jamieson, Dale. (2002) Zoos revisited. In Dale Jamieson, *Morality's Progress: Essays on Humans, Other Animals, and the Rest of Nature*. Oxford: Clarendon Press, pp. 176–189.

_____. (2005) Against zoos. In Peter Singer (ed.), *In Defense of Animals: The Second Wave*. Malden: Blackwell Publishing, pp. 132–143.

Jamison, W. and W. Lunch. (1992) Rights of animals, perceptions of science, and political activism: profile of American animal rights activists. *Science, Technology, and Human Values* 17(4): 438–458.

Jarboe, James. (2002) Domestic Terrorism Section Chief, Counterterrorism Division, Federal Bureau of Investigation, before the House Resources Committee, Subcommittee on Forests and Forest Health. https://archives.fbi.gov/archives/news/testimony/the-threat-of-eco-terrorism

Jasper, J. M. and Nelkin, D. (1992) *The Animals Rights Crusade: The Growth of a Moral Protest*. New York: Free Press.

Jasper, James and Jane Poulsen (1995) Social networks in animal rights and anti-nuclear protests. *Social Problems* 42(4): 493–512.

Jensen, Jon (2001) The virtues of hunting. *Philosophy in the Contemporary World* 8(2): 113–124.

Jerolmack, Colin. (2003) Tracing the profile of animal rights supporters: a pre-liminary investigation. *Society & Animals* 11(3): 245–263.

Kalland, A. (2012) *Unveiling the Whale: Discourses on Whales and Whaling.* New York: Berghahn Books.

Kalof, Linda. (2000) The multi-layered discourses of animal concern. In H. Addams and J. Proops (eds.), *Social Discourse and Environmental Policy: An Application of Q Methodology.* Cheltenham: Edward Elgar, pp. 174–195.

____. (2007). *Looking at Animals in Human History.* London: Reaktion Books.

Kalof, Linda, Thomas Dietz, Paul Stern, and G. Guagnano. (1999) Social psy-chological and structural influences on vegetarian beliefs. *Rural Sociology* 64: 500–511.

Kalof, Linda and Amy Fitzgerald. (2003) Reading the trophy: exploring the display of dead animals in hunting magazines. *Visual Studies* 18(2).

Kalof, Linda, Amy Fitzgerald, and Lori Baralt. (2004). Animals, women, and weapons: blurred sexual boundaries in the discourse of sport hunting. *Society & Animals* 12(3): 237–251.

Kean, Hilda. (1998) *Animal Rights: Political and Social Change in Britain since 1800.* London: Reaktion.

Kemmerer, Lisa (Ed.). (2015a) *Animals and the Environment: Advocacy, Activism, and the Quest for Common Ground.* London; New York: Earthscan/Routledge.

____. (2015b). *Eating Earth: Ethics and Dietary Choice.* Oxford: Oxford University Press.

Kennedy, R. F. (2009) Foreword. In *Righteous Porkchop: Finding a Life and Good Food Beyond Factory Farms.* New York: HarperCollins.

Kerr, Joanna. (2014) Greenpeace apology to Inuit for impacts of seal campaign. http://www.greenpeace.org/canada/en/blog/Blogentry/greenpeace-to-canadas-aboriginal-peoples-work/blog/53339/ Accessed May 25, 2017.

Keulartz, Jozef. (2015) Captivity for conservation? Zoos at a crossroads. *Journal of Agriculture and Environmental Ethics* 28: 335–351.

Kheel, Marti. (1993) From heroic to holistic ethics: the ecofeminist challenge. In Greta Gaard (ed.), *Ecofeminism: Women, Animals, Nature.* Philadelphia: Temple University Press, pp. 243–271

____. (1995) License to kill: an ecofeminist critique of hunters' discourse. In Carol J. Adams and Josephine Donovan (eds.), *Animals and Women: Feminist Theoretical Explorations.* Durham, NC: Duke University Press, pp. 85–125.

____. (1996) The killing game: An ecofeminist critique of hunting. *Journal of the Philosophy of Sport* 23: 30–44.

Kim, Claire Jean. (2015) *Dangerous Crossings: Race, Species, and Nature in a Multicultural Age.* Cambridge: Cambridge University Press.

King, Roger. (1991) Environmental ethics and the case for hunting. *Environmental Ethics* 13: 59–85.

Kitossa, Tamari. (2000) Same difference: biocentric imperialism and the assault on indigenous culture and hunting. *Environments* 28(2): 23–36.

Klein, Naomi. (2014) *This Changes Everything: Capitalism vs. The Climate.* New York: Simon and Schuster.

References

Knezevic, Irena. (2009) Hunting and environmentalism: conflict or misperceptions. *Human Dimensions of Wildlife* 14: 12–20.

Koneswaran, Gowri and Danielle Nierenberg. (2008) Global farm animal production and global warming: impacting and mitigating climate change. *Environmental Health Perspectives* 116(5): 578–582.

Kruse, C. R. (1999) Gender, views of nature, and support for animal rights. *Society & Animals* 7: 179–198.

Kupper, Frank and Tjard De Cock Buning. (2011) Deliberating animal values: A pragmatic–pluralistic approach to animal ethics. *Journal of Agricultural and Environmental Ethics* 24(5): 431–450.

Ladd, Anthony E. and Bob Edwards. (2002) Corporate swine and capitalist pigs: a decade of environmental injustice and protest in North Carolina. *Social Justice* 29(3): 26–46.

Laidlaw, Rob. (2001) Re-introduction of captive bred animals to the wild: is the modern ark afloat? In Bill Jordan (ed.), *Who Cares for Planet Earth? The Con in Conservation.* Portland: Alpha Press, pp. 64–80.

____. (2017). ZooBiz: the conservation of business? In David Nibert (ed.), *Animal Oppression and Capitalism.* New York: Praeger, pp. 71–99.

Lappe, A. (2010) Diet for a hot planet: livestock and climate change. In D. Imhoff(ed.), *The CAFO Reader: The Tragedy of Industrial Animal Factories.* Healdsburg, CA: Watershed Media, pp. 240–249.

Leaper, Russell, David Lavigne, Peter Corkeron, and David Johnston. (2009) Towards a precautionary approach to managing Canada's commercial harp seal hunt. *ICES Journal of Marine Science* 67(2): 1–5.

Liddick, Donald R. (2006) *Eco-Terrorism: Radical Environmental and Animal Liberation Movements.* London: Praeger.

Linzey, Andrew. (2006). The ethical case for European legislation against fur farming. *Animal Law* 13: 147–165.

Loftin, Robert. (1984) The morality of hunting. *Environmental Ethics* 6: 241–250.

Lorber, Judith. (1995). *Paradoxes of Gender.* New Haven, CT: Yale University Press.

Lowe, Brian and Caryn Ginsberg (2002) Animal rights as a post-citizenship movement. *Society and Animals* 10(2): 203–215.

Luke, Brian. (1998). Violent love: hunting, heterosexuality, and the erotics of men's predation. *Feminist Studies* 24(3): 627–655.

Luke, Brian. (2007) *Brutal: Manhood and the Exploitation of Animals.* Chicago: University of Illinois Press.

Luke, Timothy. (2001) The pleasures of use: federalizing wilds, nationalizing life at the National Wildlife Federation. *CNS* 12(1): 3–39.

Machan, Tibor (2012) A critical note on "animal rights." *Contemporary Readings in Law and Social Justice* 4(2): 11–14.

Machovina, Brian, Kenneth Feeley, and William Ripple. (2015) Biodiversity conservation: the key is reducing meat consumption. *Science of the Total Environment* 536: 419–431.

Mackinnon, Catherine. (2004) Of mice and men: a feminist fragment on animal rights. In Cass Sunstein and Martha Nussbaum (eds.), *Animal Rights: Current Debates and New Directions*. New York: Oxford University Press, pp. 263–278.

Magdoff, F., J. B. Foster, and F. H. Buttel (Eds.). (2000) *Hungry for Profit: The Agribusiness Threat to Farmers, Food, and the Environment*. New York: Monthly Review Press.

Magee, Siobhan. (2016) An "excess of the normal": luxury and difference in Polish fur critique. *Journal of Material Culture* 21(3): 277–295.

Mahar, D. (1989) *Government Policies and Deforestation in Brazil's Amazon region*. Washington, D.C.: World Bank.

Malamud, Randy. (1998) *Reading Zoos: Representations of Animals and Captivity*. London: Macmillan Press.

Mallon, R. (2005) The deplorable standard of living faced by farmed animals in America's meat industry and how to improve conditions by eliminating the corporate farm. *MSU Journal of Medicine and Law* 9: 389–415.

Marangudakis, Manussos (2002) New social movements: between civil society and communitarianism. *Sociological Spectrum* 22(1): 41–70.

Marietta, D. E. and L. E. Embree. (1995) *Environmental Philosophy and Environmental Activism*. Lanham, MD: Rowman and Littlefield.

Marland, Alex. (2014) If seals were ugly, nobody would give a damn: propaganda, nationalism, and political marketing in the Canadian seal hunt. *Journal of Political Marketing* 15: 66–84.

Mason, Georgia, Jonathan Cooper, and Catherine Clarebrough. (2001) Frustrations of fur-farmed mink. *Nature* 410: 35–36.

Mason, J. and M. Finelli. (2005) Brave new world. In P. Singer (ed.), *In Defense of Animals: The Second Wave*. Malden MA: Wiley-Blackwell, pp. 104–122.

Matheny, G. and C. Leahy. (2007) Factory farm welfare, legislation, and trade. *Law and Contemporary Problems* 70: 325–358.

Maurer, Donna. (2002) *Vegetarianism: Movement or Moment?* Philadelphia, PA: Temple University Press.

McCallum, Hamish and Barbara Ann Hocking. (2005) Reflecting on ethical and legal issues in wildlife disease. *Bioethics* 19(4): 336–347.

McGuire, Krista, Richard Primack, and Elizabeth Losos. (2012) Dramatic improvements and persistent challenges for women ecologists. *BioScience* 62(2): 189–196.

McKibben, Bill. (1989) *The End of Nature*. New York: Random House.

McLeod, Carmen M. (2007) Dreadful/delightful killing: the contested nature of duck hunting. *Society and Animals* 15: 151–167.

Mekonnen, Mesfin and Arjen Hoekstra. (2012) A global assessment of the water footprint of farm animal products. *Ecosystems* 15: 401–415.

Mench, Joy, Harvey James, Edmond Pajor, and Paul Thompson. (2010) *The Welfare of Animals in Concentrated Animal Feeding Operations*. Food and Agriculture Organization of the United Nations.

References

Merchant, Carolyn. (2013) *Earthcare: Women and the Environment*. New York: Routledge.

Mertig, Angela and Riley Dunlap. (2001) Environmentalism, new social movements, and the new class: a cross-national investigation. *Rural Sociology* 66(1): 113–136.

Midgley, Mary. (1998) *Animals and Why They Matter*. Athens, GA: University of Georgia Press.

Mika, Marie. (2006) Framing the issue: religion, secular ethics and the case of animal rights mobilization. *Social Forces* 85(2): 915–941.

Miller, Lance J. (2011) Visitor reaction to pacing behavior: influence on the perception of animal care and interest in supporting zoological institutions. *Zoo Biology* 31: 242–248.

Milstein, Tema. (2009) "Somethin' tells me it's all happening at the zoo": discourse, power, and conservationism. *Environmental Communication* 3(1): 25–48.

Minteer, Ben A. and James P. Collins. (2013) Ecological ethics in captivity: balancing values and responsibilities in zoo and aquarium research under rapid global change. *ILAR Journal* 54(1): 41–51.

Mirabelli, M. C. et al. (2006) Asthma symptoms among adolescents who attend public schools that are located near confined swine feeding operations. *Pediatrics* 118(66): 66–76.

Mithen, Steven. (1999) The hunter-gatherer prehistory of human–animal interactions. *Anthrozoos* 12: 195–204.

Mullan, Bob and Garry Marvin. (1987) *Zoo Culture*. London: Weidenfeld and Nicholson.

Munro, Lyle. (1997) Framing cruelty: the construction of duck shooting as a social problem. *Society and Animals* 5(2): 137–154.

Munro, L. (2001) Caring about blood, flesh and pain: women's standing in the animal protection movement. *Society & Animals* 9: 43–61.

Munro, Lyle. (2005) Strategies, action repertoires and DIY activism in the animal rights movement. *Social Movement Studies* 4(1): 75–94.

____. (2012) The animal rights movement in theory and practice: A review of the sociological literature. *Sociology Compass* 6(2): 166–181.

Muth, Robert and Wesley V. Jamison. (2000) On the destiny of deer camps and duck blinds: the rise of the animal rights movement and the future of wildlife conservation. *Wildlife Society Bulletin* 28(4): 841–851.

Nash, Roderick. (1989) *The Rights of Nature: A History of Environmental Ethics*. Madison: University of Wisconsin Press.

Nast, Heidi. (2006) Loving...whatever: alienation, neoliberalism and pet-love in the twenty-first century. *ACME: An International E-Journal for Critical Geographies* 5(2): 300–327.

Nibert, David. (2002) *Animal Rights/Human Rights: Entanglements of Oppression and Liberation*. Lanham, MD: Rowman and Littlefield.

____. (2012) The fire next time: the coming cost of capitalism, animal oppression and environmental ruin. *Journal of Human Rights and the Environment* 3(1): 141–158.

——. (2013) *Animal Oppression and Human Violence: Domesecration, Capitalism and Global Conflict*. New York: Columbia University Press.

Nierenberg, D. (2003) *Factory Farming in the Developing World*. World Society for the Protection of Animals.

——. (2005) *Happier Meals: Rethinking the Global Meat Industry*. Worldwatch Paper 171. http://www.worldwatch.org/system/files/WP171.pdf

Nituch, Larissa, Jeff Bowman, Kaela Beauclerc, and Albrecht Schulte-Hostedde. (2011) Mink farms predict Aleutian Disease exposure in wild American mink. *PLoS ONE* 6(7): e21693.

Nocella, Anthony, John Sorenson, Kim Socha, and Atsuko Matsuoka (eds.). (2014) *Defining Critical Animal Studies: An Intersectional Social Justice Approach for Liberation*. New York, NY: Peter Lang.

Norton, Bryan G. (2000) Population and consumption: environmental problems as problems of scale. *Ethics and Environment* 5(1): 23–45.

Noske, Barbara. (1989) *Human and Other Animals: Beyond the Boundaries of Anthropology*. London: Pluto Press.

Novek, J. (2003) Intensive hog farming in Manitoba: transnational treadmills and local conflicts. *Canadian Review of Sociology* 40(1): 3–26.

Nurse, Angus. (2013) Perspectives on criminality in wildlife. In Reece Walters, Diane Solomon Westerhuis and Tanya Wyatt (eds.) *Emerging Issues in Green Criminology: Exploring Power, Justice and Harm*. London: Palgrave Macmillan, pp. 127–144.

——. (2016) *An Introduction to Green Criminology and Environmental Justice*. Thousand Oaks: Sage.

Nussbaum, Martha. (2001) Animal rights: the need for a theoretical basis. *Harvard Law Review* 114(5): 1506–1550.

——. (2004) Beyond "compassion" and "humanity": justice for nonhuman animals. In Cass Sunstein and Martha Nussbaum (eds.) *Animal Rights: Current Debates and New Directions*. Oxford: Oxford University Press, pp. 299–320.

——. (2006) *Frontiers of Justice: Disability, Nationality, Species Membership*. Cambridge, MA: Harvard University Press.

Oldfield, T., R. J. Smith, S. R. Harrop, and N. Leader-Williams (2003). Field sports and conservation in the United Kingdom. *Nature* 423: 531–533.

Pachirat, Timothy. (2011) *Every Twelve Seconds: Industrialized Slaughter and the Politics of Sight*. New Haven, CT: Yale University Press.

Packer, Craig, Margaret Kosmala, Hillary Cooley, Henry Brink, Lilian Pintea, David Garshelis, Gianetta Purchase, Megan Strauss, Alexandra Swanson, Guy Balme, Luke Hunter, and Kristin Nowell. (2009) Sport hunting, predator control and conservation of large carnivores. *PLoS ONE* 4(6): 1–8.

Pardo, Italo and Giuliana Prato. (2005) The fox-hunting debate in the United Kingdom: a puritan legacy? *Human Ecology Review* 12(1): 143–155.

Patrick, P., C. Matthews, D. Ayers, and Sue Tunnicliffe. (2007) Conservation and education: prominent themes in zoo mission statements. *The Journal of Environmental Education* 38(3): 53–60.

References

Paulson, Nels. (2012) The place of hunters in global conservation advocacy. *Conservation and Society* 10(1): 53–62.

Peek, C. W., N. Bell, and C. Dunham. (1996) Gender, gender ideology, and animal rights advocacy. *Gender & Society* 10: 464–478.

Pellow, David. (2013). Environmental justice, animal rights, and total liberation: from conflict and distance to points of common focus. In Nigel South and Avi Brisman (eds.) *Routledge International Handbook of Green Criminology*. New York: Routledge, pp. 331–346.

Peterson, M. Nils. (2004) An approach for demonstrating the social legitimacy of hunting. *Wildlife Society Bulletin* 32(2): 310–321.

Plous, S. (1998) Signs of change within the animal rights movement: results from a follow-up survey of activists. *Journal of Comparative Psychology* 112(1): 48–54.

Plumwood, V. (1996) Nature, self, gender: feminism, environmental philosophy, and the critique of rationalism. In K. Warren (ed.) *Ecological Feminist Philosophies*. Bloomington, Indianapolis: Indiana University Press, pp. 155–180.

Pojman, Louis (ed.) (2016) *Environmental Ethics: Readings in Theory and Application*. Seventh edition. Belmont, CA: Wadsworth Publishing.

Ponette-Gonzáleza, A. G. and M. Fry. (2010) Pig pandemic: industrial hog farming in eastern Mexico. *Land Use Policy* 27: 1107–1110.

Posner, Richard. (2004) Animal rights: legal, philosophical, and pragmatic perspectives. In Cass Sunstein and Martha Nussbaum (eds.) *Animal Rights: Current Debates and New Directions*. New York: Oxford University Press, pp. 64–77.

Pritchard, Diana, John Fa, Sara Oldfield, and Stuart Harrop. (2011) Bring the captive closer to the wild: redefining the role of ex situ conservation. *Oryx* 46(1): 18–23.

Rees, Paul. (2005) Will the EC Zoos Directive increase the conservation value of zoo research? *Oryx* 39(2): 128–131.

Regan, Tom. (1980) Utilitarianism, vegetarianism, and animal rights. *Philosophy and Public Affairs* 9: 305–324.

_____. (1995) Are zoos morally defensible? In Bryan Norton, Michael Hutchins, Elizabeth Stevens, and Terry Maple (eds.) *Ethics on the Ark: Zoos, Animal Welfare, and Wildlife Conservation*. Washington, D.C.: Smithsonian Institution Press.

_____. (2004) *The Case for Animal Rights*. Berkeley: University of California Press.

Reichmann, J. B. (2000) *Evolution, Animal "Rights", and the Environment*. Washington, D.C.: Catholic University of America Press.

Rifkin, J. (1992) *Beyond Beef: The Rise and Fall of the Cattle Culture*. New York: Penguin.

Roberts, Rachel. (2017). China signs $300m deal to buy lab-grown meat from Israel in move welcomed by vegans. *The Independent*, September 17, 2017. http://www.independent.co.uk/news/world/asia/china-israel-trade-deal-lab-grown-meat-veganism-vegetarianism-a7950901.html

References

Rocheleau, D., B. Thomas-Slayter, and E. Wangari. (1996) Gender and environment: a feminist political ecology perspective. In Rocheleau, D., B. Thomas-Slayter, and E. Wangari (eds.) *Feminist Political Ecology: Global Issues and Local Experiences.* New York: Routledge.

Roe, Katie, Andrew McConney, and Caroline Mansfield. (2014) The role of zoos in modern society: a comparison of zoos' reported priorities and what visitors believe they should be. *Anthrozoos* 27(4): 529–541.

Rollin, Bernard. (1988) Environmental ethics. In Steven Laper-Foy (ed.) *Problems of International Justice.* Boulder, CO: Westview Press, pp. 125–131.

——. (2006) *Animal Rights and Human Morality.* Third edition. New York: Prometheus Books.

Ryder, Richard. (1975) *The Victims of Science,* London: Davies Pointer Ltd.

Scarce, Rik. (1990) *Eco-Warriors: Understanding the Radical Environmental Movement.* Chicago: The Noble Press.

Schnaiberg, A. (1980) *The Environment: From Surplus to Scarcity.* New York: Oxford University Press.

Schnaiberg, A., D. Pellow, and A. Weinberg. (2002) The treadmill of production and the environmental state. In A. P. J. Mol and F. H. Buttel (eds.) *The Environmental State under Pressure.* London: Elsevier North-Holland, pp. 15–32.

Scruton, Roger (2002) Ethics and welfare: the case of hunting. *Philosophy* 77: 543–564.

Sea Shepherd Conservation Society. (2003) WWF supports seal hunt – why? http://www.seashepherd.org/news-and-commentary/news/archive/wwf-supports- seal-hunt-why.html Accessed May 20, 2017.

Serpell, J. A. (2009) Having our dogs and eating them too: why animals are a social issue. *Journal of Social Issues* 65(3): 633–644.

Shapiro, K. (1994) The caring sleuth: portrait of an animal rights activist. *Society and Animals* 2(2): 145–265.

Shiva, V. (1989) *Staying Alive: Women, Ecology and Development.* London: Zed Press.

Silverstein, H. (1999) *Unleashing Rights: Law, Meaning, and the Animal Rights Movement.* Ann Arbor: University of Michigan Press.

Singer, Peter. (1974) All animals are equal. *Philosophic Exchange* 5(1): Article 6.

____. (1987) Animal liberation or animal rights? *The Monist* 70(1): 3–14.

____. (1990) *Animal Liberation.* New York: Random House.

____. (1993) *Practical Ethics.* New York: Cambridge University Press.

____. (2002) A response to Martha Nussbaum. The Tanner Lectures on Human Values, November 13, 2002.

Skaggs, Jimmy M. (1986) *Prime Cut: Livestock Raising and Meatpacking in the United States, 1607–1983.* College Station: Texas A&M University Press.

Smith, Liam and Sue Broad. (2008) Comparing zoos and the media as conservation educators. *Visitor Studies* 11(1): 16–25.

Sorenson, John. (2010) *About Canada: Animal Rights.* Halifax and Winnipeg: Fernwood.

References

_____. (2016) *Constructing Ecoterrorism: Capitalism, Speciesism, and Animal Rights*. Halifax and Winnipeg: Fernwood.

Stanescu, Vasile. (2013). Why "loving" animals is not enough. *The Journal of American Culture* 36(2): 100–110.

Stange, M. Z. (1997) *Woman the Hunter*. Boston: Beacon Press.

Starmer, E., A. Witteman, and T. A. Wise. (2006) *Feeding the Factory Farm: Implicit Subsidies to the Broiler Chicken Industry*. Global Development and Environment Institute.

Stathopoulos, A. S. (2010) You are what your food eats: how regulation of factory farm conditions could improve human health and animal welfare alike. *Legislation and Public Policy* 13: 407–444.

Steinbock, B. (1978) Speciesism and the idea of equality. *Philosophy* 53: 247–256.

Steinfeld, H., P. Gerber, T. D. Wassenaar, and V. Castel. (2006) *Livestock's Long Shadow: Environmental Issues and Options*. Food and Agriculture Organization of the United Nations.

Stretesky, Paul, Michael Long, and Michael Lynch. (2014) *The Treadmill of Crime: Political Economy and Green Criminology*. London, New York: Routledge.

Striffler, S. (2005) *Chicken: The Dangerous Transformation of America's Favorite Food*. New Haven, CT: Yale University Press.

Sutherland, Anne and Jeffrey E. Nash (1994) Animal rights as a new environmental cosmology. *Qualitative Sociology* 17(2): 171–186.

Szasz, Anthony. (2007) *Shopping Our Way to Safety: How We Changed from Protecting the Environment to Protecting Ourselves*. Minneapolis: University of Minnesota Press.

Taylor, Nik, and Amy Fitzgerald. (forthcoming) Understanding animal (ab)use: green criminological contributions, missed opportunities and a way forward. *Theoretical Criminology*.

Thomas, C. D., A. Cameron, R. E. Green, M. Bakkenes, L. J. Beaumont, Y. C. Collingham, B. F. Erasmus, M. F. De Siqueira, A. Grainger, and L. Hannah. (2004) Extinction risk from climate change. *Nature* 427: 145–148.

Thomas, Keith. (1996) *Man and the Natural World: Changing Attitudes in England 1500–1800*. Oxford: Oxford University Press.

Thompson, F. M. L. (1968) The Second Agricultural Revolution, 1815–1880. *Economic History Review* 21: 62–77.

Tietz, J. (2010) Boss Hog: the rapid rise of industrial swine. In D. Imhoff (ed.) *The CAFO Reader: The Tragedy of Industrial Animal Factories*. Berkeley: University of California Press.

Tilman, D., and M. Clark. (2014) Global diets link environmental sustainability and human health. *Nature* 515 (7528): 518–522.

Tovey, H. (2003) Theorising nature and society in sociology: the invisibility of animals. *Sociologia Ruralis* 43: 196–215.

Trend News Agency. (2010). Zoo staff convicted in Germany for culling hybrid tigers. http://en.trend.az/world/other/1706329.html. Accessed September 7, 2016.

References

Tribe, Andrew and Rosemary Booth. (2003) Assessing the role of zoos in wildlife conservation. *Human Dimensions of Wildlife* 8: 65–74.

Tuohey, John and Terence Ma. (1992) Fifteen years after "Animal Liberation": Has the animal rights movement achieved philosophical legitimacy? *Journal of Medical Humanities* 31(2): 79–89.

Twine, R. (2010) *Animals as Biotechnology: Ethics, Sustainability and Critical Animal Studies*. Washington, D.C.: Earthscan LLC.

_____. (2012) Revealing the "animal-industrial complex": a concept and method for critical animal studies. *Journal for Critical Animal Studies* 10(1): 12–39.

US General Accounting Office. (1999) *Report to the Honorable Tom Harkin: Animal Agriculture Waste Management Practices*.

Uyeki, E. (2000) Diffusion of pro-environment attitudes? *American Behavioral Scientist* 43(4): 646–661.

Van Dyke, Nella and Holly McCammon (eds.). (2010) *Strategic Alliances: Coalition Building and Social Movements*. Minneapolis: University of Minnesota Press.

Varner, Gary. (1994) Can animal rights activists be environmentalists? In Christine Pierce and Donald VanDeVeer (eds.) *People, Penguins, and Plastic Trees*. second edition. Belmont, CA: Wadsworth, pp. 254–273.

Verge, XPC, C. De Kimpe, R. L. Desjardins. (2007) Agricultural production, greenhouse gas emissions and mitigation potential. *Agric Forest Meteorol* 142: 255–269.

Vitali, Theodore. (1990) Sport hunting: moral or immoral? *Environmental Ethics* 12: 69–82.

Wade, Maurice (1990) Animal liberationism, ecocentrism, and the morality of sport hunting. *Journal of the Philosophy of Sport* 17: 15–27.

Warren, Karen. (Ed.) (1997) *Ecofeminism: Women, Culture, Nature*, Bloomington, Indianapolis: Indiana University Press.

Warren, K. (2000) *Ecofeminist Philosophy: A Western Perspective of What It Is and Why It Matters*. New York: Rowman and Littlefield Publishers, Inc.

Warren, Mary Ann. (2000) *Moral Status: Obligations to Persons and Other Living Things*. Oxford: Clarendon Press.

Wasley, Andrew. (2009) Signed, sealed, delivered... *Ecologist* 39(4): 30–33.

WAZA (2010) Statement on behalf of the World Association of Zoos and Aquariums (WAZA) in reference to the recent conviction of staff of Zoo Magdeburg for the management euthanasia of three hybrid tigers. http://www.waza.org/files/webcontent/1.public_site/5.conservation/code_of_ethics_and_animal_welfare/Magdeburg%20tiger%20statement%20REV2.pdf

_____. (2014) WAZA Statement – Euthanasia of a giraffe at Copenhagen Zoo. http://www.waza.org/files/webcontent/1.public_site/5.conservation/code_of_ethics_and_animal_welfare/WAZA%20Statement%20Giraffe%20Copenhagen.pdf

_____. (2015) Committing to Conservation: The World Zoo and Aquarium conservation strategy. http://www.waza.org/files/webcontent/1.public_site/5.con

References

servation/conservation_strategies/committing_to_conservation/WAZA%20
Con servation%20Strategy%202015_Portrait.pdf

Weis, T. (2010) The accelerating biophysical contradictions of industrial capitalist agriculture. *Journal of Agrarian Change* 10(3): 315–341.

Wenzel, G. W. (1991) *Animal Rights, Human Rights: Ecology, Economy, and Ideology in the Canadian Arctic.* Toronto: University of Toronto Press.

West, B. M. et al. (2011) Antibiotic resistance, gene transfer, and water quality patterns observed in waterways near CAFO farms and wastewater treatment facilities. *Water, Air and Soil Pollution* 217(4): 473–489.

White, R. (2008) *Crimes against Nature: Environmental Criminology and Ecological Justice.* Portland, OR: Willan.

Wilkie, R. (2005) Sentient commodities and productive paradoxes: the ambiguous nature of human–livestock relations in Northeast Scotland. *Journal of Rural Studies* 21: 213–230.

Winders, B. and D. Nibert. (2004) Consuming the surplus: expanding "meat" consumption and animal oppression. *International Journal of Sociology and Social Policy* 24(9): 76–96.

Wise, Steven. (2000). *Rattling the Cage: Toward Legal Rights for Animals.* Cambridge, MA: Perseus.

_____. (2002). *Drawing the Line: Science and the Case for Animal Rights.* Cambridge, MA: Perseus.

World Animal Protection. (2014) Animal Protection Index. http://www.worldanimalprotection.org/news/ground-breaking-animal-protection-index-assesses-animal-welfare-around-world

World Bank. (2017) The World Bank in agriculture and food: Overview. http://www.worldbank.org/en/topic/agriculture/overview Accessed July 12, 2017.

Wyles, Kayleigh, Sabine Pahl, Mathew White, Sarah Morris, Deborah Cracknell, and Richard Thompson. (2013) Towards a marine mindset: visiting an aquarium can improve attitudes and intentions regarding marine sustainability. *Visitor Studies* 16(1): 95–110.

Yearley, S. (2002) The social construction of environmental problems: a theoretical review and some not-very-Herculean labors. In Dunlap, R. E., F. H. Buttel, P. Dickens, and A. Gijswijt (eds.) *Sociological Theory and the Environment: Classical Foundations, Contemporary Insights.* Lanham, MD: Rowman and Littlefield, pp. 274–285.

Zande, K. (2008) Raising a stink: why Michigan CAFO regulations fail to protect the state's air and great lakes and are in need of revision. *Environmental Law Journal* 16(1): 1–53.

Zarkadas, I., G. Dontis, G. Pilidis, and D. Sarigiannis. (2016) Exploring the potential of fur farming wastes and byproducts as substrates to anaerobic digestion process. *Renewable Energy* 96: 1063–1070.

Zimmerman, M. E. (2005) *Environmental Philosophy: From Animal Rights to Radical Ecology,* New York: Pearson/Prentice Hall.

Index

Index

Britain 23, 39, 54, 57, 70
British Fur Trade Association 127

Callicott, J. Baird 11–12, 49, 62, 83, 86, 160
Canada 11, 51–52, 58–59, 66–67, 69–70, 73–74, 77, 89, 111–112, 114–118, 120–122, 125–129, 136, 177, 187
Canadian Association of Zoos and Aquaria (CAZA) 89–90
capitalism 19, 66, 124, 134; *see also* Inverted Quarantine; Treadmill of Production
Carson, Rachel 15, 60
Cecil the lion 54–55
China 115, 123, 146
coalition building 10, 15, 40–41, 44, 48–49, 137, 156, 160–161, 183–185
cognitive dissonance 2
colonization 87
companion animals 1, 12, 18, 23, 25, 37, 42, 60, 98, 112, 164–167, 180, 188
condensing symbols 47, 157
confined/concentrated animal feeding operation (CAFO) 64–65, 137–149, 156, 184–185
conservation 15, 44, 55–61, 64–75, 78–80, 85–88, 90–110, 113, 127, 146, 166, 168–175, 182, 186–187
ex situ 90–100, 108, 171
in situ 90–100, 104, 108, 171–172, 174–175
criminology 21
green criminology 8–9, 17, 182
culture/nature dichotomy 4–5, 20–22, 36, 50, 78, 83–84, 89, 106, 156, 171, 185–189

Darwin, Charles 57
"death of nature" 83–84, 180–181, 186
deforestation 96, 140, 145–6, 151, 182

Denmark 123
Dietz, Tom 13, 137
Dizard, Jan 63, 70, 76, 83–84, 170
Donovan, Josephine 3, 12, 35–36, 50, 161, 163

Earth Liberation Front 163
Earth Summit 95–96
ecocentrism 61
ecofeminism 8, 19–20, 42–44, 77–78, 84, 89, 106, 123, 129, 156, 171, 182–189
ecological justice 8–9, 78
endangered species, *see* threatened/ endangered species
environmental ethics 6–8, 11–12, 48, 78, 61–64, 91–92
environmental movement; *see also* global climate change; Inverted Quarantine; level of analysis; Treadmill of Production
as a new social movement 43
environmental justice 8–9, 44, 78, 137, 156, 184–185
phases in 15
Europe 23, 43, 56, 58, 70, 89, 115, 117–118, 120–123, 126, 138–140, 144
European Association of Zoos and Aquaria (EAZA) 89
European Union 94, 115, 120–122, 129, 133–134, 140, 144, 177
evolution 7, 57, 60
"in reverse" 73–75, 79–80, 82, 168

feminist care ethic 35–36
Finland 123–124, 126
fishing 7, 50, 59, 66–67, 102, 118, 129, 146
Food and Agriculture Organization of the United Nations 135–136, 141, 145, 151–153
France 8, 54, 56–57
fur 15, 27, 45–46, 111–134, 154, 175–178, 182, 184, 188
animal welfare concerns with 120–121, 130

213